D1188199

Beyond Myself

*It's not about us, but what
God can do through us.*

By
Heather English

PRESS

Copyright © 2015 by Heather English

Beyond Myself
It's not about us, but what God can do through us.
by Heather English

Printed in the United States of America

ISBN 9781498457477

All rights reserved solely by the author. The author guarantees all contents are original and do not infringe upon the legal rights of any other person or work. No part of this book may be reproduced in any form without the permission of the author. The views expressed in this book are not necessarily those of the publisher.

Unless otherwise indicated, scripture quotations are taken from The New King James Version (NKJV). Copyright © 1982 by Thomas Nelson, Inc. Used by permission. All rights reserved.

www.xulonpress.com

God bless you!

Heather English

Ps. 71: 15-18

Dedication

This book is dedicated to my loving Mother, who was always there for me in every sense of the word. Without you urging me on through all of my awkward years, molding me into the Godly woman I am today, I don't know where I would be.

To my amazing husband, Dale English, who has been my stronghold and the love of my life for nearly thirty years. Thank you for your love, patience, and support. My life would not be complete without you.

To my sons, Daniel and Christian, who have brought joy unspeakable into my life. You will never know the love I have for you both and what an honor it is for me to be called your Mom.

To all of my family who have patiently put up with me through the years and loved me no matter what. I love you all more than you could ever know.

To everyone who has ever sat under our ministry and/or supported us. You all will forever be our extended family and we appreciate everything you've ever done.

Finally, I dedicate this book to my Heavenly Father, for without You, this book would not even be possible. Thank You for giving me the words so that they may help someone else. May You get all the honor and glory!

Introduction

There are many songs that I love so it's hard to pick just one as my favorite. I guess it really determines on what is going on in my life at the moment as to which one sticks out more to me. For the sake of this book, I would have to say that the song "Lifesong" by Casting Crowns has a real impact for a couple of reasons. One being that since I'm a singer, song writer, and musician, I want my music to honor God in every way possible. The line "Let my life song sing to You" means something deeper to me.

Another reason is that I want my life, my song, my testimony, to ring true and give Him praise at every opportunity. My purpose is to magnify Him with every breath, every word, every step, every action. I want to look back at my life and have as few regrets as possible. I want to make a difference in my world of influence.

My goal is to point as many people to Christ as possible by the life I live, and not necessarily the words I say. Like the old saying goes, "Preach the gospel, and if necessary, use words."

"Wow! You should write a book!"

That's usually what I got after sharing different testimonies of what God has done in my life. I already knew in my heart that God was calling me to write one, and every time I heard someone tell me that I should, it was only confirmation. So why did it take me so long to write one?

Fear of failure. Fear of saying the wrong thing. Fear that I may offend someone. Fear that no one would want to read it. Take your pick from any of these excuses. Thankfully, I listened to God instead of the devil in my ear. I always knew that God was going to use different portions of my life to help minister to others. I just never realized how much of my life until I began writing this book.

I pray that God blesses this book in such a way that His Holy Spirit comes to you as you read it, helping you through whatever your struggle may be—past or present. I pray that somehow He speaks to you through the pages that have been carefully written just for you. Above all, know that God is good and He loves you very much, right where you are. Happy reading and hope you enjoy the journey with me!

Table of Contents

Chapter 1

Innocence Lost

*"And the Lord, He is the One who goes before you.
He will be with you, He will not leave you nor forsake you;
do not fear nor be dismayed." Deuteronomy 31:8 (NKJV)*

Looking out the window of the car, with my head resting on my fist, I remember the awkward silence as I'm watching the trees quickly pass by. Daddy and I were on the way back home from visiting Grandma and Grandpa's house in Arkansas over the weekend. I'm angry and confused but really not understanding why. So many questions running through my little five-year-old mind. What just happened? Why do I feel this way? Why did Daddy do those things?

After the divorce, my time with Daddy was usually either going to my Grandparents' house, roller skating at the local Hot Wheels, or a day at Hamel's Amusement Park in Shreveport, Louisiana. These were always fun times and I really enjoyed being with my Daddy. It was our special time to be together.

Daddy was an excellent skater and taught me how at a very young age. We used to do tricks together, most that you would only see with ice skating couples. I loved it when he picked me up in the air and I posed like a flying ballerina. Although Hamel's Park is now closed, the amazing memories of the birthday parties, the rides, seeing the animals while riding the train, they will always stay with me. However, there would be no fun today.

A few moments before, Daddy and I were heading back home to Bossier City, Louisiana after a weekend visit at his home near my Grandparents. The trip back to my Mom usually took a couple of hours with mostly wooded, quiet roads, going through a few small towns along the way. So many times on these weekend trips to Arkansas, Daddy would have to use the restroom in the middle of no where. He would find a wooded area along the route, pull over, go deep into the woods where I couldn't see him, and soon returned to continue the trip home. Today would be very different.

As Daddy pulled over on what looked like a hunting access road to a wooded area, I prepared myself for another boring few moments alone in the car. Instead of walking far into the woods for privacy as usual, he only walked a few feet to the front of the car on the driver's side. Facing away from me, I wondered why he was staying at the car. Didn't he need to potty?

After a few moments, Daddy turned his head toward me.

"You can get out of the car if you want to."

I thought this was strange but it sounded better than just sitting alone in the car, so I got out and began walking toward the front of the car. While feeling a little apprehensive I also began to get a little curious as to what Daddy was doing. I continued walking toward the woods, when he called out my name. Without thinking, I turned around to see what Daddy wanted. I just stood there in shock of what I saw.

My mind was racing, trying to grasp what was happening. As a five-year-old, I was very innocent. I wasn't even aware that boys and girls were different "down there." Now I'm looking at my very exposed father standing by the car and I'm not sure what to think.

Daddy called for me to come over to him and I really didn't want to, but my curiosity is pulling me to go. I didn't want to get in trouble for not obeying him.

I thought to myself, "What is that? What's wrong with my Daddy?"

I was confused. He was so different from me and my private area, as Mom called it. I thought he may be deformed. Fear and nervousness began to overwhelm me. Something wasn't right.

I've heard how sometimes we can block out very traumatic moments in our lives as a coping mechanism. There are some moments that I cannot recall on that day, but other moments are just as vivid to me today as the day it all happened. I thought about writing the details of what happened so you could fully understand what I went through, but I don't want to have to rate this book as a PG13 read.

It's very hard to read details about a little five-year-old girl being molested by her own father. You can only imagine what took place over the next several minutes, but I did have one thing that was in my favor. Daddy didn't have intercourse with me.

After he was done, we both got back into the car to continue our trip back to my Mom. At this point, it's very quiet in the car while we're going down the road. Daddy finally breaks the silence.

"You can't tell anybody about what just happened. If you tell anyone, I will never take you anywhere again. They won't understand."

To a little girl that knows that's the only time she gets to see her Daddy, this is a big threat. Even though I didn't fully understand what had just happened, I knew it wasn't right, but I still loved and wanted to be with my Daddy. I was so confused. I thought if I told, I would get in trouble.

Did I do something wrong? Would I get punished for what just happened? I decided out of fear and shame that I would keep my mouth shut and not tell anyone. I kept my secret for at least three years before it was pulled out of me. Unfortunately, this wouldn't be the only time I'd have to keep this kind of secret.

A God Moment

Life happens to us all. We have the "why" questions and sometimes we get those questions answered, while at other times we don't. When we're young, it's hard to look at your situation and see how anything positive or good could possibly come out of it, but if we trust God and have faith that He has our best interest at heart, we'll see Him work wonders through our trials. Ask God to show you what you can learn from this or how you can turn this trial into a triumphant victory for the Kingdom of God. More times than not, your victory, as well as the struggle to get there, can be your testimony, which can then help someone else who may be going through the same situation.

Chapter 2

The Good, The Bad, & The Ugly

"For I know the thoughts that I think toward you,
says the Lord, thoughts of peace and not of evil,
to give you a future and a hope." Jeremiah 29:11 (NKJV)

When you're young, there's so much that is hard to recollect before the age of five and that's true for me as well, but I remember snap shots, feelings, things that are etched in my memories. Not everything was bad. I have some good memories that I like to recall from time to time. I've always, and forever will be, an optimist—trying to find the good in every situation, every person, if possible. But our memories can haunt us when things of our past aren't so good. Until I was twenty-three years old, I wouldn't know how to escape my memories, my nightmares, but that's for a later chapter.

Before I go any further, I would like to say that every character mentioned in this book are real people but for privacy reasons, some names have been changed. If you know my family then you'll know which names are made up and which aren't.

The Good

My mother, Pat, married my father, Bill, when they were both very young. Mom has described how charming Bill was but the

Vietnam war changed him. Bill enlisted in the Navy after they were married and was later stationed in Rhode Island at the time of my birth. Yes, this country, southern girl was born in the North, but we were only there for one year before moving back to the Shreveport/Bossier area of Louisiana. I know. . .don't hold it against me. . .I got home as fast as I could, but I'm getting ahead of myself.

I was almost named Christina instead of Heather. When Bill was on a Naval ship, he read a book that had a character named Heather in it. At that time, no one had really heard of that name so he wrote to Mom saying that if they had a girl, she should be named Heather. Mom agreed but not long after that, a new movie came out and the lead character was named Heather. Bill was afraid that everyone was going to name their little girl the same thing so he decided to change his future daughter's name to Christina.

When Mom went into labor in the local Naval Base hospital, it took them three days to figure out that I was double breach, which means I was trying to come out rear-end first. With every contraction I was pushing up toward my Mom's chest and she had to push me back down with both hands. The doctors joked that I was trying to enter the world while letting it know what I really thought about it.

They finally decided to take me by C-section and discovered that the umbilical chord was wrapped around my neck three times. Mom wasn't surprised considering how active I was in the womb.

After seeing how much pain and struggle Mom went through to have me, Bill decided she could name me anything she wanted. Mom really loved the first name they had picked out so I became Heather Lynn. Bill was right about my name because it wasn't long that many little girls were named Heather and it became very popular for years.

While in the hospital, Mom carefully walked to the nursery only to find the nurses rocking me every time.

"Y'all are going to have her so spoiled before I even get her home."

"We have to keep her quiet because she'll wake up the entire nursery," the nurses informed her.

"What do you mean?"

"This little girl is going to be a singer with the set of pipes and lungs that she's got! She doesn't quietly cry like the rest of the babies. She screams her lungs out!"

Mom just laughed it off, thinking to herself, "Yeah, right." Little did she know that I would indeed become a singer at an early age, but I'll get into that later.

As Mom slowly walked back to her room to feed me, she noticed as I laid in her arms how I patiently waited with my mouth wide open like a baby bird waiting to be fed. When she finally got to the room it took her a little while to get situated after her surgery so my patience eventually ran out and I got fussy. Everyone said that I was a beautiful baby.

After I was a year old, Mom and Bill decided to move back to the South where both of their families were. It was a long trip so they laid the back seat down in their yellow Volkswagen Beetle, laid blankets down, and surrounded me with stuffed animals and toys to keep me occupied. This was way before car seats were mandatory.

Everything was fine until someone slammed on their brakes right in front of our car. What happened next had to be a God moment. I flew through the air, in between the front seats, head first toward the windshield, but Bill miraculously intervened. He caught me with his right arm and gently laid me down in his lap while swerving the car to avoid an accident with his left. Even then God had His hand on my life.

Once we got back to Louisiana, I remember living in the left side of a duplex, across from a public park right off of Jewella Avenue in Shreveport. It was small but just the right size for our small family.

My and my parents' bedrooms were right across from each other and I sometimes ran and jumped in bed with them. I tumbled around with Bill until I finally just laid there between them both, all of us giggling and laughing. Those moments may seem simple but I remember feeling loved, a time of warmth that didn't come very often, so I cherished those memories.

There were some good times and one in particular almost involved the police. Bill played hide and seek with me and taught me how to be a good hider. I giggled if he got close to my hiding place and he would find me. He taught me to keep very still and quiet so I wouldn't give away where I was hiding.

"I give up! You can come out now."

After his surrender, I came out of my hiding place.

"Ha! I got you!"

I learned to ignore Bill when he said he was giving up.

One particular game of hide and seek, when Dad tried to find me, I was no where to be found. He yelled out that he gave up but I stayed still and quiet. I wasn't buying it. Mom and Bill both began to get a little nervous, questioning if I had slipped outside without them knowing. They both were frantically looking everywhere, calling out my name but I never answered.

Just in case, they went outside and got a couple of the neighbors to help look for me around the immediate area, but they couldn't find me anywhere. Bill finally made the decision to go back in the house to call the police but before he dialed, he yelled out for me.

"Heather Lynn, if you're in this house you better tell me where you are or I'm going to call the police to come find you!"

It was then that he heard a faint giggle coming from the kitchen. I had managed to pull a big pot out of a bottom cabinet, crawl into the cabinet, pull the big pot back in front of me, and then close the cabinet door. Mom and Bill both had already opened that cabinet door but never saw me hiding in the darkness. Bill taught me to be very still and quiet, even when he was close, so I was able to not give myself away. After that day, he regretted teaching me how to play hide and seek so well, but I loved those moments when he took time with me.

The Bad

Mom seemed to be the responsible one that comforted me, while Bill tried to be the "fun" one, at least when he took the time to be with me. For the most part, Bill was still growing and maturing as a man, as well as a father. He was trying to figure it all out but still having those selfish tendencies along the way. You know those moments when it's all about "me" and nothing else really matters? When things just get in the way of our quest and zest for life? Yeah,

I think that's where Bill was, while trying to deal with the memories and demons of his own past.

Looking back, Mom felt that Bill wasn't really ready to be a father. After fighting in the Vietnam war, Bill wasn't the same. He struggled with the memories of what he experienced in Vietnam but he had another problem. Bill had a sexual appetite that he couldn't seem to get enough of. Mom made sure that she was the dutiful wife, being there when he needed her, but even then Bill strayed from their marriage bed.

After getting caught cheating with another woman the first time, Mom decided to stay with him for my sake so I could still have a father and a complete family. Mom gave him another chance and explained that if it ever happened again, she would leave him. How long he stayed faithful until he was caught again is uncertain.

Mom recalls one particular night, when I was around six months old, how I was very fussy. No matter what she did, she couldn't get me to settle down and rest. They were trying to go to bed but when I kept crying it was really irritating Bill.

"Just let her cry. She'll eventually stop."

When I kept crying, Mom got up to check on me again, but Bill had a different plan.

"I'll take care of this. You stay here."

Mom wondered what Bill was going to do. Suddenly, she heard loud "whacking" sounds and then me screaming out even more than I already was, which made her jump up to see what was wrong.

Mom ran to my bassinet and noticed there was a small amount of blood on the bedding. She picked me up and checked me from head to toe, trying to find the source of where the blood came from, only to find nothing. Bill denied that he had done anything but Mom knew something happened. For my protection, she threatened to leave him if he ever abused me like that again. Mom began to worry about what kind of father Bill was going to be after that night.

When looking through some of my baby pictures, I ran across a few professional portraits taken when I was around a year old. My grandmother on Mom's side, Grandma James, really liked spoiling me so she paid to have some nice pictures taken.

While looking at the pictures, Mom asked, "Do you want to know why you're not smiling in any of those pictures?"

I really hadn't thought about it or noticed until she said something. After looking them over once again, there were no smiles in any of them. Mom explained that just before we left to take the pictures, we were at Bill's parents' house and I had done something. She couldn't recall exactly what I did but it made Bill angry, so he took me into one of the bedrooms and locked the door.

Mom and Grandma heard me screaming but couldn't tell what was transpiring on the other side of the door. Grandma was beating on the door, yelling at Bill to let her in and to stop hurting me, but he wouldn't open it. Mom and Grandma were both crying and trying to get to me but they couldn't. They both felt so helpless. Bill eventually opened the door and they both comforted me, but it was too late. Bill had hurt me so much that I refused to smile for the photographer, no matter what they did.

The Ugly

After seeing what kind of husband and father Bill was turning out to be, Mom decided not to have any more children for a while, so I remained an only child. That made things pretty lonely for me and unless I was allowed to play with the neighbors' children, I pretty much had to play by myself. There were times when Bill didn't want to be bothered so I was told to stay in my room unless he allowed me to come out.

I was not allowed to watch television as long as there was something on that Bill wanted to watch. Only if there was nothing on that interested him was I allowed into the living room to watch anything. There was some physical abuse that happened from time to time and I'm not talking about a good old fashioned spanking. There was slapping me across my face, pulling or grabbing my long, blonde hair, as well as other forms of abusive punishment when he got angry.

I have permanent scars, mostly on my face, from contracting chicken pox and being allowed to scratch my scabs. Bill wasn't working at the time but going to college to be a Registered Nurse, while Mom worked as a commercial artist. Mom arranged for a lady to watch me, ensuring that I would not scratch, creating scars on my face.

There were no classes on one particular day so Mom asked Bill to watch over me so she wouldn't have to pay a babysitter. Mom didn't want me to grow up having scars, especially since the majority of my chicken pox sores resided on my face. Bill agreed to watch me but he didn't want to be bothered so while he stayed in his bedroom reading a book, he sent me to mine to play alone. Needless to say, when my Mom returned home to see that I had been left alone to scratch at so many scabs on my face, she was livid and heartbroken.

"I hope you're happy! She's now going to have to live with permanent scars all over her face! Now every time you look at her and see those scars, I hope it reminds you of what you've allowed to happen today and how a book was more important to you than your daughter and her future! You did this to her!"

I have one more scar on my face but it was my own doing. While taking a nap on my Grandmother's bed, I happened to fall off while turning over too close to the edge. When I fell off, my left eyebrow hit the wood-frame holding the mattress, cutting into it and creating a permanent scar. I've tried to cover it up, but I usually just leave it alone and go on with my day, not worrying about my little battle scar.

There were so many times that I felt alone but there was one particular day that I recall feeling so desperate for my mother's time and attention. I thought I would just melt into a puddle of my own tears if she didn't color with me. Mom was gifted in art and drawing and I remember as a little girl being very careful with my coloring, loving it when Mom colored one page while I took on the other in one of my coloring books.

She came into my room to put up some of my clothes when I begged her to stay and color a page with me. Since Mom was busy she gave the excuse that she needed to finish her duties, but when she heard the desperation in my voice and saw tears welling up in my eyes, she couldn't help but drop everything for at least a few minutes to spend with me. I felt so relieved and loved at that simple moment, knowing that my Mom was there for me. For a small child, my world felt like it was going to fall apart if she didn't color with me at that moment, but Mom passed the test with flying colors, literally.

There are so many things that I could say, so many events to recall, but I want to move on so let's start another chapter, shall we?

A God Moment

God entrusts us with our children, to raise them to know and love God. Every little moment in their lives means something much bigger than we could understand. Make every moment count with them, loving on them, praising them often. "Catch" them being good instead of only the bad things they inevitably will venture into. Bring them to church instead of sending them or dropping them off. The family unit has drastically changed by definition through the years, especially when it concerns spiritual matters. We only have a few short years to train them up so let's make every opportunity to do our best for our children. After all, time is running out before Christ's return and we don't want to be responsible for anyone left behind.

Chapter 3

Fun Facts

"Be glad in the Lord, and rejoice, you righteous; and shout for joy, all you upright in heart!" Psalm 32:11 (NKJV)

Habits And Attachments

At the time of this writing, I am forty-five years old and I still have an ugly habit of picking at my nails. At least I don't bite them anymore like I did as a kid. As long as I can remember I've done this and I can only guess that it's due to being anxious and nervous the majority of my young childhood.

I remember lying in my bed when I was very little, trying to bite my toenails as well. Yeah, I know. Nasty right? You have to be pretty limber to pull that off. Well, now I can say that my toes look much better as I've finally allowed my toenails to grow out and I don't feel embarrassed by how my feet look. I've managed to stop picking at them so I can get pedicures or have my daughter-in-law have fun painting my toenails. My fingernails, on the other hand, are a different story.

I also had a blanket that never left my side and it was my comfort piece. It was the same blanket that they brought me home wrapped up in from the hospital. The blanket had a soft layer of stuffing inside, wrapped in very soft fabric on the outside, so I rubbed a section in between my fingers until it created a hole in the fabric. All the while doing this, I was sucking my two middle fingers with the other hand.

Anybody remember Linus on the cartoon Peanuts? He was inseparable from his blanket and I was just like him. Nothing could separate us and my nick name became "Heather Linus" instead of Heather Lynn because of that hole-ridden blanket. Eventually, the blanket was in pieces and while Mom saved a piece for herself, she also gave a piece to both grandmothers to keep once I finally gave it up.

So how did they get me to finally give up that permanent attachment of mine? Bribery always works well but only if you're bargaining with something that is totally irresistible to a five-year-old. I had a best friend that lived next door named Tracy. If I remember correctly, I think her last name was Whitaker or Whittier but I couldn't pronounce it correctly so I called her Tracy Wigger. Tracy came home one day with her ears pierced and I thought that was just the most amazing thing. Naturally, I had to have mine done. I ran home to ask Mom and she sat me down to explain how only big girls get their ears pierced, but big girls don't carry around blankets everywhere they go. I wanted my ears pierced so bad that I agreed to give up my blanket.

We all went to the mall and found this jewelry store that would grant me my wish. The only problem with all of this is that I had never seen this process done and didn't realize that pain was involved. It didn't grasp me what had to be done to be able to wear those pretty little earrings that Tracy had on.

I crawled up in the seat and waited for my first ear to become as pretty as Tracy's when I suddenly heard this "gun" go off, followed by unexpected pain I had never felt before. I jumped out of that chair, screaming and running for my life down the hallways of the mall, followed by everyone else trying to catch up with me. Once this refugee was finally caught, they brought me back, but this time they all had to hold me down, kicking and screaming, so they could finish the job. When I finally settled down, I looked in the mirror and was satisfied that I was now just as pretty as Tracy.

Art School

Mom knew she was good at drawing and was always told that she should do it for a living but she lacked confidence to search for a job in the commercial art field. Mom decided to enroll in a local art class but not long after she started the class, they ended up asking her to teach it. Bill always knew she was good and told her she should be teaching the class instead of taking it. Bill just laughed when he heard about them wanting her to teach.

"I told you so."

Mom struggled when it came to being confident in herself in just about anything.

When Mom sat at her art table, instead of making me go away and leave her alone like Bill usually did, she pulled up a chair and gave me my own paper to draw on. She gave me little pointers and I enjoyed watching her draw beautiful people with amazing detail. I was in such awe of how she could draw them so life-like.

One day Mom took me to her art class and announced to all of her adult students that I would be teaching the class. Of course, everyone laughed but they decided to humor me as I walked around the room, observing their work.

They stopped laughing when I told one of the students, "You're foot is wrong."

The student carefully looked at his work again as my Mom came over to inspect my judgment call. They both agreed that I was right. I got some strange looks after that, like they were thinking I was some sort of art prodigy or something.

Mom went on to work as a commercial artist for several major companies like Montgomery Ward, Rubenstein's, The Fashion, and more. Her job was to draw with different colors of ink for advertisements in the newspapers. Mom mostly drew people with different clothing lines for adults and sometimes children. She made a decent living and still today I enjoy looking through her portfolio, admiring her amazing art work.

Growing up, it didn't take long for others to find out that Mom and I had artistic abilities so we were generally asked to help out with any face painting booths or class room door decorating contests.

Being able to draw sometimes had its advantages and I used this gift throughout the rest of my life for many important purposes.

A God Moment

We are all unique and wonderfully crafted by the hand of God Himself. None of us are a mistake and God has a plan for every one of us, no matter how messed up you may think you are or insignificant. Each one of us has bad habits, but they can be overcome with prayer and faith in God. Embrace what makes you different and sets you apart as long as it's God-honoring. Remember that God doesn't make junk. . .only original masterpieces.

Chapter 4

Performance Based Love

"And now abide faith, hope, love, these three; but the greatest of these is love." 1 Corinthians 13:13 (NKJV)

It is no secret that parents are supposed to love their children no matter what, even when they want to pull their hair out during the stubborn times of raising them. It is universally understood that children should know they are loved, including when they're being corrected or punished. The structure and boundaries that parents place their children in to help shape and mold them are much needed and actually craved by their little ones, although they will certainly deny that later on when they're older.

This is not always the case with every parent. Becoming a mother or father doesn't always click on the maternal/paternal button inside your brain, making you a runner up for the best parent of the year award. It takes great sacrifice and patience to be a good parent, but for some, not only is it a hard step, but can become a step they're unwilling to take; not realizing the damage they're not only doing to themselves, but mostly to their children.

While a mother's love is vital to any child, a daughter truly needs and craves the love and strength of her father. She longs for that male role model in her life that will stay with her when she grows older and begins to date, picking out her future husband.

While mothers generally bring the comforting, nurturing, softer side of things, fathers are there for support, strength, and stability.

My mother was my comfort and still is. I've always had a very close relationship with her, knowing that I could go to her and talk about anything, at any time. Although Bill had his "great daddy" moments, he often seemed to be Daddy only when I was worthy and it was convenient for him.

Yes, there were times of great happiness and joy with Bill. Those are the moments that I cherished the most as a child; the ones I most longed for. I learned at a very early age how to gain his love and affection in between the moments that just naturally happened.

I noticed if I did something extraordinary that a little girl my age normally wouldn't be able to do, I got the attention and love I craved.

Bill said things like, "Now, that's my girl!"

That made me push myself hard on a daily basis, looking for any and every opportunity to gain his affection. This became part of my character that made me continue to push myself to the limit just to prove myself to others while growing up and even into my adulthood.

I will have to say that I'm very blessed that God gave me the gift of learning new things easily and usually doing them well. Artistry runs in my family and I noticed that I had a good eye of looking at things and was able to draw like my mother and grandfather. This artistic eye helped me become a talented florist later as well.

Music also came easy to me, including reading music, playing any instrument that I wanted to learn, and singing. I've often been asked if I ever had singing or voice lessons, to which I will have to say that I have not.

Cooking became a hobby after I married, especially baking pastries, and I became pretty good at it. I love the idea of creating something that I know my family can enjoy.

These talents and gifts became assets throughout my life and I used them to my advantage to gain the respect and love of my father as a child, as well as others later in life. It helped me make friends, and unfortunately at times, enemies as well. I had to learn humility, which is not an easy virtue to acquire and master.

Although several things came easy to me through the years, I had some things that I had to work through. Being right all the time, having to admit I was wrong, and having to have everything perfect were just a few. You would think I was overly compulsive about some things and I probably was. I still struggle with some of these issues even today but through the grace of God, I am much better in many areas.

I've learned a lot through the years and have come face to face with my inner demons that have tried to destroy me from the inside out. Understanding that I don't have to perform for love and acceptance of others proved to be a long, hard lesson to learn and mindset to change. We often get ourselves caught in these traps that we lay out for ourselves, unaware of the damage that can be done, not only to just ourselves, but to others around us that care about us.

I've also learned to just be myself, knowing that I will never be able to make everyone happy, no matter what I do. As long as I know that I'm in God's will and making Him proud of my daily choices, I know I'll be alright. Trying to please everyone for the sake of my own feeling of outward acceptance is something that took a while to change but the journey to get to this point has been, let's just say, interesting, but liberating.

A God-Moment

The world around us is changing and it's not for the better. Watch out who you keep company with since they have the power to bring you closer to God or drag you away from Him. 1 Corinthians 15:33 says, "Do not be deceived: 'Bad company ruins good morals.'" When we try to please others, it can be a nasty trap if we're not careful; especially if it's for the wrong kind of people. Our first goal should be to please God. When we do this, then everything else will always fall into place. If our hearts are in line with Him, then we will want to please Him with our choices in life as well as love our neighbor as ourselves.

Chapter 5

A Divorce and the Blanket

"When my father and my mother forsake me, then the Lord will take care of me." Psalm 27:10 (NKJV)

My blanket was my world; the one possession that would outrank anything else. I say this to help you understand the significance of what is to come later in this chapter. They say that desperate times call for desperate measures. For a little girl wanting her parents to stay together and for her father not to leave, it was time for me to pull out the heavy artillery. But before I get into all of that, I have to back up a little bit first.

Mom grew up with dogs all her life, with most of them living in the house and sleeping with her, so when she found out she was allergic to them, she was shocked. Mom and Bill had just gotten a puppy for me when Mom started having trouble breathing. The diagnosis was if she came in contact with any kind of animal hair that her throat would swell to the point of possibly closing off her air way, suffocating her.

When the doctor gave the bad news, they both knew they would have to do something with my puppy. Thankfully, our neighbors agreed to take the dog and I was allowed to play with it at any time I wanted. That helped ease the disappointment of having to give my puppy away.

Now back to the year 1975. Bill was caught cheating again and Mom remembered her previous warning. She told Bill that she would kick him out if he kept committing adultery, but now she wasn't sure what to do. Does she stick it out for my sake, or leave him and hope for the best as a single mother? Mom needed time to think so Bill took me outside to play with my puppy while Mom stayed inside the house, pacing in the living room with her thoughts.

Bill was on edge, wondering what the fate of his marriage and family would be within the next few minutes. He knew he messed up but there wasn't really anything he could do about it at this point. While retrieving my puppy from the neighbors, Bill warned me to be careful with it and not hurt it. Things took an awful turn in our front yard in a matter of minutes.

We lived right across the street from a nice public park that had a lot of big trees and playground equipment. While we were playing, the puppy noticed a squirrel just across the way from us. His attention was so focused on the squirrel that when I came up behind him to pick him up, it startled him and made him "yip". Bill had his back turned and didn't see what just happened but from what he heard, he thought I hurt the puppy. In an instant, reacting out of frustration, Bill spun around and kicked me in my ribs with such force that I rolled across the yard.

Mom was inside and just happened to be looking out of the window to see what had just happened. She was horrified that I might have had a broken or cracked rib, or even a possible punctured lung, so she ran out of the house, picked me up and examined me immediately for any damage. After making sure that I was physically alright, she switched her focus from me to Bill. With me in her arms, she walked straight up to Bill, looked him square in the face and said, "If this is the kind of father you're going to be to our daughter then neither of us need you. You just made up my mind. Get out!"

After that, they both knew that breaking the bad news to me wasn't going to be easy. I remember that day very well; where everyone was sitting, the room, everything. Mom was sitting on the couch across from me with Bill sitting next to her on the arm of the couch. They carefully chose their words as they tried to explain what divorce was and what it meant for our family. It was a lot for my little mind to consume so I began to cry. All I knew is that I didn't want my Daddy to leave so I offered a bribe.

"I'll give you my blanket if you don't leave!"

That statement made both of them speechless and upset. Mom and Bill carefully tried to choose their response that would help ease the pain somehow. Neither really knew what to say but offered as much comfort as possible. They tried their best to explain that it wasn't my fault and nothing I did would change the situation.

It amazes me how many children blame themselves for their parent's divorce. No matter how much you try to explain it, most kids take that with them for many years as they grow up; not realizing that it had nothing to do with them at all. That alone is a hard lesson to learn and can be a liberating experience when we can let that go.

A God Moment

Divorce in any family is always a horrible experience for everyone involved, but especially if there are children. It's hard enough for the adults, but much harder for the children to understand why. We try to protect our children from the troubles that marriage brings sometimes but as they grow older, they become wiser and the problems in the relationship cannot be hidden any longer. Be honest with your children, only answering the questions they ask, and in a way they can understand. Don't "bash" the other parent, no matter how awful you may think they are, because to your child, it is still their parent and possibly their hero. It will only backfire on you and make your child grow to resent you instead. Help a stressful time go more smoothly by being civil toward one another for the child's sake. Then pray for God to help you let go and forgive one another. God is able to heal all wounds.

Chapter 6

A Different Life

"Do not remember the former things, nor consider the things of old. Behold, I will do a new thing, now it shall spring forth; shall you not know it? I will even make a road in the wilderness and rivers in the desert." Isaiah 43:18-19 (NKJV)

Mom decided to look for another place to move to for a fresh new start for us both. She found a place to rent in Bossier City, Louisiana on the same street where Grandma and Grandpa James lived. It was the perfect little house for us and Mom didn't waste any time decorating and making it into a beautiful home for a new beginning.

It was a white, two bedroom house with an attic that I loved going up into for a little adventure. There was a slatted board opening for ventilation that overlooked the back yard and I discovered a bird's nest with eggs waiting to hatch inside. That excited me and I made frequent visits to check on them, waiting anxiously for the baby birds to hatch. The attic was an escape that I went to often but life was pretty good with just Mom and me.

With us living so close, it was real convenient for us to spend more time with Grandpa and Grandma M&M's. Grandma James always had a candy dish full of M&M's so that was how I identified her. Oddly enough, she was a diabetic and couldn't have any sweets but she always made sure there were plenty around for me.

She later switched to Hershey's Kisses so I would grab a little hand full, crawl up in Grandpa's lap, and we shared them together. Grandpa James always had a big belly so we lined the Kisses up across it, taking turns unwrapping and eating them together. That was something special the two of us shared for many years until I got too big to sit in his lap.

Grandpa James was a retired Major in the Air Force and he always kept his military hair cut. I remember having a great time as he sat back in his recliner and I tried my best to "fix" his hair by placing bobby pins in whatever hair was long enough to put them in. I hid behind his chair and he played the game of trying to grab me with his arms behind him.

Someone else that I dearly loved was my Uncle Larone, Mom's brother. He was also in the Air Force so when he got to come home, it was always a thrill for me because he was so fun to be with. Uncle Larone was there for several of my mile stones growing up and introduced the "creature" to me. He created this thing with his hand that looked like a spider but only he stuck out his middle finger for the neck and head of the creature. The creature loved sniffing and crawling up my arm, then around my neck, which tickled. I loved playing "creature" with him but another thing he did was the voice of Cookie Monster and other Sesame Street characters. Uncle Larone was one of my favorites to be with and he always had a loving and giving heart.

It was Uncle Larone that helped me get over my fear of walking. In the process of learning to walk, I had fallen and hurt myself. After that, I wouldn't walk by myself without at least touching something around me, just in case. It didn't matter what it was, as long as I had a finger on it, I felt more secure about walking.

One day Uncle Larone gave me two toys, one in each hand, and then Mom called me to come show her the toys. Without thinking, I began walking without holding on to anything. They had fooled me, but about half way, I realized I wasn't holding on to anything and began to squat down in the middle of the floor. Uncle Larone and Mom told me to get back up and finish what I started.

Grandma James loved spoiling me and made sure I had everything that I ever wanted or needed. Mom was now a single mother trying to provide a living as a commercial artist but couldn't afford the nicer things in life. When she said she couldn't afford something I wanted, I knew where to go.

"That's okay because Grandma will get it for me."

That always hurt Mom but I didn't understand that until much later in life.

Grandma sewed beautiful dresses for me and made sure that I was always in the nicest clothes. She was also determined that I had plenty of activities to do, including tap and ballet. At first I thought I might like it and I tried it for a while, but I quickly became bored and dropped out. I did get to dress up like a beautiful ballerina and my class performed in front of a huge crowd as part of a special presentation. That was the only highlight that I can remember from being in that ballet class. I later had remorse for dropping out and wish I had stayed.

Because Grandma was always taking pictures, I became a camera hog and a bit of a show-off pretty early on. I loved posing and acting out for the camera, making sure that she got a great shot. I got to perform on stage at times and I never had a shy bone in my body. I was the type that would be like, "Look at me! See me?" I craved the attention and did anything to get it.

I wasn't just spoiled by one set of grandparents, but two sets. Bill's parents also equally spoiled me, although I didn't get to spend as much time with them since they lived in Arkansas. I was the only grandchild on both sides of the family for about seven years so you can imagine how spoiled I must have been. Sometimes I got duplicate items for Christmas and birthdays because when my grandparents asked me what I wanted, I didn't know to ask for different things from each set. I just rattled off my list to both sets and they granted my wishes just about every time.

Going to Grandpa's and Grandma's house in Arkansas was always a treat when Bill came to pick me up for his visitation time. It was also the time that I got to spend time with my Uncle Gerry, Aunt Audrey, and Namaw (Grandma's mother). I loved going to visit with Namaw out at her farm.

The court awarded Mom full custody with the ability to allow, or not allow, Bill visitation rights. She knew that I still loved my father and didn't want to punish me for something that I had nothing to do with, so when Bill asked to spend time with me, she never refused for my sake. Bill always tried to make sure that our time together was fun so we often went to the local Hot Wheels skating rink or Hamel's Park like I mentioned earlier. I always looked forward to seeing Bill because I missed him and being with him always meant I got to do something exciting. At least that's the way it was most of the time.

A God Moment

When things don't go the way we expect in life, don't worry or fret over it. Take it to God in prayer, but make sure you're not doing all the talking. Sometimes we need to be still and quiet; listening to His voice speaking back to us. Is it an audible voice? No, but when His Spirit is speaking to you, you can tell the difference between your mind just coming up with something on its own and God getting your attention. The Bible says that His sheep know His voice. In other words, if you stay close to Him, spend time with Him in prayer, and read His Word, you'll know His voice when He speaks. There won't be any guessing if its Him or not. Let Him guide you into something better than your current circumstance.

Chapter 7

The "Uh-Oh" Moments

*"In God I have put my trust; I will not be afraid.
What can man do to me?" Psalm 56:11 (NKJV)*

I started out this book with one of the first, most devastating moments of my life; a moment that started a downward spiral that I would struggle with for many years. It's amazing how a single moment in time can transform your entire life, your character, your everything.

Have you ever watched the movie *The Green Mile*? One of the main characters in the movie is a very large black man named John Coffey with the gift of helping, or "taking it back" as he calls it. He not only "heals" two people in the movie and brings a dead mouse back to life, but he also seems to have insight into others around him. All of this takes place in a prison, a section only for those sentenced to death, that they call "The Mile." John ended up there because of a big misunderstanding due to circumstantial evidence against him.

In one of the movie scenes, as some of the guards are bringing in a new inmate, the lead guard is standing ready to receive him and he suddenly hears John quietly say from his own prison cell, "Careful. Careful." John knew something bad was about to happen. He had an uneasiness about the situation and the new inmate being brought in.

Have you ever had that feeling, that uneasiness deep in your gut? Ever been introduced to someone and there was just something about that person that didn't feel quite right? Or maybe it was just a situation that made you feel very uncomfortable. I used to call those feelings my "Uh-Oh" moments because in my mind I would be thinking, "Uh-Oh. Something's not right here." I would immediately put my guard up, being very cautious with every move I made and every word I said.

I ended up second guessing every male figure in my life, giving them a good examination of whether I could trust them or not. Some passed the test while others failed miserably. On one hand I longed for the loving touch of a father figure, while at the same time the very thought of a man actually touching me would make me want to vomit. What a confusing mixed bowl of emotions to have growing up.

If certain men just simply hugged me, I had all kinds of questions running through my mind.

"Why is he touching me? What else does he want from me? Is he going to do something to make me feel uncomfortable?"

This gut feeling we get around certain people can help us avoid danger sometimes. It's smart to listen to our "gut" because that feeling or thought process could, in fact, be the Holy Spirit guiding us, warning us of something or someone to avoid. But if we've ever been hurt, those feelings can grow into an unhealthy fear that we eventually live with on a daily basis. We end up questioning everything or everyone around us – will they hurt me like the others?

As we grow up, if we've ever had someone hurt us, whether it was physically, emotionally, or spiritually, we tend to start building "that wall." You know what wall I'm talking about. That barrier we build brick by brick, that gets thicker and higher with every offense. We eventually shut down and shut out everyone in our lives thinking that this will prevent us from ever getting hurt again. The problem with this theory is that it doesn't work. We only damage ourselves slowly over time, making us distant, cold, having a "no-man-shall-pass" attitude toward everyone except a select few. We become a paranoid fortress that not even God is allowed to penetrate. Pride sets in and we defend our actions out of survival mode, saying that we are justified since, after all, they don't deserve our forgiveness, let alone our time or affection.

If I were to take a poll with all of my readers, everyone would say that they've been hurt by someone very close to them, no matter what your age. The difference between living in fear or living in freedom is how you react and handle the situation. Who do you run to? What do you do? How do you go on with life? How do you get past the past?

These are all questions that I had and I didn't find the answers until I was around twenty-three years old, and I'll share these answers with you later in this book. I wish I had someone share these revelations with me at a much earlier age because I could have prevented a lot of heartache for myself, as well as those closest to me. Healing, understanding, forgiveness, and even true love became a reality to me in God's timing but I had to do my part by trusting God totally with my life, not holding anything back. I had to learn how to let go and that was one of the hardest lessons to experience.

A God Moment

We all get hurt but we can't wallow in our pain and self-pity forever because it just gets annoying to everyone else around us. People find us not so fun to hang around with after a while. We become the "fun suckers" and eventually we find ourselves alone and miserable. You don't have to be very old to find out that life isn't fair, but then again, God never promised us it would be. I find examples all throughout my Bible of people that had horrible things happen to them unfairly but there was always a purpose behind it. The ultimate example, of course, would be Jesus Himself. Jesus understands our human struggles so run to Him, ask for strength and understanding. Be careful when praying for patience though. He'll give you opportunities to be patient.

Chapter 8

The "No-No" Zones

"Peace I leave with you, My peace I give to you; not as the world gives do I give to you. Let not your heart be troubled, neither let it be afraid." John 14:27 (NKJV)

Being introduced to the sexual side of things at such an early age made me start to explore my body and how things work way too soon. Since I couldn't tell my Mom what had happened to me, I couldn't ask her the important questions I needed answered and had to figure things out on my own. I look back at how young I was and what my friends and I were doing at the ages of five to seven years old. The crazy thing is that most of this stuff happened at a very prominent day care with plenty of adult supervision. Don't think for a second that young children won't do things they shouldn't when you're not watching, even things of a sexual nature.

It's unfortunate that we're having to raise so many children that have been sexually molested and abused at very young ages so it's no wonder they know, or want to know, more about their sexual nature. They're continually bombarded with music, commercials, cartoons, television shows, and movies that are loaded with sexual content so what do we expect? We have become too accustomed to half naked, scantily dressed images that we are allowing our very young children and teens dress in a way that would even make Jesus blush with embarrassment.

We might laugh a little to ourselves when we hear someone jokingly chant, "Stop! Don't touch me there! These are my No-No squares!" We do, however, need to teach our children what is acceptable and what's not when it comes to touching, hugging, and even kissing.

Since the majority of sexual molesters are going to be related to you or very close family friends, you need to stay on your guard and listen to your children when they try to tell you, "Uncle Fred creeps me out." There may be something there that needs your attention. The majority of sexual predators don't look like sexual predators but are sometimes well-dressed businessmen or women, upstanding citizens, and very friendly. Sometimes they're the very person you love and trust the most; never suspecting they would ever be capable to do these unspeakable things, especially to a child.

I can't tell you how many times I've counseled with kids or teens that were scared to tell their parents of someone hurting them because they were afraid their parents wouldn't believe them. It is extremely rare for a child to actually lie about something like this. It's taking every ounce of courage and strength they have to finally trust you and tell you what someone may have done to them. Please parents, listen to what they have to say and take the necessary steps to begin investigating the whole situation. You don't know the damage you can do to a child by making light of what they're saying, not listening, or not believing them. They need you to come to their rescue and be the hero.

A Couple of Bad Moments

Fear had already set in after Bill threatened me to never tell anyone, especially my Mom, so I managed to keep my secret for about three more years. In the mean time, I sought after my own answers and started down a path that I'm not proud of. I discovered some things by myself but then I started experimenting with other children my age or younger. It didn't matter if it was a boy or girl. Although I was curious about the boys and how they were different than me, I felt more comfortable with other girls because I decided they couldn't hurt me and girls felt safer.

Like I said earlier, a lot of it happened at my daycare. There was a big slide on the playground that had a tower and it held around ten kids at a time, but it was underneath the tower that many things happened beyond the teachers' watching eyes. Ever played the "I'll show you mine if you show me yours" game? Yeah, that was played a lot underneath that slide tower and I was a participant on one occasion.

There's always this one really cute boy or girl at daycare or school that everyone else crushes on (or hates because they're jealous). We had a very cute, blonde-haired boy that all the girls at daycare swooned over and the game was if you caught him, then you got to hold him down and kiss him. This is the same boy that I found myself with, along with a couple of his buddies, underneath the slide tower one day.

A few days after that, it was picture day at school so I wore a dress. The boys thought they would take advantage of this rare opportunity. They kept trying to lift my dress to see my panties and wouldn't stop so I ran away from them. They chased me until I was cornered into a fence and all three or four boys began pulling at my dress. They kept lifting it up and grabbing at my panties, trying to pull them down, all in front of the rest of the daycare kids. I was scared to death and very angry, screaming at them to stop. Only after slapping and kicking them did they finally leave me alone, but not before screaming hateful words back at me. They all promised to make my life miserable after that. This was all coming from five to seven-year-old kids.

I felt so violated at that moment and I still remember the helplessness and fear that began to overwhelm my body as they were all grabbing at it. All the memories of my father came flooding back to me and I quickly ran to the bathroom to cry where no one else could see. There were more episodes very similar to this that happened throughout my life and each one made me want to crawl up in a corner, in a fetal position, while crying my eyes out. Somehow, I had to learn how to get my past out of my head where it couldn't haunt me anymore, but that didn't come until years later.

A God Moment

Sometimes I see parents laugh at their very young child behaving badly, saying how cute it is. Actions like cursing, flipping someone off, being disrespectful or smart-mouthed. This behavior isn't cute or even funny. When you laugh at them and do not discipline them while they're young, you're actually teaching them that doing these crude things gets them positive attention. Later on, you try to correct them but the damage has already been done. You've already taught them a life-lesson without even realizing it. By the time they're teenagers, you're going to have your hands full. You'll be trying to raise an almost adult that's disrespectful, who won't listen to you, or respect you. Start teaching your children while they're very young how to be respectful and compassionate toward others. Just those two things alone go a long way in your child's character development. It has been proven that a child's character and habits are usually set upon the age of five so start early.

Chapter 9

First Love

"Charm is deceitful, and beauty is passing, but a woman who fears the Lord, she shall be praised." Proverbs 31:30 (NKJV)

Do you remember your first crush—your first boyfriend or girl-friend? I think it's hilarious how young we are when we begin to say that we have a significant other in our lives. If I remember correctly, my first boyfriend happened in first grade at an elementary school in Bossier City. I remember it all like it was yesterday and it brings a silly grin to my face just thinking about the innocence of that time in my life.

When I was a small child, before the awkwardness of puberty came along, I was a pretty cute little girl. I had bright blue eyes and long, natural blonde hair. There was this little boy that had caught my eye named Jed, I think, and the flirting began. During lunch in the cafeteria one day, I remember leaning over to get a good look at Jed, who was sitting with his class across the aisle.

"I'm Heather."

I remember that I was saying it in a way to confirm the rumors of who I actually was.

"You're Heather?"

I nodded my head in confirmation and he gave me a look of approval.

We finally met officially on the playground since he was a grade ahead of me. Yes, I had my eyes set on an older man and I liked it. He was a cute, blonde-haired boy and he introduced his best friend to me. This cute boy was named Garland and he instantly liked me, too. What's a girl to do when you suddenly have two boys after you at the same time?

Garland was much more open with his advances and flirting than Jed, so eventually Garland won my heart. Of course, that made Jed furiously jealous. Remember that we're talking about six and seven-year-old kids here. Ah, the perils of dating.

Around Halloween, our school had a fall festival on campus and the older students created a walk-through haunted house. Garland asked me if I wanted to go through it with him, so I agreed. Close to the end of the tour, Garland made his move. He put his arm around my shoulder, like he'd probably seen guys do in the movies, trying to act like a man on an official date. At first it shocked me so out of impulse, I quickly got out from under his arm and ran out of the haunted house. Garland thought I ran out because I was scared of something on the tour, but it was actually his advances and touching that scared me.

Our "relationship" was over the next year after my Mom and I moved to Shreveport and I had to attend a different school. I missed Garland so much and thought about him often, wondering if I'd ever get to see him again. Little did I know that I would get that chance about three years later.

While playing at a local park, I saw some kids walking home from a local school and one particular boy caught my eye. Could it be Garland? I wasn't quite sure so the next day I waited to see if I saw my long lost love, but with no luck. One afternoon as I was playing there again, there were a couple of boys on the other side of the park and one of them looked like Garland. Is it really him? I had to know. My friends and I hung around and we could tell that he was curious as well. Did he notice me? Would he remember me? I decided to test him out, just to see if it was really him.

It wasn't until he and his brother got up to go home that I got up the nerve. I told my friend to yell out my full name in a sentence as we played, loud enough where he could hear it. After she screamed out my name, we both turned to see his reaction. His back was toward us as he was walking away, but in hearing my full name, he immediately stopped and slowly turned around. There was an awkward silence as we both just stood there staring at one another from a distance in disbelief.

We didn't speak again until the following school year. Garland and his brother moved, began attending my school, and was placed in my class. We started talking again, but since I already had a boyfriend at the local skating rink, we just remained friends. It's funny how things happen the way they do sometimes, isn't it?

I didn't have too many boyfriends growing up. Eyeglasses became a permanent part of my daily wardrobe after the third grade since we discovered that I took after both of my parents and their poor eye sight. Being hefty was never a problem either since I was always bone thin. People thought that I was anorexic and unhealthy because of my tiny figure but I ate constantly. Finding clothes to fit me was always a problem, all the way into my high school years. Even my shoes had to be bought at specialty stores since my feet were so skinny and narrow.

The cute little girl certainly went through that awkward stage of growing up and the cuteness became the "not-so-cute." My looks didn't help me in the popularity department and my attitude wouldn't help much either.

A God Moment

The innocence of growing up several years ago isn't quite what it's like for most children today. Kids have so much knowledge about things that they should never know about until they're much older and mature enough to process it correctly. Some are becoming sexually active by choice at ages as early as ten and eleven, mostly out of curiosity since it's portrayed in front of them so much. They're being taught what a sexual relationship is by television, movies, and music, but not so much from the church, or sometimes the parents. It's hard being a parent in these last days but it's not impossible. Be watchful over your children and teach them the way of God and His Word at a young age. Never have the attitude, "They would never do that. They're too young. They're good kids." You'd be surprised what your children are capable of doing at a very young age, especially if they're hanging around the wrong people and given the opportunity to be alone.

Chapter 10

"Will You Be My New Daddy?"

"Being confident of this very thing, that He who has begun a good work in you will complete it until the day of Jesus Christ."
Philippians 1:6 (NKJV)

After the divorce, it seemed that my Mom's well-meaning friends thought they had to set her up on dates and find her a new man. One particular guy, named John, would try to win both of our hearts at the same time.

Once Mom and John started dating, he said things like, "Heather and I are going to Six Flags. Are you coming with us?"

John knew the fastest way to Mom's heart was first through her daughter's. I liked John because he was a lot of fun but there was always something about him that I didn't quite trust. They dated for a while and I can't remember exactly what it was about John, but Mom finally put an end to that relationship and wasn't interested in dating anybody else for a while. Of course, Mom's friends wouldn't have any of that.

They tried to persuade her to go out with this new guy that had also recently divorced and had three young girls of his own, but she wasn't interested. Eventually, Mom was invited to a party and reluctantly went where this guy, that was supposed to be perfect her, was also invited.

Joe really didn't want to be at this party either but these mutual friends convinced him to get out and try to have a good time. Mom and Joe finally met, and though it was awkward at first, they found themselves talking all the way into the very early morning hours. They both felt a connection and had so many things in common between their pasts, but they were nervous about pursuing a relationship any further.

Mom gave Joe her number and decided to see if he would call. Several days passed and there was no phone call. Mom was certainly disappointed and wondered why he wouldn't try to contact her. Didn't he enjoy her company the other night? Didn't he feel what she felt as they were sharing and talking? Just when Mom was about ready to give up, Joe showed back up in her life and explained that he tried many times to call her but chickened out every time. He finally got the courage to drive up in his T-top Corvette and they began dating. The more Joe was around, the more I liked him and felt comfortable with him dating my Mom.

Being an only child for so long, you get really lonely and want siblings to play with, so I was always begging Mom for a baby brother or sister. After Mom saw what kind of father Bill was, she didn't want to bring another child into the world. I didn't understand that after the divorce, having another baby was out of the question. The wonderful thing about Mom dating Joe was that he had three girls and I remember the day we all met for the first time.

Joe's parents had eighty acres in the country setting of Longstreet, Louisiana, and we all took a day trip to meet them. This was our first meeting as possible future siblings and I couldn't wait to meet and play with them. I could hardly contain my excitement as I was getting ready for them to finally show up at our house to pick us up.

When they arrived, I thought they were all pretty with their tanned complexions and near jet black hair. Amy was the oldest of the three, being eight and a half years old. Mary had just turned seven years old and we found out that our birthdays were only two months and two days apart, with her being the oldest. Stacey was a very cute little two year old.

I felt like I was in heaven! I suddenly had three girls to play with, especially Amy and Mary since they were so close to my age.

I could tell they were just as excited as I was about our meeting and we got along that day very well.

When we arrived at Tom and Bet West's home in Longstreet, I took a deep breath of fresh, country air and fell immediately in love with their place and everything it had to offer. I wasn't used to being around this much land with big gardens and plenty of animals to take care of, but I knew I loved it there.

A Proposal And A Wedding

The more Mom and Joe dated, the more I was liking this guy and how he made my Mom happier than I'd ever seen her. There was just something about Joe that I trusted and that meant a lot to both me and Mom. One day I got brave as he and I were outside of our home in Bossier City.

"Will you be my new daddy?"

Joe was pretty shocked at my blunt question but it made him happy that I accepted him so fully into my life so he replied

"Well, I'll have to ask your Mom about that first."

Mom was washing dishes in the kitchen as Joe walked in with a big grin on his face.

"Why are you smiling like that?" she asked.

"Heather just proposed to me."

"How sweet. So Heather wants to marry you, huh?"

"Not exactly. She asked if I would marry you and be her new daddy."

Of course, she said "yes" and we all began to plan for the wedding that would change all of our lives forever. I was Mom's flower girl at their small, but beautiful outdoor wedding. Joe wore a nice suit and Mom found a beautiful floor-length, light blue dress that really made her blue eyes sparkle. Family from both sides, as well as mutual friends, were invited to celebrate their happy day, including the couple that set them up at the party. Everything went fine until the preacher asked the question that every couple doesn't like.

"Is there anyone here that objects to these two uniting in holy matrimony?"

Suddenly, their guy friend said, "I was paid $100 to object!"

Everyone got a good laugh because this guy was known for doing crazy things, but especially since most of them knew that it was Mom's ex-boyfriend, John, that paid him to object.

I knew God existed and I knew about prayer at that age, so I prayed many times for a brother or sister, and possibly even a new daddy. God heard both my Mom's and my prayers. He answered in His timing with just the right people. I had an instant family, more than I had ever thought or asked for, and after the wedding was over, we all began planning our new lives together.

Everything wouldn't always be great and smooth for all of us, but it was through those difficult times that made us all stronger. We were a family unit that nothing, or no one, would ever be able to break apart.

A God Moment

When we pray, God hears us. I've always been told to speak to God as if He is standing right there, like a best friend. He's not interested in fancy words, just for you to be yourself and spend time with Him. He's interested in having a full-time relationship with you, not part-time custody. Be specific with your prayers, no matter how silly or insignificant you think they are. God has our best interest at His heart and definitely wants what is best for His children. However, what we think is best versus what He knows is best, can totally be two different things. That's when we have to trust Him to direct our paths to what He's trying to get us to—a better life with His blessings in tow.

Chapter 11

A Fresh Start

"Behold, children are a heritage from the Lord, the fruit of the womb is a reward. Like arrows in the hand of a warrior, so are the children of one's youth. Happy is the man who has his quiver full of them; they shall not be ashamed, but shall speak with their enemies in the gate." Psalm 127:3-5 (NKJV)

Starting out on a new path in life, especially as a little seven-year-old girl, can be scary but yet very exciting. I now had a new daddy with three new sisters, which meant that Mom and I had to move into our new home.

Joe had a small house in Shreveport not far from the St. Vincent Mall and I can still remember every inch of that place. I ended up having my own room since Amy, Mary, and Stacey were still living with their mother, Lynn, at the time of the wedding. It was always exciting when my new sisters got to come and stay with us for a few days.

Joe started looking into getting custody of the girls and he and Mom began looking for a bigger house in preparation. They found a duplex that was actually the exact house right next door to the duplex that I had lived in at the time of Mom's and Bill's divorce. It had the same park across the street and a neighborhood with plenty of kids our age to play with.

Since Joe was working in the oilfield and made pretty good money, he was able to afford buying the entire duplex. They knocked the wall out in between, making it one big four bedroom, two bath house. They remodeled one kitchen and turned the other kitchen into a large dining room. The two living rooms became a very large great room. Although we had two front doors, Mom rearranged the living room and switched which front door we used from time to time, just to make things different.

Meet the Rest of the West Family

I already introduced Joe's parents, Tom and Bet, but they were best known by Papa and Gammy, or Gam for short. They were very different than either set of my grandparents but I loved them.

Joe had one brother named Jerry, but everyone called him "Uncle Pie" from a nick name that stuck from childhood. He also had a sister named Betty, but we all called her "Aunt T-Honey."

Uncle Jerry had one son named Jerry Dale, Jr. and he also had a nick name that followed him until he was an adult. Because he watched and loved the cartoon "Scooby Doo" so much as a child, he was able to sound just like the dog. He was then dubbed as "Scooby."

Aunt T-Honey also had one child, a daughter named Kristen, but we all called her Krissy. Scooby was the same age as Mary and me so you usually saw the three of us together more often than anyone else, although Amy was usually mixing it up with us, too. Krissy was a couple of years older than Stacey but she hung out with us when she could.

Papa and Gammy lived on a farm of eighty acres in Longstreet just off of Woodsprings Road. It was famously named "The Funny Farm", after a newspaper column that Gam wrote called "The Funny Farmer." There was always something interesting going on at the Funny Farm and I enjoyed going to visit. Papa was usually all business and work, while Gammy was the humorous, fun one, but still just as hard-working. She really knew how to cook and sometimes allowed us in the kitchen to help.

All of the grandchildren were lovingly labeled as Gammy's "Honeybuns" and we loved sleeping over on the "honeybun beds."

They were no more than just twin mattresses that were laid out on the floor, but we thought it was the most amazing place to sleep.

Sometimes we all drove down from Shreveport for the weekend and when we did, we usually went to church with Gammy and Papa at Longstreet Baptist Church. All of the girls would get special hair treatments the night before by Gammy herself after our baths. She rolled our hair in sponge rollers and then we all tried to sleep in those things, looking forward to all of the pretty curls by morning.

One unique thing about the Funny Farm was Gam and Papa had two houses that served two different purposes throughout the year. The main house was their comfortable, and somewhat modern, place they stayed in during the spring through fall months, but just next door was what they called the "winter house." It was like going back in time to the pioneer days. The amazing smell of the large wood-burning stove cooking Gam's home-made "cat-head" biscuits in the morning or brewing a pot of sassafras tea in the evening, will always be great memories in that house.

There was no television in the winter house but we always found something to do or just visited together as a family around the other wood-burning stove in the living room. I loved the warmth of getting cozy by the fire and I now have one similar in my own home today.

Gam had another amazing talent and it turned into a nice little enterprise right there on the Funny Farm. She turned the winter house into her sewing house where there was plenty of room to create her many masterpieces, especially her beautiful lingerie. Before the sewing house, Papa built her a room off of the main house that was her sewing room for several years. There she lovingly sewed amazing dresses and other clothes for all of her Honeybuns.

Gam was famous for her "Gammy panties", as we called them, because they were not only gorgeous but very comfortable and long lasting, and women everywhere loved them. She could give Victoria Secret a run for their money if she were still alive today. All of us girls eventually got old enough to learn under the instruction of Gam, and some amazing memories were made with her in that sewing house, especially learning the secrets of how to make our very own Gammy panties.

Papa was a very no-nonsense, hard-working man that worked on trains at the train yard for years. I still have my old train engineer hat that each of the Honeybuns got from him. He believed in rising early in the morning and working hard until dark, including growing numerous, huge gardens throughout his nearby acreage. When I say huge, I mean at least three football field sized gardens, carefully placed in certain spots around the Funny Farm that were within walking distance of his house. A few of our summers were spent working those gardens but we made some good money so we didn't mind the reward of hard work in the end. Although we usually griped and complained a lot, we really loved and appreciated the example Papa was for us. He taught us to appreciate everything we had, not taking anything for granted. Laziness was never an option on the Funny Farm, but at least we were never bored.

A God Moment

Cherish God's creation around you. Never overlook it's beauty. The simple moments of taking the time to look up and gaze at the stars, or admiring a landscape created by God's hands. Sometimes we make our lives so busy that we rarely slow down long enough to enjoy the wonderful things that God has prepared for us. Sitting with your family around a fire, roasting marshmallows, or going for a nature walk together for no apparent reason are wonderful. Enjoy His creation. Enjoy each other.

Chapter 12

Siblings

*"Blessed is every one who fears the Lord, who walks in His ways.
When you eat the labor of your hands, you shall be happy, and it
shall be well with you. Your wife shall be like a fruitful vine in the
very heart of your house, your children like olive plants all around
your table. Behold, thus shall the man be blessed who fears the
Lord." Psalm 128:1-4 (NKJV)*

Life was definitely becoming different but in a good kind of way.
I adjusted easily in certain areas, but had a hard time in others.
After being an only child for so long and spoiled with so many
toys by both sets of grandparents, it was hard for me to learn that it
wasn't all about me anymore. It didn't take me long to discover how
different my sisters and I actually were, but we made it work.

Joe eventually got full custody of Amy and Mary, while Stacey
chose to stay with her mother. We were slowly becoming a family
and a few years later, Stacey came to live with us, too. But for
now, we needed to learn how to go from two separate families to
becoming one. Let me introduce you to my new step-sisters.

Amy was the oldest and the strongest of us all, with the muscles
to prove it. She was rough around the edges and more like a tom boy,
but very pretty at the same time. Amy had dark brown, nearly black,
hair and beautiful hazel eyes. She had a leader quality about her and

was generally the boss when it was just her, Mary, and Stacey, but she could be a bully if you didn't obey.

I was used to being my own boss so Amy and I had issues at times. I recall on one occasion when Amy wanted to play with one of my toys and I wouldn't let her. She drew back her fist getting ready to hit me when Mom passed by and put a stop to it. Amy learned that hitting others to get her way wasn't going to work anymore and I learned that I couldn't be stingy and sharing wasn't so bad. Amy and I loved each other but we fought like sisters normally do. Amy liked stretching the boundaries and I was the tattle-tale. Well, I didn't always tell on her but I caught a lot of flack for that until we both grew up and got a lot wiser about life. We eventually became close, but not quite as close as Mary and I were when we were younger.

Mary and I were only a couple of months apart in age so we got along pretty well. We used to call each other "the step twins," and we got some strange looks on that one. We both loved horses and played together for hours with our Briar horses, making home made bridles and saddles for them all. Mary was the quiet, shy one out of the three of us, unless she was comfortable and really opened up. She loved making people laugh and acted goofy when she had the opportunity. Like Amy, Mary & Stacey had dark hair, but Mary had beautiful blue eyes with long dark eyelashes. Her eyes got her voted "best eyes" in a high school paper our senior year.

One problem that Mary had was that she was generally clumsy. When something was broken in the house and Mary wasn't the guilty one, she hollered out wherever she was in the house, "It wasn't me!" We always got a good laugh out of that.

While Mary and I acted crazy together sometimes, Amy generally thought we were too childish to hang out with her. Secretly, Mary and I thought she was pretty cool and wished we could spend more time with her. Amy spent much of her time to herself in her room listening to rock and roll music while playing solitaire on her bed.

There were times, however, that Amy did hang out with us and we always had a great time together when she did. Mom and Joe frequently called us the three musketeers because we were usually doing something together. When one of us got in trouble, the other two were usually getting in trouble right along with them.

When I say we got in trouble, I mean that we got our rear ends tore up with a belt, and that alone kept us out of a lot of serious trouble. We got a spanking if we did something bad enough to warrant it, but if we lied about it, then we'd get another one. Joe couldn't stand anybody to lie to him and he was determined to make sure he raised some honest kids.

I still remember Joe telling us, "Line up." Amy, Mary, and I would all bend over, side by side, on one of our beds, waiting for judgment to fall. Amy could generally take it better than the rest of us, while Mary squirmed everywhere. Remember me saying how skinny I was? They used to call me "tiny hiney" or "thimble butt" because it was so small. When it came to me getting a spanking, I learned quickly that I had to be very still or I'd end up getting it on my legs or back.

Now don't misunderstand, we weren't abused in any way, but simply disciplined in love, the way the bible instructs us to as parents. We never enjoyed getting disciplined but we appreciated that our parents loved us enough to correct us when we were wrong. That discipline made us all the women we are today.

We could come up with some pretty crazy things together and one of them is when we formed our own singing group called "The Ruby Diamonds." We got the name off of a board game called "Stop Thief" where one of the thieves was named Ruby Diamond. We had to have our own original song so I wrote our first, and only, hit single "Ruby Diamond." I know, it's original right? But not bad for a fifth-grader. We announced our upcoming concert to Mom and Joe and performed in the living room for them. I don't know how they kept straight faces but we're all very thankful that camera phones and YouTube didn't exist back then.

Something else that we loved to do was making forts inside the house with sheets, blankets, and any structure or piece of furniture that we could use to drape the sheets over. If we weren't building forts in the house, then we took it outside, making our own little houses with trails in the woods.

All of us loved the rock and roll of the eighties and we were all pretty good at dancing. We loved it when Joe put his record album of *Aerosmith* on and played "Walk This Way." This was the time of turn tables for vinyl 45's and 33's, before cassette tapes. A dance called "The Hustle" was popular at that time. We line danced together in the living room and tried out new moves to the latest hits of the day.

Prince, Madonna, Ratt, Bon Jovi, Van Halen, Aerosmith, Michael Jackson, and others were just a few of the hottest music stars at the time. I remember when we all had a huge crush on the group *Duran Duran*. Those were the days when MTV first started and they actually played music videos around the clock. We eventually all ended up with our own stereo system in our rooms and loved playing our music loud. I don't know how Mom and Joe lived with three teenage girls growing up at the same time, but they did it with flying colors.

Our cute little Stacey was growing up and finally came to live with us when she was around the fifth grade. After she told Joe that she really wanted to start living with us, he immediately began taking the legal steps to getting full custody of Stacey and it wasn't long before she began to move in. It took her a little while to get used to the new life of living with us everyday instead of the occasional visit, as well as the new set of rules that came with staying in the West household. We all adjusted from being a family of six to a family of seven. Wait, where did the extra kid come from?

Jody and Joey

A few months after Mom and Joe got married, they discussed the idea of having a child together, making it a "yours, mine, and ours" family. Mom knew about the infant son Joe had lost before Stacey was born, and prayed that God may give Joe another son. After all, they already had four girls so it was time for a little brother to join the family. It wasn't long before we discovered that Mom was expecting, and yes, we were going to have a little brother, which made us all very excited.

Amy and Mary were still very young but old enough to remember what happened that awful day when they lost their little brother, Jody. He was born on October 31, Halloween of all days, and he was named Joe Thomas West, Jr., but they called him Jody. Joe was working as an Emergency Medical Technician and driving ambulances at the time, but little did he know that he would get a call to his own home.

It was December 22, and the girls were getting ready for Christmas. Their mother, Lynn, had just laid Jody down for a nap on her bed, after Joe had warned her not to since he had witnessed Jody already trying to roll over.

Joe's mind was running a million miles an hour trying to grasp that he was called to his own house to save his son's life, but when he arrived, it was too late. It's unclear as to how Jody passed away since there were conflicting stories. One was that he died of Sudden Infant Death Syndrome and the other was that he rolled off the bed on his head and never recovered.

Joe remembers having both Amy and Mary in his lap, all three of them crying together over the loss of little Jody. Halloween and Christmas was hard for the next few years for all of them.

Now Mom and Joe were expecting their own son together and they were about to find out when the hospital was going to schedule her C-section. Joe was unable to go to the doctor with Mom that day, so when she got home she couldn't wait to tell him the good news. Mom knew that Jody had passed away close to Christmas but Joe never told her exactly what day it was.

"Well, we know what day we're having our baby boy!" Mom said.

"Oh yeah? What's the date?" asked Joe.

"December 22nd!"

Joe immediately became quiet with a ghostly white look on his face as he heard the date. Mom knew something was wrong.

"What's wrong Joe?"

"That's the day Jody died."

Mom quickly explained that she had no idea and would call the doctor to try to get the delivery date rescheduled.

"No. Don't change it. This must be God's way of giving my son back to me in His way, His timing. Don't change anything."

Joe Thomas West, III, or Joey as we called him, was born on December 22nd, on the same day, within the same hour, that Jody had passed away a few years earlier. Although Jody's death would never be forgotten, the 22nd of December would now be a happy day instead of one of mourning.

While Amy, Mary, and Stacey were visiting other family, I was with my father, Bill, during Joey's delivery. I was lucky enough to be the first sister back home after Joe and Mom brought Joey home from the hospital. I bragged how I was the first sister to get to hold him.

We all instantly fell in love with Joey and he ended up having not one Mom, but five. With Joey being the baby of the family and the only boy, you can imagine how spoiled he was. Of course, as he grew, he aggravated us all, as little brothers are so famous for, but we loved him anyway.

As Joey got older, he noticed how all of his sisters went off to see their other sets of parents or family but he always stayed home. He wondered why he didn't have an extra set of parents like we all did. It took him a while to understand why we left but he later understood how fortunate he was to have his parents still intact as a family unit. After a few years, I stopped going to visit my father so it was just me and Joey at the house when the other girls went to see their mother.

Because Joey was so much younger than the rest of us and the only boy, he often played alone. I remembered how miserable I was having no one to play with when I was little so I went into his room and began building sophisticated roads, highways, and towns for all of his Hot Wheels cars that he collected. We both played together for hours and I felt a special bond with him when we spent that time together, just the two of us. All of us girls had our own special relationship with Joey and still do to this day.

There are so many wonderful memories of us all growing up together. Although we weren't all blood related, we always considered ourselves a genuine family and we loved it. I've seen so many families that were like ours, and they just couldn't make it through the tough times, but somehow, we made it work. We fought for our family, pushing past the flaws, differences, and mistakes that we all made, and tried to focus on the love and positive side of everything we could find in each other. Family became a different meaning for us, but we were still a family, then, and now.

A God Moment

Making a new family come together and work well can be a chore, but yet very rewarding when God is allowed to lead in that family. No matter what you may go through in life, as an individual, or as a family unit, if you put God first and fully trust Him with your lives, God can work on your behalf and for your favor. Honor and love Him by being obedient to His Word.

Chapter 13

The Secret Is Out

"And you shall know the truth, and the truth shall make you free. . . .Therefore if the Son makes you free, you shall be free indeed." John 8:32, 36 (NKJV)

I'd like to tell you about a couple of other people that were very important to me as a child. Bill was the oldest of three children. He had a sister, Audrey, and the youngest was a brother named Gerry, and I loved them both. People thought I was Aunt Audrey's "mini me" since we both had long blonde hair and we spent so much time together when we could. Aunt Audrey was a lot of fun and I have so many wonderful memories with her. I always thought of Aunt Audrey as the cool, much older big sister that I never had, until Amy and Mary came along later.

Uncle Gerry was also a lot of fun to be with and would always call me his sidekick. Whenever Bill had me for his visits, no matter where Uncle Gerry was going, he put me on his shoulders and we hung out as buddies.

We had this routine every morning when I happened to be spending the night with Grandma. While Grandma cooked a big breakfast for everyone, Uncle Gerry waited in his bed, pretending to still be asleep, so I could come wake him up. I anxiously awaited for Grandma's signal to go get Uncle Gerry up. I quietly entered his room, sneaked up to his bed, and then pounced on him.

"It's time to get up! Breakfast is ready!"

His part was to act totally surprised and then a tickle fight always ensued. It was the highlight of my day.

I love to recall these good times, these fun memories of my father's family. The only problem with memories is that you remember the bad stuff, too. As much as we would like to, it's hard to forget our past, whether it may be things that we regret we've done on our own free will, or things that have been done to us by others. Although there are things that we all wish we could do over, it seems that the memories of pain caused by others are the hardest to escape from and to forgive. We can't control everything that happens to us in this life, but we can control how we handle the hard times as they come along.

I've been asked why I still love and trust a God that allows bad things to happen to good people. It's simple really. God created us with free will, but man chose to bring sin into this world. This means we have some bad people that choose to do bad things, whether it was carefully thought out, or a huge mistake. God gets blamed for a lot of things that He has nothing to do with and I'm very thankful that I had enough forethought to know not to be angry with Him about my past. The question is how do we move past our memories, our nightmares?

So far, I had managed to keep my secret from everyone but it overwhelmed me one night as I laid in my bed. I couldn't go to sleep due to my mind bringing up all sorts of images that I didn't care to recall. I began to cry as everything that had happened on that dirt access road with my father only a few years earlier crept back into my thoughts, persecuting me every passing minute. Moments like this happened often but I had learned to cope by crying for a while and then pushing the pain of the memories to the furthest back corner of my mind.

What I didn't know is that Mom heard me crying while walking past the door of my room. Walking into my room and sitting on the edge of my bed, Mom began to try to comfort me, asking me why I was crying. Fear immediately took over. I couldn't tell her. How do you tell your Mom, the closest person in your life, something that will surely break her heart? So many questions began running through my mind: What would happen if I told? Would I ever see my Daddy again? What about his side of the family? So many questions that I didn't have an answer for.

"Nothing, Momma. Nothing's wrong." I replied.

"Then why are you crying? Something is wrong Heather and you know you can tell me so please talk to me."

"I can't Momma. I can't tell because he said he would never take me anywhere again if I did."

Mom began thinking quickly about who I may be talking about. The only person she could think of was Bill but she wanted to see what I would say.

"Who said you can't tell?"

I just couldn't tell her. Mom didn't want to push me too hard so she made a suggestion that I come in the living room where Joe was and I agreed. Joe was sitting in his recliner and I crawled up into his lap, as Mom sat across from us on the couch. At first I still didn't want to say anything but I think I knew that there was no way out of this without saying something. Even though I knew Mom was sitting right there, I felt more comfortable telling Joe, looking at him, not her.

I slowly began telling everything in detail as I remembered and I began thinking that they were handling everything a lot better than I expected. What I didn't understand in my young mind is that they didn't want to react to this horrible news right in front me so they both kept their composure until I finally settled back into bed and fell asleep.

After discussing what to do, Mom called Bill to see what he had to say about everything I had just revealed. To Mom's surprise, Bill readily admitted what he had done.

"Yeah, I did it. My new wife is helping me get through it."

"Help you get through it? What about Heather?"

After giving him everything she had and more, Bill knew he would be lucky if he was ever allowed to see me again. Mom didn't make any promises until she had time to pray and think about everything. Right now her stomach was in knots and her mind was whirling of what to do next.

Mom then called Grandma, Bill's mother, to explain what I had just told them. Everyone was so upset but Mom knew she had to think smart about this whole thing. Her first reaction was to kill him or, at the very least, have him thrown in jail, but then she thought of me. She knew that I had already been through enough and didn't want me to feel that any of it was my fault or be punished for something that I had no fault in.

She knew that she couldn't completely take my father away from me because even through everything that happened, I still loved him. To this day, I thank her for putting her motherly instinct and personal agenda aside, thinking only of me and my well being, not only physically but emotionally and mentally. At the same time, however, she knew that she had to do something to prevent this from ever happening again, to protect me.

While on the phone with Grandma, Mom gave the stipulation that if any of them ever wanted to see me again, they would all have to assure her that I would never be left alone with Bill, ever. Grandma agreed that she would see to it and watch over me. Mom would rather have locked me away where no one could ever hurt me again, but she knew that wasn't possible. She had to trust the family to protect me and that worked, for a while.

It wasn't long after that, that we found out Uncle Gerry had died in a head-on collision in his small sports car with a large truck. He was coming back home to Arkansas from Colorado, round trip with no sleep. Trying to get back to his fiance, he fell asleep at the wheel and never made it back. We were all devastated by his death, including me. I had never been to a funeral before; never seen a dead body lying in a casket. It was also my first time to see my father cry.

This was the first time that Mom and Joe had the chance to see Bill after me telling them about what he had done to me. They didn't want to cause a scene with the family so they kept quiet and respectful. Once the funeral was over, we all went to my Namaw's house to eat and visit with the family. While there, Mom found a time to be alone with Bill.

"If you ever so much as look at her the wrong way, I swear I will throw you in jail so fast it will make your head spin!"

Mom meant every word and Bill knew it.

A God Moment

God always watches over His children. He never neglects you or fails to protect you. The Bible describes God as an emotional God. He gets angry, He gets jealous, and I can imagine He cries as He looks upon us and what we all have to go through in life sometimes. That's why He sent His Son, Jesus. There was no other way to save us from ourselves, our sin, our fate. . .hell. Never blame God for your troubles. Sometimes the mess we're in is the mess we've made for ourselves, while other times it's no fault of our own, simply because of sin being in the world. Instead of getting angry with God, turn to Him for your healing and strength to make it through another day. The Bible says, "You have not because you ask not." That's not meaning that God is our Santa Claus in the sky and all we have to do is ask Him for our every wish to become a reality. This refers to more spiritual matters so crawl up into His arms and let Him love on You while you ask for wisdom on what to do in difficult situations.

Chapter 14

Texas, Here We Come

"For the eyes of the Lord run to and fro throughout the whole earth, to show Himself strong on behalf of those whose heart is loyal to Him." 2 Chronicles 16:9a (NKJV)

Even when you think your life is falling apart, you can always pick up the pieces and keep going. Yes, your life will be different now, but sometimes different can be a new adventure, if you look at it that way. It's like taking broken pieces of colored glass or pottery and creating a whole new masterpiece. Something else that these pieces really weren't meant to create in the beginning, but in the end became something beautiful. It's all in the eyes of the creator, the vision of the artist. We can choose to stay broken or allow God to pick up our pieces, put us back together the way He sees us and not the way we see ourselves.

I wasn't healed of my past yet but I learned how to move on, despite my inner pain. I knew and loved God but didn't fully understand my relationship with Him. I accepted Jesus as my Lord and Savior at the young age of around eight. Mom and Dad (Joe) found a large church in Shreveport that ran a bus route in our neighborhood and allowed them to come get us for their amazing children's ministry every Sunday. That was my first real experience with God, although my Namaw and Grandma James took me to their church from time to time.

I felt so excited about going to church and even at that age, I felt God tugging on my heart in such a powerful way. I understood what Jesus did for me and I broke down crying at the thought of His sacrifice for us all. God put something inside my heart to love and truly care about other people. I wanted to help others in any way I could, and became a good listener. Now that I look back, I can see how God was preparing my heart for ministry, all those years ago.

Have you ever looked back and examined how all the little puzzle pieces that once never made sense suddenly created a full picture that amazed you? Never second guess what God is doing for you, even through the struggles and tests of life. Those are the times that define our character and strengthen us. We need to run to God, while trusting Him and allowing our faith to stretch to new boundaries we never thought we could go.

The important thing about those times in the valley is to learn the lesson that is required, not just pouting and throwing yourself a big pity party. Those parties are no fun for anyone except you. They're definitely not productive, so pick yourself up, including your bottom lip that you've been dragging on the floor, and allow God to guide you where He wants and needs you.

The Move

Life began to slowly get back to normal and Dad (Joe) was still working for the oil field, making pretty good money. At first, he delivered drill bits to the oil rigs and he liked for us to tag along to "help" him find the rig locations. Later on we figured out that Dad just liked having us around to keep him company, but we didn't mind.

Before the laws changed, Dad secured an old bus bench seat to the bed of the truck, directly behind the cab, where all three of us girls rode many times. We wore our shorts and rolled our shirt sleeves up, hoping to get a tan, with the wind blowing through our hair.

Later, Dad got a promotion at another oil field company but it required us to move to Liberty City, Texas. We had never heard of Liberty City but it was in between Gladewater and Kilgore, only a couple of hours away from Shreveport. We were all excited about a new life, a new school, and a new house. We moved into a beautiful, large brick house in a nice subdivision that had plenty of other kids around our ages. It was here that I met my first best friend for life.

My first day of walking into that fourth grade class was scary but the kids surprisingly welcomed me with open arms. One pretty girl, named Tammy, and I quickly hit it off and found that we both had a lot in common, including the love of horses. We became inseparable and visited each other at our homes often. Tammy made my time in Texas an adventure and I loved her like a sister.

Mary and I were separated into different classes and Amy was on a different campus with the older kids where she got to be in the band. This school was a lot larger than what we were used to but I really enjoyed the extra opportunities it offered. Since we arrived at the school in the middle of the year, we missed out on a few things at first but fifth grade had several defining moments for me. My singing and love for music was really discovered that year by my music teacher, who was also the gifted and talented teacher.

Music and Singing

My first singing solo happened in my fifth grade class Christmas play, where I was chosen to play the role of Rudolph the red-nosed reindeer. They held auditions because this role required a singing solo of the intro to the Rudolph song. You know, the part that goes, "You know Dasher, and Dancer, and Prancer, and Vixon. . . ." I know, I'm sorry. You're singing it now, aren't you?

Anyway, I was discovered as having a great voice for my age and I loved being out front. I always enjoyed singing to the rock and roll music that we all grew up with on the radio but now I actually understood that I had a gift and wanted to pursue it more.

My music breakthrough happened during a routine test in music class; a test that I thought was crazy. They were determining who was gifted and talented in music by allowing every student to take this test. Whoever passed by a certain percentage of correct answers became a part of the elite group of young musicians.

I remember thinking that the test was so easy that everyone would pass it and really wouldn't work, but it did. I didn't understand that everyone doesn't hear tones and pitches the same way. The test consisted of blocks of smiley faces with one block containing faces that were the same, and the other with faces that were different. As we listened to two separate tones, we had to determine if the two tones were the same or different by circling the corresponding smiley faces. I found it very easy to hear even the slightest difference in tones and passed with a perfect score.

I was so excited to learn that I had made one of the coveted spots in the gifted and talented music program. We started out learning how to play recorders and I ended up flying through the music book that we were given. I already knew how to read music from a former music class in Louisiana.

We were also taught how to play the piano but only with one finger. It was then we were assigned to different sized xylophones that formed a "choir". I played one of the metal ones that had the lead melody tones and it sounded really great with the others playing the harmony. We all had the opportunity to play in front of the Dillard's at a local mall for a special Christmas program. I absolutely loved playing music for an audience. Little did I know how much this class would prepare me for my future.

Another thing that I loved about living in Texas was that we were able to take twirling classes. Amy had gotten in trouble and was grounded so she wasn't able to take the classes, but Mary and I taught Amy everything we learned when we got home anyway. I really loved twirling and even thought about trying out for a twirling position once I got into high school later. I changed my mind once I saw the extremely small uniforms they had to wear.

We loved it in Texas but only after a couple of years, Dad's job moved us all back to Shreveport again. We still had our old house that we remodeled on Penick Street so we got to move back into familiar surroundings. Leaving Tammy was the hardest part of the move and I'll never forget my last day at school with her.

Everyday my class had a leader for the day and although it wasn't my turn yet, they moved my name up the list to make my last day special. Any time I needed a helper I always picked Tammy to be with me. It was so hard leaving that classroom after I saw her hiding, crying inside her lunch box. Tammy's family and Mary's best friend all came to see us off that afternoon at our house and we all had another good cry together. We promised to keep up with each other and we did.

A God Moment

Having a great best friend is something to be cherished but yet hard to find. Someone who you can always trust to keep your secrets, to be there for you no matter what, even on your worst day. God knew we needed that companionship, that special relationship. After all, He did create us. We all have a hole in our spirit-man that only God Himself can fill. Yes, human friendship is amazing, but it is also flawed, since we are sinful by nature. Only God's kind of friendship is perfect and He offers that kind of relationship to us all. All we have to do is ask for it. Getting saved, or born again, is much more than "fire insurance" or a "get out of hell free" card—it's a real relationship with God.

Chapter 15

Oh No! Not Again!

"For the eyes of the Lord are on the righteous, and His ears are open to their prayers; but the face of the Lord is against those who do evil. And who is he who will harm you if you become followers of what is good?" 1 Peter 3:12-13 (NKJV)

After the divorce between my Mom and Bill, he tried to move on with his life. He went through a period of growing his hair and beard out really long, looking like he was trying to get back to the sixties time period. He shortly married again to a very young and pretty lady named Kate. I remember that she was nice and had very long, thick reddish brown hair. She looked like she was a hippie herself, but it didn't last very long after Bill found out that she was cheating on him.

Ironically, Bill called Mom, crying to her about what Kate had done to him. He began apologizing to her for what he now understood that he had done to her a few years earlier. Mom wanted to laugh but she kept her cool and remained the lady that she always was.

Bill later found another lady who he eventually married. I thought Carol was pretty and she had short red hair. I think Bill had a thing for red-heads. We seemed to hit it off pretty good. Carol was different and seemed to make Bill happy so things were pretty good when I went to visit.

They lived their lives in a laid back way, not as strict as it was at Mom and Dad's house. I liked that they let me break the rules sometimes when I was there. They kept wine, as well as marijuana, in the refrigerator and sometimes watched shows that made me blush. They didn't smoke marijuana all the time but occasionally Dad asked me to go get the baggie so he could make himself a pipe.

I got to get away with things that I would never try back home, although I never really pushed the envelope much. About the worst thing I ever tried was smoking cigarettes. Carol was a smoker like my Mom but one day she just casually said something that blew me away.

"If you ever want to smoke a cigarette, just ask me and I'll give you one."

I had never even thought about trying to smoke a cigarette, but now that she gave me an open invitation, I thought I might give it a shot, just to see what the big deal was. I got up the courage and asked for a cigarette. I hacked and choked with my first drag. I felt so embarrassed but I knew I had to finish what I started so I faked like I was actually smoking. I was just keeping the smoke in my mouth and then blowing it out. I decided then and there that smoking was definitely not for me, but I never really liked it anyway. Mom smoked at the house and I always hated how the smell got all over everything.

I started growing up and my body began changing a little at the age of eleven. Since I was so skinny, there wasn't much change to speak of but I didn't care because I finally started feeling like a young lady. I wanted to fit in and grow up like the other girls around me. These changes in my body started a downward spiral all over again with Bill.

Every summer I spent two weeks with Bill and his side of the family in Arkansas and I was usually spoiled by everyone while I was there. After time had passed, everyone forgot all about the agreement that I was to never be left alone with Bill, and that was a big mistake.

Without going into detail, within a two week period, things happened that should never have happened, but it all progressed very slowly. Everything he did was so gradual and slick. I ended up so brainwashed and wasn't myself by the time the two weeks were over. I was pretty modest when I showed up but by the time I left, I had no problem taking my clothes off in front of anyone.

It started with Bill looking at a book of anatomy, I think, and began this conversation about our bodies and sexuality. He was a very intelligent man and was talking very professional. It was like he was trying to be a real father, explaining things since I was growing up. I'm assuming he noticed some physical changes with me and thought he'd capitalize on it.

I can't recall how we ended up in his bedroom but I remember feeling scared and very nervous. He started showing me graphic pictures out of a dirty magazine he had. Inappropriate touching then progressed to other things. Intercourse never happened but what he did do was damaging enough. I just laid there looking toward the door at my left, thinking of a plan of action, but I didn't have one. I wanted to run away, but where would I go? I couldn't run back home since it was so far away, but I desperately wanted my Mom. I wanted to cry so bad but I tried to just stay numb to what was happening.

After it was all over, Bill told me to get dressed and treated me so nice. He reminded me that I couldn't tell anyone what was happening because they wouldn't understand. It would be our little secret. He was acting like it was normal for him to "love" me this way. He bought me a lace bra and panty set and said it was for a late birthday present because I was growing up into a young lady. Bill made sure that I stayed happy so I wouldn't have any reason to get mad at him and possibly tell on him.

These inappropriate times with Bill were nearly a daily occurrence now and each day that passed, I was slowly becoming someone else. I slept in the living room and one night Bill crawled into bed with me, did what he came for, and then disappeared back into his bedroom, with his wife never knowing what had just happened.

The only time he actually hurt me was when he tried to have intercourse but when I screamed out in pain, it scared him and he quickly stopped. He didn't want to hurt me, especially when he knew that this whole thing could blow up in his face quickly with one word from me.

I felt so dirty and ashamed of everything that was happening and I was scared to tell in fear that no one would believe me, or worse, blame me. There were times that I felt so guilty or angry about everything that I would go hide and slip into a temporary depression. I was angry at the world. One such time, Carol came outside where I went to be alone and began really getting on to me for my attitude.

I remember thinking, "Lady if you only knew what your husband is doing to me behind your back, then I'd have the last say in this conversation. Maybe then you'd understand my attitude!"

I just took it and kept quiet. It seemed simpler that way.

Bill thought he was doing me a favor by educating me in the ways of sexual behavior and even taught me how to kiss correctly. Needless to say, it was very awkward to have your own father kissing you, showing you all the techniques on how it's done. Can you say, "Gross!"? Yes, I thought you could. No matter how disgusted I was with anything he did, I felt like I had to go along with it because I was too afraid to know what might happen if I didn't. Not to mention the awkwardness and embarrassment of it all.

One day Grandma had everyone over to her house and as usual, she went shopping and bought some cute outfits for me. We were all hanging around as she told me to go try the clothes on but instead of heading toward to the bathroom to change, without even thinking, I began taking off my shirt in front of everyone like it was a normal thing to do. Bill immediately walked out of the room and everyone else started yelling at me.

"No, wait! What are you doing?"

I looked around and was thinking, "What am I doing wrong?"

I felt so uncomfortable and ashamed at that moment but it also made me realize how far I had gone down in nearly two weeks with Bill. I was later scolded by Carol again.

"Why did you try to do that? Don't you know that you embarrassed your father so bad that he had to walk out of the room to keep from seeing you take your shirt off?"

I didn't say anything. What could I say? I didn't want to hurt her. She wouldn't believe me anyway.

The two weeks were finally over and it was time for Bill to take me back home. I had bought a diary while I was there and for the last couple of days I began to write in the past dated pages just to fill them up with stuff noteworthy. I knew better than to record what had been happening with Bill in it and he kept asking what I was writing, in fear that I might incriminate him in my diary. About half way home we stopped at a rest area and that's when Bill started manipulating my silence.

"You know you can't tell anybody what happened, right? Your Mom said that if anything happened between me and you that she would throw me in jail. Do you know what they do to guys in jail?"

I shook my head as he then started giving me a series of horror story situations. I began to cry, which is what he wanted. He wanted me to feel sorry for him so I would never tell anyone his dirty little secret.

Bill asked, "You don't want that to happen to your daddy now do you?"

"Of course not."

He hugged me and assured that everything would be alright as long as we kept the past two weeks to ourselves. I kept our secret for about a couple of years before Mom caught me crying again.

A God Moment

The devil is a clever liar. He knows how to get us to sin and which buttons to push. It usually takes a gradual fade, deceiving us a little at a time. He even helps us with the excuses that we need to justify our actions, helping us to feel better in the middle of our sin. We become desensitized to what we once knew was wrong, then believing it's not so bad after all. Be careful how you allow the devil in to deceive you, little by little, until he has you fooled and hooked. We won't be so easily deceived if we stay close to God and His Word.

Chapter 16

"Will You Adopt Me?"

"Whoever receives one little child like this in My name receives Me." Matthew 18:5 (NKJV)

As bad as I wanted to talk to someone about my summer and what happened with Bill, I knew I couldn't say anything. There were so many emotions and my mind was going crazy, thinking about everything. I felt so alone in my pain and confusion. I learned once again to push back my thoughts and try to avoid anything that reminded me of the past. I desperately wanted some positive back in my life.

One day I was talking with Mom and I don't remember how or who started the conversation but the subject of adoption came up. Mom told me that Dad would love to adopt me if I wanted him to. I hadn't thought about adoption but now I was intrigued and began asking questions as to what would happen if he did. I always felt like the odd one in the family since I was the only fair-skinned, blonde-haired kid in the bunch, with a different last name. I liked the idea of having my name changed to fit in with the rest of the family and I considered Joe as my Dad already anyway.

Mom suggested that I go ask Dad personally so I crawled up in his lap and asked if he would adopt me. I remember watching the biggest smile come across his face and he gladly accepted. They both started the legal steps after they called Bill for his consent and he graciously agreed. Mom thought he wouldn't have any problem with it since he wouldn't have to pay his child support every month anymore, but Grandma didn't like the idea at all.

"Well, if she changes her last name then I'm cutting her out of my will! She won't be part of this family anymore."

That hurt me a lot. I later learned more about the history of Bill's parents when I was old enough to understand. Grandpa had an issue with infidelity and since Grandma knew about it, she drank alcohol to help herself cope. Grandma had an explosive temper and it was worse if she had been drinking. Bill had to learn how to have quick reflexes to dodge whatever object was within Grandma's reach that she could hurl in their general direction, no matter who she was mad at.

I had a bad habit of coming behind my Mom, drinking from her coke cans or glasses of coke, so when I tried to take a drink from Grandma's glass, she said, "You don't want to drink any of that. That's Grandma's special drink."

I always went shopping with Grandma and sometimes we went through the drive through of a local liquor store to pick up her drink of choice. She always said how Grandpa didn't need to know about our trip or what she got. I never told a soul. I began to understand that just because Grandma said something, didn't necessarily mean that she actually meant it. Chances were that she wouldn't remember half of what she said the next day.

Moving to the Funny Farm

While the adoption process had started, Mom and Dad began thinking about moving all of us out to the Funny Farm in Longstreet. Gam and Papa had divided up the eighty acres between the three kids and Dad had already picked out a great spot to put a house. Mom and Dad found an old house to be moved for a great price so we got busy clearing the land and getting it ready for the house to be delivered. It was a simple wood frame home that was way too small for our family of seven but Dad was going to use the money from the sale of the other house to add on and make it much bigger.

School was about to start but the house wasn't ready to move into yet so Dad gave us a choice. Our first option was to go ahead and start school in Shreveport while we got the house ready to move into and then transfer to Logansport High School later in the year.

There weren't many good schools to choose from where we lived. Mom and Dad thought the best option for us was a Catholic school, even though we weren't Catholic. For two years we learned all about the Catholic religion and it's rituals. Although it was interesting in a way to watch how they did things, none of us felt the Spirit of God there and we disagreed with several of their beliefs.

It seemed that everyone felt that by sending their troubled kid at that school that somehow they could straighten them out. In a lot of ways, the kids in that school were worse than public school so we were glad to have the chance to get out of there.

The second choice was to move into the house with no running water, no electricity, and little furniture but start school at the beginning of the year at Logansport with everyone else. We were excited about starting a new school and we figured moving into the house early would be a lot like camping so we took option number two.

Dad used a generator to run a small window unit inside the dining room since we were moving in during the hottest part of the summer. We piled all of our mattresses on the floor in that one room so we could at least sleep in the cool with no mosquitoes. Without us being able to cook anything we ate a lot of bologna or peanut butter and jelly sandwiches. We brushed our teeth out of several red Solo cups. We used one to rinse the toothbrush, one to rinse out our mouth, and one to spit in.

There was a natural running spring just down the hill and through the woods from the house, so we used it to fill up a few five gallon buckets each morning and hauled them back up to the house for our water that day. Dad put out a big wash tub in the front yard and we filled it up with the freezing cold water from the spring in the morning, hoping that the sun would warm it up by the time we took a bath in it that night. We waited until it was pitch black outside and each of us kids took our turn going outside to take our bath with Mom helping us. I remember being buck naked and screaming as Mom poured the still ice cold water over my skinny little body.

We quickly learned to appreciate running water, electricity, and all of the other little things that we generally take for granted. The house was really cute but Mom had a special touch for decorating and it didn't take her long to get the place looking great. The first rooms they built onto the house were a huge 48' x 24' family room and a very large bedroom for me and Mary to share. Dad ran out of money before he could build Amy's room so he made the hard decision to sell our ski boat to make sure Amy's room was built. Stacey hadn't come to live with us yet at this point but when she did, we turned the back breakfast room into her room.

Now that I've mentioned the ski boat, there's a funny story about one of our ski trips. We didn't live too far from Cross Lake in Shreveport so a lot of times, we would be waiting for Dad to get home from work to take us water skiing. Amy, Mary, and I got really good at it and was just learning how to slalom ski when Dad sold the boat.

On one windy day, it was my turn to ski when I thought Dad was playing around with me. I was trying to get in position for him to pull me up but it was hard since the boat kept pulling me. I fought against it, finally got situated and was already half way up when I kept signaling for him to go faster. They all just laughed because Dad had the boat in neutral the whole time and wasn't trying to pull me at all. I was so light that the wind pushing the boat was enough to pull me out of the water.

Now, where was I? Oh yeah. . . .the house. Mom and Dad still live there in that house, and some things have changed since we've all grown up and left the nest. At first, Mom was concerned about having such a large house, especially the huge family room, but Dad reminded her of what was coming.

"Have you forgotten that we have five kids and one day they're all going to get married and have their own kids? We'll need every inch of this house when they all show up at once, like during the holidays."

He was right. We now have twelve grandchildren between all of us and that's not including all the cousins that show up for holidays, too. We always have a great time when we all come together. Instead of cousins, they feel more like brother and sister to us.

Shortly after we got settled in to Longstreet, the adoption went through with no problems and I remember the day we all showed up in the Judge's chambers to seal the deal.

"Well, you know that Mr. Joe can use his parental rights now don't you?"

We all knew what the judge meant and got a good laugh out of it since Dad had been punishing me for years with old fashioned spankings, or as we put it in the South: "butt whoopin's." It felt so good walking out of that office knowing that I was now officially a "West" kid and I had my new birth certificate to prove it.

Church Life

After we moved to Texas, we found a church that we all loved and went together as a family for the first time on a regular basis. We really enjoyed going to church, loved our hilarious Pastor, and actually got involved a little bit. We hated losing our new church family when we moved back to Louisiana but after we moved to Longstreet, we found another church family that we quickly fell in love with.

We had already visited Longstreet Baptist Church several times with Gam and Papa when we came to visit but now we were getting to go every Sunday. I loved watching our family get involved and it wasn't long before all of us joined the church choir. At the time, they allowed the teenagers to sing with the adults as long as there was enough room in the loft to hold us. It was there that I learned a lot about myself and my singing talent.

At first, it was pretty simple since we just sang along with the congregation out of the hymn book. Every now and then someone would sing a special. Soon things changed when we got a new choir director and he started helping each of us reach our full potential. I was classified as one of three first sopranos since I could sing so high. That meant that we sang on the front row but I didn't mind as long as I got to stand beside Penny Smith who quickly became a great friend, even though she was older.

Between Mom, Penny, the choir director, and Aunt T-Honey, who was our talented piano player, they all had a hand in bringing me to where I am today with my singing. At the house, Mom critiqued me, pushed me to do better but with love, support, and encouraging words. Aunt T-Honey saw my potential and we sometimes sang together around the piano with her alto harmony.

Other than Mom, Penny was one of the first people to notice my voice. She continually elbowed me in the choir, telling me to sing out and not hold back. She helped me have the confidence I needed to take that extra step with my singing. As I got older and my voice was getting stronger, Penny told me to remember who first discovered my talent when I made my first million. I just laughed and agreed that I would give her a share of my riches.

Our choir director worked with me and said that I was singing through my nose, especially on the high notes. I needed to open up my throat to get a clearer sound but I had no idea what he was talking about, no matter how he tried to explain it to me. I got the concept but didn't know how to actually do it until one day it happened by accident.

In the middle of practicing for our first Christmas cantata, I was hitting a very high note when suddenly my throat opened up and I felt, as well as heard, the change in my throat and voice. Still singing, I turned to the choir director who heard it from several feet away and turned to look at me.

I pointed at my throat with a facial expression that asked, "Is this it? Is this what you've been talking about?"

He ran over to me and said, "That's it! You've got it!"

My first solo in church with our choir was when I was about eleven or twelve years old and it was the song "Standing On Holy Ground." I remember how I felt having the privilege of singing one of the verses alone and I was hooked. I started singing more solo specials whenever I could. Eventually I got up the nerve to start singing at school special events and assemblies. I found what I thought was my main destiny in life: to sing for God.

A God Moment

God creates us all very uniquely and there is something special that God gave you to use to honor Him. It's up to you to figure out what that special something is. If it's not obvious then pray and ask God to show you exactly what your calling is. You could be a prayer warrior, an encourager, counselor, teacher, or many other things that can be useful for the kingdom of God. As Christians we have a two-fold purpose on this earth: (1) To worship God, having a relationship with Him, and (2) to spread the good news of the Gospel (the Bible), telling others of the goodness of God, helping them to come to Christ. Find your calling and begin using it. It's there for a reason.

Chapter 17

The Scary World of Junior High

"Yet in all these things we are more than conquerors through Him who loved us." Romans 8:37 (NKJV)

Once we got moved into our house in Longstreet we began preparing to start our new school in Logansport. At that time, the elementary portion, called Rosenwald Elementary, was located on Hwy 5 a few miles away from the high school, which was located on Gum Street. The high school was an old two story building that smelled of floor wax from constantly buffing the hard wood floors in the big, open hallways.

Since the building wasn't air conditioned we raised all the large windows and prayed for a breeze. We were used to not having air conditioning at our house. Before Mom and Dad were able to afford central air and heat, we had an attic fan and carefully placed wood-burning stoves throughout the house. While everyone at school was dripping wet with sweat, we were pretty much used to the heat.

The junior high classes and cafeteria were placed in other buildings beside the high school. I started my seventh grade year there and it was hard for me to make many friends. I was going through my most awkward time of growing up and figuring out who I was. I sometimes tried too hard to make friends, which only pushed them away, but I eventually learned what it meant to be a good friend. One of those lessons was for me to just be myself and respect the

Christian young lady I was trying to become no matter what people said about me. Another lesson was to remain humble while I loved and respected everyone around me.

I think there is a time in every person's life that we have to look at ourselves in the mirror. I mean really look at ourselves for who we are on the inside. Sometimes that can be one of the hardest things to do because we don't always like what we see, or even admit there's anything wrong. It's hard to see the faults in ourselves but that's where change begins. I remember the day I had my awakening to my true self.

Among all the problems I was having at school, some of it was my own fault with my attitude toward others. I couldn't see that I was actually asking for some of it by how I was unintentionally coming across to people. I had a bad day and came home complaining and upset so Mom called in reinforcements. Mom asked Amy and Mary to be very honest about how they see me at school and they unloaded a list that was bitter to take.

I got so upset and began being defiant, screaming out that it wasn't true. I didn't want to hear that I had faults, that I was wrong. I was a good girl that tried to stay out of trouble. How could I be this self-righteous, judgmental, and awkward person they were describing? I knew Amy and Mary weren't trying to hurt me but I got angry with their honesty and didn't want to accept anything they had to say.

While I was losing it, Mom had to lightly slap my face to get me to settle down. That was the first and last time Mom had ever done that. It didn't hurt but it startled me enough to get me to calm down, which was what she wanted. I felt cornered and wanted to run but I knew I had to sit and listen to what she needed to say.

That night was when I learned that I could be a good girl without having the wrong attitude along with it. I had to learn patience, compassion, and understanding. It didn't happen overnight but I slowly took strides in the right direction.

Ever read the book *The Ugly Duckling*? That is exactly what I felt like when I was in junior high school. I was accused of being anorexic since I was bone thin but I kept telling everyone that I ate all the time. I really did eat frequently but I was also very active and had a high metabolism so I burned off the calories just as fast as I ate them.

Clothes were very hard to find since I wore size 00 in my pants and I had more of a boyish figure, with no girlish assets to brag about. My nickname from a few of the guys was "Feather" since I was so skinny. Puberty wouldn't fully hit me until around the age of fourteen so I guess you could say I was a late bloomer.

I got bullied and picked on a lot and how I reacted really didn't help anything. I didn't have the best hair and didn't really know how to fix it correctly until much later. I had oily skin with pimples everywhere and wore cheap glasses that didn't compliment my facial features much. I had a complex concerning my looks and the boys at my school constantly played cruel games with me.

They acted like they were coming on to me and even sometimes "complimented" my clothes or what little make-up I was allowed to wear, but I knew they didn't mean it since they laughed together at me right after. I even had a couple of guys pretend to ask me out, but when they thought I was going to say yes, they quickly retracted.

"No, never mind. I don't want you."

I quietly walked away when I really wanted to run and hide the tears that eventually fell.

Getting put down and picked on became a way of life for me and I still remember the names and faces of those who really hurt me. It's interesting the things that you take with you as an adult, even things so far back as your school days. There is one particular moment that I will never forget from a guy that picked on me frequently.

He was the son of our typing teacher and was only one grade older than me. His family wasn't necessarily rich but they had enough money where he got pretty much anything he wanted and his attitude reflected it. He hung around several other guys and girls that were considered part of the cool group of their class and I wished some of their coolness would rub off on me, even if I was just seen hanging out with them.

My birthday had just passed so I was carrying a few of the small gifts I received in my new purse, including five little sample bottles of perfume that I wanted to show my friends. It was the last period of the day and a bunch of us were hanging out in the new gym on the bleachers. Amy was hanging out with some of the cool kids and I went up where they were to see how long I could be with them before they told me to leave. Some of the girls were actually being nice and I was showing them my birthday gifts. Suddenly, the boy grabbed my purse and dropped it down a hole at the top of the bleachers.

"Hey Heather. . . .go fetch!"

It was dark and very dirty under the bleachers. Where he had dropped my purse was way down in the middle so I had quite a ways to crawl under there to retrieve my purse. What I didn't know is that he had been dipping snuff and spitting down that same hole. Once I reached where my purse had landed, it was covered in his spit and all of my perfume bottles were now busted. I was so upset but then the boy called my name again so I looked up at him. Just as I saw his face, he spit on me.

I stood there in disbelief as I wiped his skoal-drenched spit off of my face, hearing everyone around him laughing. I immediately ran to the bathroom to cry uncontrollably. I had never been so humiliated and I swore I would hate that boy forever. I'm not sure what happened to this boy since his family ended up moving from the area but I remember being so thrilled that he was gone.

I don't think bullies really understand the damage they can do to their victims. The majority of bullies act the way they do from something that's missing way down deep inside and most have been bullied themselves. I've always told my kids to look beyond the mask that people wear because everybody acts the way they do for a reason. There's always an underlying reason. It's up to us to have the patience and understanding to find out why and try to help them instead of lashing back out and causing more pain to others.

There are so many young people out there that are hurting badly on the inside but hide it well when they're in the presence of others. You don't know what these people are going through behind closed doors and one wrong act or word can cause someone to snap. Wouldn't our world be a much better place if we spread loving and encouraging words instead of hurtful ones?

With all the boys picking on me you would think that I wouldn't want to have anything to do with any of them, but I still longed for a boyfriend of my own. I watched other girls that were much prettier than me land any guy they wanted and I was so jealous. I wanted to be noticed and important. I wanted to matter. I wanted to be loved by someone that didn't have to.

There was one particular boy that lived not far from us that I ended up having a crush on. Our families were good friends so we spent a lot of time together, but at school it was very different. We never ended up more than just friends, just like several other guys in my class that I liked.

I eventually began to change into a different young lady and found true love fit for the fairytale story books, but that's for a different chapter so hang on. Things are about to get worse for me on a whole new level.

A God Moment

God's Word tells us to be careful with the most unruly muscle in our body—our tongue. It's a very powerful muscle that is extremely hard to control, but not impossible. As we get close to God in our relationship with Him, it gets a little easier every day to keep silent when you really want to lash out or gossip about someone. Before speaking, messaging, texting, etc., pray and think about what these words will do. Will it bring honor to God? What will these words do to my personal testimony? Is it beneficial to the other person? Will it build them up or tear them down? Ask God for help concerning this difficult part of us and He will.

Chapter 18

Deja Vu, But Worse

"Be of good courage, and He shall strengthen your heart, all you who hope in the Lord." Psalm 31:24 (NKJV)

Living life on the Funny Farm was much different than the city life we had lived much of our childhood, but it was a welcome change for all of us. Our house sat so far off the road that if anyone came down our driveway we knew they were either in the right place or they were completely lost. It was quiet and peaceful back in the woods and we all went down to the spring frequently to either play in the water or just hang out as a family.

The spring was my quiet place to pray and just get away from everybody. A huge tree had fallen across a section of the spring so I would take off my shoes and sit on the tree with my feet dangling over the water. After collecting my thoughts, I then invited Jesus to come sit beside me for a chat. Jesus and I had many long conversations there and I always felt His presence with me.

When we were all in school, we mostly concentrated on our school work and normal chores around the house. It was a different story when it came to the weekends. Since Joey wasn't quite big enough to handle a lot of the tasks that needed to be done around the property, Dad said that his girls were boys on the weekends.

We could all sling an ax with the best of them. After a long day of cutting, splitting and stacking wood for the winter, Dad took us to the local convenience store for a treat. I remember one day in particular where we all walked in, dirty from head to toe.

"Come on boys, let's get a coke," Dad said.

This older man gave us all a strange look, but we just laughed it off. We learned to not be afraid of a little dirt and hard work.

When it came to the summer months, there was no time for a lot of playing. One summer Papa had three gardens that were about the size of a football field each. We all pitched in and helped plant, fertilize, and take care of them until harvest time. I even got to use the tiller, which was pretty funny to watch because it was much stronger than I was and it took all I had to control it.

Papa showed up early before we were even out of the bed, making sure we were ready to get out in the gardens to work before it got too hot. After we worked hard all summer, it was time to start making some serious money out of what we grew in the gardens. We sold a lot of vegetables that summer and we all made over $300 each, after we split the profits four ways. Mom and Dad took us to the mall to buy whatever we wanted and that made all the hard work worth while.

One of the things that Mary and I wanted to buy was contacts so we could ditch wearing glasses. Mom and Dad wanted to make sure that we would take care of them so they made a deal with us. We had to buy the first set, along with the eye exam, and if we were responsible with them, they would buy the rest as we needed them. I started my Freshman year in high school with no glasses and it felt so good to not have to worry about being picked on anymore, at least about that anyway.

Dad was an excellent mechanic and always had some pretty amazing cars around to be worked on. Our favorite was his rare 1969 Chevy Z28 Camaro Rally Sport that he was slowly restoring. It was red with black racing stripes and it was absolutely beautiful. We helped Dad work on the interior and the engine so we learned a good bit and had fun doing it. To keep from jacking up the car, Dad would just slide me right underneath with a wrench in hand. Since I was so skinny it was no problem.

We loved sticking our heads under the hoods of a roaring engine and the smell of burnt rubber at the race track. Dad sometimes drag raced his Chevy 2 Nova that he fixed up and we were his "pit crew." We got so good when we watched and listened to the burn-outs that we could predict the winner nearly every time. I'll never forget the time we got to watch top fuel dragsters and funny cars race. I still love the sound of heavy American muscle cars with their big block engines. Maybe that's where I got my lead foot.

We ended up getting two Welch Shetland horses given to us and Mary and I instantly fell in love with them. The mother of the two we called Nellie and since she was more laid back, Mary claimed her as her own. The baby had one glassy blue eye so we called her Blue Eye. I know, it's not really that original but it fit. She was more high strung so she became mine.

We loved going riding and taking care of our horses together. There were plenty of days that we would go search out the horses, saddle them up, and ride for hours. Sometimes we rode down Woodsprings Road but most of the time we stayed on the Funny Farm property.

Spilling the Beans

Even with us staying busy and having fun living on the Funny Farm, my memories still haunted me. My past kept creeping in when I wouldn't expect it and I had to fight from slipping into a depression. I didn't want people to start asking questions, especially my Mom, so I developed the ability to wear my mask that covered up my pain and I wore it well.

For what reason, I can't recall, but I remember sitting in our living room alone and my thoughts got the better of me. I began to cry when Mom unexpectedly walked in and found me. It was too late to try to hide it from her and she knew me well so I couldn't easily make her believe that everything was fine.

Mom began asking me what was wrong and as soon as I told her that I couldn't tell her, she knew. She continued asking what was wrong until I finally broke.

"If I tell you, you have to promise me that you won't throw him in jail."

Her greatest fear was coming to life right in front of her and she felt so helpless. Mom reluctantly promised for my sake so I began to pour my heart out in detail of what had happened that awful summer with Bill.

I made sure that I gave enough information so Mom would know that I couldn't possibly make it all up in my mind. After we talked everything through, Mom called Bill to confront him, but this time he reacted totally different than he did before. He denied everything and acted like he didn't know what Mom was talking about.

I was standing there listening to the conversation and I could tell he was lying so I angrily grabbed the phone from Mom. I confronted Bill as he acted clueless, while apologizing to me at the same time. I didn't understand until later that he was not only protecting himself but his wife who was now pregnant with his second child, my brother. He couldn't go to jail with her about to have their baby so he made it appear that I was the one lying.

There was a point while Mom was on the phone with Bill that I remember the look on her face, questioning if I was really telling the truth. After all, the first time she confronted Bill, he readily confessed but now he's emphatically denying everything. For a moment, she began to think that I may have been making it all up for attention based on the past, but then she looked into my eyes and remembered the details of everything I told her. How could I know so many details and make up such an elaborate story just to stir up trouble for everyone including myself?

When I saw doubt in her face, that she was questioning my story, I felt my stomach drop and my world beginning to crash all around me. I thought I would die if she didn't believe me. Mom was my rock, my strength, and if I didn't have her behind me, then I didn't know what I would do.

Maybe it was the look of horror on my face that caused her to rethink her doubt in me but I remember exhaling in relief as soon as I realized that she was backing me up all the way. I can't remember how the phone conversation ended with Bill but I do know that Mom then called Grandma. Mom confronted her as to how I was left alone with Bill after everyone promised to protect me. I wasn't prepared for what happened next.

There was a family secret that much of us didn't know about Grandma until later. We knew that Grandma had the occasional drink but we didn't know that her drinking was a much bigger problem than we thought. When she drank too much, she did and said things that she normally wouldn't when she was totally sober.

After Mom explained everything over the phone, Grandma began defending Bill and attacking me instead.

"Heather is lying. We've all caught her in a bunch of lies around here. If Heather can't behave herself no better than that, then we don't want her here!"

I don't know where she got that I was a big liar but I do know that I was very hurt and angry after both phone conversations. I determined then that I would pull away from that side of the family. If they didn't want me around then I would grant them their wish.

Mom always left it up to me if I wanted to go visit so she backed me up with my decision to stay away for a while. I eventually went back a couple of times but when the time was right, I cut them all off completely. I had enough pain in my life without allowing the people that were supposed to love me, to only hurt me even more. My plan was working out nicely, or was it?

A God Moment

Statistics show that the odds are high that you either know someone, or have gone through a sexual abuse situation yourself. Maybe it was incest, rape, or improper touching. Any of these can be devastating to anyone. It is up to you on how the end of your story will look like. Take your pain to God and ask for His help, then find someone you trust to talk to. Christian counseling can be a good thing because they can help guide you through more than just the emotional side of things, but the all-important spiritual side. Holding it all inside isn't good for you physically, emotionally, or spiritually. There is a whole new world out there waiting for you to discover that doesn't include your past pain so what are you waiting for?

Chapter 19

High School and Boyfriends

"Fear not, for I am with you; be not dismayed, for I am your God. I will strengthen you, yes, I will help you, I will uphold you with My righteous right hand." Isaiah 41:10 (NKJV)

There were so many crazy and wonderful things that happened during my high school years. It was like every year that passed, everything kept getting better and easier for me. I was finally growing up and maturing. I was learning who I really was and what I wanted out of life. My drive and ambition pushed me to become active in almost everything I could get involved in, including becoming an officer in several clubs that I joined. I figured if I was stuck in high school for four years I might as well have fun while I was at it.

My Freshman year I started actually caring about how I looked and I was allowed to wear a little more makeup. Dad never really bought us hair products other than hair spray and curling irons so it was a real challenge to figure out what to do with my naturally frizzy, curly hair.

It made me feel very proud after my class voted for me to represent them in the Student Counsel, but it totally shocked me when the club voted me as their Homecoming Sweetheart. Back then was the time of the toilet tissue flowers. We didn't have the money for a nice car so we just used my Mom's Chevy Caprice Classic. My artist ability helped me to make my own posters and we did everything we could to decorate the car with what we had, which was mostly our imagination. My dress was borrowed and was a little too big for me but we made it work. I had never felt prettier or more special than on that day.

I didn't have a boyfriend to escort me but Amy was dating a very nice guy named Keith so he agreed to escort me at the end of the parade. The parade route used to start at the riverfront, then go down Main Street turning by the old Stark's, which later turned into Dairy Queen, finally ending in front of the old high school. Our escorts helped us off of our vehicles and walked us to the front steps, awaiting for the rest of the parade participants to arrive so we could take our group picture for the local newspaper and yearbook.

That wouldn't be my first parade to be in. During my Senior year, I almost got Student Counsel Sweetheart again. The voting became a continuous tie between me and one of my good friends, Amy, until someone said they had heard that I really wanted the Miss Noel Senior Candidacy. I don't know where that rumor came from because I hadn't even thought about it, but it was enough to sway the vote in Amy's favor. Although I was a little disappointed, I was more thrilled for Amy and offered to help decorate her car. Another good friend named Mary, was also in the homecoming parade so I offered to help her decorate, too. I thought it was funny how two of my closest friends had the same names as two of my sisters.

A couple of months later I was called to the office to find out that my class had voted me to represent them in the Miss Noel contest, which also meant that I got to ride in the Christmas parade. I worked very hard to raise the most money but another friend in the Junior class beat us all out to be crowned Miss Noel that year. Although I didn't win, I had a lot of fun participating and representing my class.

I wouldn't say I was the smartest kid on the block but I did put a lot of effort in my studies which made me stay either on the honor roll or superintendent's list. Some of my friends asked if they could copy off of my papers and I usually let them.

One day in Biology class, one of my guy friends got aggravated with me because I was taking the test in pencil instead of pen, which made it harder for him to see my answers. In a different class, another guy friend of mine, Stacy, sometimes sat beside me and we had a system. As I finished a paper, I slid it over to him, he copied it, then took both of our papers to the teacher. We did that throughout the whole class and the teacher never said a word, even though we figured she knew exactly what was going on.

During my Senior year I also was part of the year book staff. I created most of the layout design for the ad section and took most of the pictures. It was a lot of fun going around taking a lot of the funny and candid shots around campus.

I gained the trust of my teachers and other faculty so I sometimes got out of class to either work in the office or other extra curricular activities. I even got to make some announcements over the school intercom. I remember having to announce that the old gym was on fire and for everyone to immediately move their vehicles away from it. As soon as I made that announcement it felt like an earthquake from all the driving high school students running on both levels to get to their vehicles.

The entire school halted as everyone hung out of the north side windows, watching as a big piece of our history was completely going up in flames. I later went out to the rubble and found a singed piece of wood and taped it inside of my Senior memory book.

It wasn't long before others discovered my singing ability and I started getting asked to sing more and more for school functions. I loved being in front of everyone doing what I really loved to do, which was sing my heart out. I always sung inspirational, Christian songs so I could use my talent for God, even in front of my peers at school, hoping that I could make a difference somehow.

My Senior year I fooled everybody during a Christmas program when I played the character "Jingle Bell Rock". Several of us played the parts of different popular Christmas songs where "O Holy Night" won out as the most important. My part required me to dress up as a cool rock star type so my friends helped me dress the part.

I had the eighty's hair, wild makeup, black high heels, black pantyhose, short leather mini skirt, leather jacket, and cool shades. We also made a string of jingle bells to strap around the mini skirt so I jingled when I walked. No one knew who I was since I was dressed completely out of my character. It wasn't until close to the end of the play when I had to take off my shades that everyone finally realized who I was. For a while I had a few people call me the "Jingle Bell Rock" girl, and they thought I had a cool side, even if it was small.

My love for music caused me to join the band my seventh grade year. I had never played an instrument like these and really didn't know which one I wanted to try. The band director suggested I try the french horn since he didn't have any yet. Scooby and I were the only two french horns and it didn't take me long to learn it and love it.

I didn't know what to expect but a few of us went to the Northwestern State University campus in Natchitoches, Louisiana to try out for their annual Honor Band concerts. Although I was the only one who made it, we all had so much fun being there together that day. I ended up making third chair in the junior high concert band and it was an experience that I would never forget.

When I graduated up into the eighth grade, I got the privilege of marching with the high school band. At our practices we worked really hard in the heat so when we got a break, we all walked or piled up in the back of pickup trucks to go to the local Stark's. That was the place to be and the local hang out for many, especially on weekends. Our band was so big at that time that it took three school buses just to haul us all to the games. Besides our band, we had a majorette line, flag line, and rifle team.

My Freshman year was a great year for me in band and I tried out for the NSU Honor Band again for the second time and made second chair. The only problem was that my band director had forgotten and didn't show up in time to take me down there. I can't remember being as mad and disappointed as I was that day. Because of his incompetence, I missed out on one of the biggest things that happened to me that year. I didn't have much respect for the guy already but his brownie points plummeted after that day.

The band was gradually falling apart because we had several students joining just to get an easy credit. They weren't really trying or didn't care about how we looked or sounded at our games or competitions. It made those of us that cared about our performances really upset and frustrated, which caused more and more drama throughout the band members. Enough of us got tired of the drama and began not signing up anymore each year that passed.

My Freshman year was my last year in band, but my music didn't stop there.

The Dating Game

It was my Sophomore year that I began to gain a little weight and start actually having a little bit of a girlish figure. Remember, I said a little bit, but even graduating from a size zero to a size half, and then to a size one was enough to throw a party at my house. Dad started saying that I was actually a whole person when I started wearing a size one.

I watched all of my friends continue with their dating relationships and sometimes I wanted to laugh. It was like a game to most of them. They would date someone for a couple of weeks, break up, then started dating someone else just a couple of days later. I didn't want that, but then again, having a boyfriend wasn't exactly something I knew about either. My luck soon changed, or so I thought.

Amy, my sister, never had a problem having boyfriends. She had the looks and the attitude to go with it. At one time she was dating one of four brothers that lived in Longstreet named Tony. All of the brothers liked coming over to our house since we had a pool table. Out of no where, the youngest of the four, Roger, asked me to be his girlfriend. I was dumb-founded.

My first reaction was if this was a joke or not. Did he really mean it or was this just another stunt like all the other guys in the past? On the off chance that he really meant it, I said yes. I was so taken back and happy that I actually had a boyfriend that I forgot about my standards, but then I really never sat down to think about what my standards were concerning a boyfriend.

How much did I really know about Roger? Who was he and what was he about? What did he believe? Was he even a Christian? I couldn't answer any of those questions—questions that I should have asked before I ever agreed to be his girlfriend. At the time, I was all in the moment and proud to be part of the dating pack. I felt like I was finally included.

I started making extra sure that I looked good for my boyfriend, making him proud to call me his, but I think I embarrassed him more than anything. You see, he wasn't a Christian and I started learning more about him and his family life. Even then, I thought that I could influence him, help him be a better young man.

When his friends asked if we had "done it" yet, before he could reply, I proudly spoke up.

"No. I'm a virgin and I'm going to stay that way until the day I get married."

It felt good saying that openly. That was the first time of many for me to take a stand for my purity and keeping it. Of course I always got funny looks, like I was some kind of circus freak for saying it, but I didn't care.

That relationship didn't last very long. I began to feel Roger slowly pulling away from me and soon I was handed a note from one of his brothers at school. It was a break-up letter and it crushed me. At first the only thing I could do was cry, but then I got angry. All I wanted to know was why.

I saw Roger walk toward the baseball and track field with a friend so I took off running after him. I know it was a mistake but my pride was already out the window. He saw me coming and just kept walking away. It was then that I stopped, gathered what pride I had left, and accepted my rejection. Later on Amy finally told me that the whole relationship was a set up from the very beginning.

Her now ex-boyfriend Tony, wanted Roger to date me to further enable all of them to come over to play pool and help Dad to trust us to go over to their house, out of his watchful eyes. Roger never really liked me and that crushed my heart. I had been used and I didn't want another boyfriend for a while.

Later on I realized what a blessing it was that we broke up. Roger had a very rough life and would have drug me down with him if we had stayed together. If I would have gone to God in prayer over that relationship before agreeing to date him in the first place, my heart would have been spared the agony of rejection. I'm just glad that God helped me see my mistake and I learned from it.

I wondered if any boy would ever really fall in love with me. I longed for that kind of love. For a guy to truly love me and I would give him my whole heart back. I finally went to Mom out of frustration.

"When do you know you've found 'the one'?"

She just smiled and replied, "You'll know in your heart. God will let you know but you just have to listen to Him when He tells you. You know you can pray for who you're gonna marry, right?"

I didn't understand what she meant so I asked her to explain.

"You can go to God and ask Him to send the right guy, but be specific. Make out your wish list in what you want in a man and simply ask Him to bring the right guy when it's time."

I'll have to admit that I thought her advise was trivial but I figured it couldn't hurt so I started out with my list.

I never actually wrote any of this down on paper but I had it deep in my heart. Number one on my list was he had to be a Christian and love God with his whole heart. Next, he had to have a sense of humor and love to have good, clean fun. Then I asked for him to be into music like me and want to sing as much as I did. I wanted him to be kind hearted, compassionate toward others, and trustworthy. At the end, I laughed a little at my last request. I thought it might be too much but I asked God for a guy that was at least a little good looking. I figured I'd help God out with that one. God soon started putting the wheels in motion to bring me my knight in shining armor.

A God Moment

Being patient isn't always easy but God wants us to wait for Him to bring about His will in our lives. He wants what is best for us but sometimes waiting for Him to bring it all together can be hard. We want what we want, and we want it now. Our prayers should be patterned after Christ's. Remember Jesus prayed, "Nevertheless, not My will but Yours be done." Jesus was in a bad position, knowing that He was about to be tortured and killed. His prayer started out asking the Father for another way if there was one, but then Jesus said, "not My will, but Yours be done." Ask for God's will to be done in your life instead of your will. His plans for your life are far better than your own.

Chapter 20

Looking for Prince Charming

"Rejoicing in hope, patient in tribulation,
continuing steadfastly in prayer." Romans 12:12 (NKJV)

I had a Geography class my Sophomore year that was extremely boring. We really didn't have a teacher but a coach that basically babysat us. Since I had good handwriting, the coach frequently asked me to write a bunch of multiple choice questions for everyone to copy off of the black board. I'm not sure if he ever figured it out but I tipped off the class that I was actually giving them all the answers by completely circling the correct answers but only putting the rest in parenthesis. Naturally, everybody loved me in that class.

Out of no where, the coach suddenly decided to rearrange the class with new assigned seats. The first seat in my row was now occupied by a guy I barely knew named Kenny and I was assigned the seat right behind him.

I had seen Kenny on campus but didn't know much about him. To make time pass in Geography class, Kenny turned around and we talked, played squares, S.O.S., or compared handwriting since I was a "rightie" and he was a "leftie". It didn't take long for us to become good friends. What I never expected was for him to start liking me.

One day he asked me to write my name as pretty as I could on the front of my notebook, so I did. Then he asked me to write his name as fancy as I could below it, so I did. Kenny then turned my notebook around and filled in between our names "loves." After I saw what he wrote, I quickly scratched it out.

"No, no, no."

"Why not?" Kenny asked.

"Because we're good friends and that's all."

Kenny quietly turned around and grabbed a note that he had already written and then gave it to me. I got real nervous as I opened it up and began to read that he really liked me and wanted to ask me out. I guess Kenny noticed the look on my face.

"Please don't answer yet. Just go home, think about it and I'll call you later."

I wouldn't give him my phone number at first but then he talked me into it with his sad puppy dog eyes. I didn't know what to do. I got on the bus to go home and my mind was whirling with all sorts of questions. My sisters, Amy and Mary, as well as a mutual friend named Brenda, all saw the strange look on my face as they got on the bus and began to ask me what was wrong.

"Somebody just asked me out."

They quickly started screaming in unison, "Who? Who asked you out?"

They were so excited for me since they knew my history of being dateless for so long.

"Kenny."

"Kenny? Go with him! He's a sweet guy."

"I know he's a sweet guy but I just don't like him like that. I just like him as a good friend."

"Just go with him. You'll end up falling in love with him. So what did you tell him?"

"I told him that I would think about it. He's supposed to call me tonight to get my answer."

All three of them kept telling me that I should go out with him, so I started thinking of the reasons that I might say yes.

First on my list was that he had to be a Christian and Kenny was a Christian. He seemed to have a great sense of humor so that was a plus. He was also a very nice guy but I wanted to make sure that not only would I not get hurt again, but I didn't want to hurt him either. I didn't want to go out with a guy that I didn't know if I could fall in love with. That wouldn't be fair to either of us, so I was trying to be very careful with my answer.

When I got home I began praying about what to do and something inside of me felt that I was supposed to say yes. When the phone rang I began to get butterflies in my stomach. After some nervous general conversation, Kenny finally asked if I had an answer for him. When I told him my answer, there was a short, awkward silence on the other end of the phone line. Kenny questioned if he heard me right.

He was in disbelief that I actually said yes, because he didn't have a history of girls flocking to his doorsteps either. Both of us were considered somewhat misfits, not quite cool or good looking enough for the rest of the in-crowd.

It was right before Valentine's Day, which made me excited that this would be my first year to actually have a Valentine of my very own. I liked the idea that I had someone that would be waiting for me to arrive at school. I thought it was sweet how we walked to class together down the halls holding hands, but others didn't think we were so cute.

I remember how some said things behind our backs, picking us apart on how we looked.

"Look at that. That is the weirdest couple I have ever seen. She looks like the boy in the relationship with her skinny, no-figure self, and he walks like he should be the girl."

I know if I heard it, Kenny must have too, but neither of us ever said anything about the rude and hurtful comments. At first I was upset, but the fact that I wasn't alone seemed to make it much more tolerable. I just held his hand and we both kept walking proudly to class.

Our first official date was to a Valentine's Banquet that Kenny's youth group was hosting at his church, South Oak Grove Assembly of God in Stanley, Louisiana. I had never been on a date before so I was very excited. At the age of fifteen, I was finally catching up with the rest of the dating world. Since it was more of a formal banquet, I picked out my favorite dress that Gam had made for me. I wanted to look my very best to make Kenny proud to have me as his date.

Kenny had two older brothers but Jerry Allen was the only one I knew of since he was still in high school and in the same grade as Amy. I got to know Jerry Allen pretty well since he had to drive me and Kenny everywhere on most of our dates. If it wasn't Jerry Allen driving us then it was usually his Mom. Although Kenny was almost eighteen years old, for some reason that I can't remember, he couldn't get his driver's license yet. I really liked Kenny's parents and enjoyed spending time with them at their home on some of our future dates. But let's get back to our first date.

I felt so grown as my date picked me up and walked me out to Jerry Allen's truck. The ride from Longstreet to Stanley was pretty fun since Jerry Allen was making the awkwardness of our first date more lighthearted and funny. He turned sharply on curves to sling my light weight frame right on top of Kenny and we all got a good laugh out of it.

"That's what you call a 'come-over-to-me-baby' curve," Jerry Allen explained.

I didn't know what to expect when I got to the church but there were a lot more teenagers than I had expected. I only recognized a couple of them since the majority of them went to Stanley High School. Several of the guys kept staring at us, whispering as if they were trying to figure out who this girl was with Kenny. It was like they were surprised that Kenny actually had a date. I made sure that I acted like a young lady and didn't do anything that may embarrass Kenny. I wanted to be a good girlfriend that could make him happy.

We were having a great time when a young man and a girl named Tonya got up to sing a couple of songs together. I remember thinking they both sounded so good. As a singer myself, I appreciated good music and loved to admire others that could sing, too. I went to school with Tonya but I turned and asked Kenny who the guy was. He told me it was his cousin, Jerry Dale English, who happened to be the preacher's son.

I know what you're thinking but don't get too ahead of me here. After the banquet was over, Kenny started introducing me to his friends and then to Jerry Dale. We shook hands, said something nice, and it was over. I never gave him a second thought after that and I'm pretty sure he didn't either.

Jerry Allen drove us back to my house and all the way there I started getting butterflies again because I knew our first kiss was coming. I really didn't want our first kiss to be awkward, but I wondered if he was a good kisser or how he would kiss me. The first kiss is always the hardest but also the most exciting to experience. I could tell Kenny was nervous too as we reached my front porch but our first kiss was actually nice and we were both glad that we got that awkward moment out of the way.

During the next two months, we enjoyed spending more time together and getting to know each other on a deeper level. I loved meeting more of his family and always had a great time with all of them. Most of our dates were either at his or my house, but a lot of times our dates involved youth functions at Kenny's church.

I got to make a lot of new friends with their youth and they mostly had a bunch of boys, but I didn't mind. At one youth function they started choosing teams for a game of capture the flag. What Kenny and I didn't know is the guys had predetermined to make sure we were on opposing teams. Jerry Dale was a captain and voted for me to be on his team. It ended up that we were the last two left but we lost after Kenny's team outran us.

During spring break, Kenny's youth group and another church group planned a Six Flags trip. Kenny invited me to go with him, but I really didn't think Dad was going to let me go. It shocked me when he said I could. I was so excited and counted the days until we left.

The bus ride up there was interesting. Kenny and I sat together in the back seat but several of his friends ended up sitting around us, visiting the whole way there. They thought it was cool how I could sing so high and played different songs on their boom box, asking if I could hit the high notes. I could tell Kenny started getting aggravated so I asked him to join in with us since he had a good singing voice, too. I think he was getting jealous that all the guys were taking up so much of my time and attention away from him.

Once we got to Six Flags everybody started breaking off into groups of who would hang out together all day. It ended up that our group consisted of me, Kenny, Cody, and Jerry Dale. It felt a little awkward at first with me being the only girl but the guys made it fun and I trusted them so I had a great time.

Most of the day had passed and there was something that I hadn't noticed. We were standing in line for a ride where Kenny was first, then me, followed by Cody and then Jerry Dale. Suddenly I turned around and Jerry Dale was right behind me instead of Cody. Cody started pushing Jerry Dale back to where he was originally standing.

"No, man. You've been sitting by her all day so it's my turn now."

I could tell that Jerry Dale was a little embarrassed and didn't saying anything, but that did get me to thinking. Jerry Dale had always been the guy on the other side of me on every ride.

For a second, I thought about the idea of Jerry Dale possibly liking me but it really didn't matter since I was dating Kenny. I never gave it a second thought after that. I did notice, however, that Jerry Dale often volunteered to drive me and Kenny to my house after youth functions. Mom was always the one to wait up for me and the other girls when we went out, so we all sat around visiting and laughing together until the guys had to leave.

Mom and I thought that Jerry Dale's laugh was so different and funny, as well as his lamb noise that he made. Even during this time of getting to know Jerry Dale, I never thought about liking him more than just a friend and a cousin of Kenny's. I found out later that Jerry Dale was beginning to like me but he never interfered with Kenny's relationship with me. He remained silent about his possible feelings for me.

One time after a youth function, Jerry Dale volunteered to drive us to my house. He wanted to stop by his house on the way to change since everyone had been getting sweaty from playing around outside at the church. When we all went inside I finally got to spend a few minutes with Jerry Dale's parents, the pastors of his church, Bro. Doyle and Sis. Sarah English. I thought they were really nice people. At one point Bro. English and I were sitting in the living room together talking when I noticed that he had a strange smile on his face. I'll tell you why later.

A God Moment

Life can be pretty interesting when we sit back and let God work on our behalf. Sometimes He answers our prayers totally different from how we expect Him to. If we're patient, we'll see that His way of doing things is much better than we could have ever imagined it ourselves. The Bible says that His ways are not our ways and our thoughts are not like His. Isn't it better to trust in Him to answer our prayers the way He sees is best for us instead of us getting upset with Him when He doesn't do it to our liking or on our time schedule?

Chapter 21

And God Said, "Not That One"

"Scarcely had I passed by them, when I found the one I love. I held him and would not let him go." Song of Solomon 3:4a (NKJV)

Everything was going fine with Kenny, and I was starting to think that my feelings were beginning to go from a strong like to possibly loving him. I enjoyed being with Kenny and I loved his big heart, but he suddenly started acting out of character. One day he made me angry about something that I can't remember but we quickly made up. I figured our first real fight was out of the way, but not long after that we fought again.

Kenny called me one night and I thought everything went fine by the time we hung up, but when I got to school the next morning, Kenny wouldn't have anything to do with me. I asked him what was wrong with him but he refused to even talk to me. I had no idea what was wrong and tried to think of what I might have done to get him so angry with me. I started getting pretty mad myself with how rude and ugly he was treating me with no explanation, so I finally left him alone.

I decided to wait and see what happened at lunch time, so I waited for him by the coke machines as I always did. When Kenny finally showed up he passed me a note that he had written earlier. Neither of us said anything as I started reading it, and the more I read, the angrier I got.

When I'm very angry I end up crying. Since I didn't want anyone to see me cry, I quietly just folded the note, put it in my back pocket, and slowly walked away to go hide in the girl's bathroom in the high school building. As I walked away, Kenny asked me if I was going to say anything

"No."

While in the bathroom I finally composed myself and decided I needed to blow off some steam, so I went upstairs to the typing room to practice. The more I thought about Kenny's actions and the words in the note, I reminded myself that I didn't have to put up with any guy treating me that way. I made up my mind that I was done so I walked back downstairs to the office where I knew Kenny's jacket was and placed his ring in his jacket pocket.

I immediately started feeling better about my decision as I walked back upstairs to the typing room. I didn't feel like talking to Kenny, but he knew where he could find me and eventually joined me. We didn't talk much but he knew it was over and asked for his ring. I calmly let him know that I had already put it in his jacket pocket. I could tell that surprised him at first, but then after saying a quiet, "OK," he left.

I was hurt but tried to find some sense into what just happened. The only thing that I got out of Kenny was he thought I said something negative about his mother during our phone conversation the night before, but I hadn't. I didn't have time to play those games with everything I had going on with school and church so I tried to put it behind me.

That same night my youth choir was scheduled to sing at a community wide revival at Maple Springs Baptist Church in Logansport so I had to get my mind focused on that instead of the breakup.

Our youth choir arrived at the church a little early to get ready for our performance that night so we hung out as other people started arriving. As I walked to the door I met Jerry Dale walking in. After a quick greeting I found out that he was scheduled to sing for the revival, too. He asked how my day had been and when I told him that Kenny and I had broken up, he was trying hard not to smile.

"Oh really?"

Before I go any further, I have to tell you about Jerry Dale's dating experiences. Jerry Dale didn't date much because he wasn't interested in dating girls just for the sake of dating. Good Christian girls, even back then, were hard to find in high school, even after he graduated and went off to bible college. There were a couple of girls he seriously dated but all it took was a couple of his friends flirting with them to sway them away from Jerry Dale.

It really hurt him to lose his girlfriends like that. He felt cheated on, second choice, left-overs, and stabbed in the back by his so-called guy friends. Jerry Dale chose to stay away from the dating scene until he knew he had the right girl, which turned into a two-year time frame.

Jerry Dale prayed the same prayer I did, asking God for the right one. He was feeling lonely but didn't want to make a big mistake of ending up with the wrong kind of girl, especially since he knew he was called into the ministry. While praying, he felt God tell him in his heart, "The girl you will marry won't be anyone that you already know or grew up with." That made Jerry Dale nervous.

"God, you know how shy I am. I'm afraid I'll miss her so You're going to have to get her to make the first move."

It wasn't too long after that when I came into the picture.

Now let's get back to the revival. A group of teenagers were hanging out close to the front of the church and I was sitting in a pew directly in front of Jerry Dale. While we were all talking we realized that the service was about to start. Before I knew it, I did something that I would have never normally done.

"Do you mind if I sit with you?"

I immediately gasped quietly to myself because I couldn't believe that I had just asked that. It was as if my mouth flew open like I was a puppet, with no mind of my own, not thinking before I spoke. I later figured out that it was the Holy Spirit playing match maker for the both of us. I just knew that Jerry Dale thought I was a flirt, or worse. I looked at his face and at first, he looked at me in shock to my question, but then it quickly softened, with him slowly smiling.

"Sure."

I really didn't know why I said it, but I was so glad that he didn't think bad of me or make a big scene over it. Even at that point I really didn't like Jerry Dale as more than just a friend but I felt comfortable talking to him. Most of the teenagers sat toward the front and several of them crammed into the same pew Jerry Dale and I were sitting on so we were sitting very close.

We both took our turns singing and complimented each other on a job well done. At first everything was pretty normal but the longer I sat there, with our bodies sitting so close to each other, it was like God struck me with a cupid arrow. I had never felt anything for Jerry Dale but suddenly I was. I start feeling guilty about my feelings that seemed to have come from no where.

I didn't hear very much of what the preacher said that night, which was unusual for me since I loved soaking up the Word. My mind was running in circles and I began praying.

"God, what are you doing to me? I'm not supposed to be feeling this way! I just broke up with Kenny today. His cousin! This isn't right!"

I didn't feel God respond at that point but He did speak to me later that night.

As the service went on, I told myself that if this was real and something was supposed to happen between us, then Jerry Dale would stick around and talk with me after the service. I do remember that a couple of teenagers walked forward for salvation so we all stood to take our turn shaking their hands after the service was over.

As we were filing out of the pew, I turned around and Jerry Dale was standing in the same spot at the end of the pew where he had been sitting, talking with another guy. At first I felt disappointed because I knew that God was doing something with my heart, but I turned around and convinced myself that it just wasn't meant to be.

What I didn't know is that an old high school buddy saw Jerry Dale and quickly ran to him after service to catch up since he hadn't seen him since graduation. The whole time Jerry Dale was keeping an eye on me so I wouldn't get away and finally made an excuse to cut the visit short.

After a while I turned around and saw Jerry Dale right behind me. My heart skipped a beat as I turned back around to collect myself and the excitement that was about to burst out of me. He asked me to go with him and a few friends for a quick ice cream run and then take me home. I was screaming and jumping up and down on the inside but remained calm on the outside. I told him that I'd have to ask my Mom.

Mom and my sisters were already in the car as we walked up to her window to get permission. Mom didn't have a problem with it since she had already gotten to know Jerry Dale over the past few weeks and really liked him. Amy and Mary were happy for me but started picking at me like sisters do.

"Heather's got a date! Heather's got a date!"

Jerry Dale started walking me to his truck and asked if I wanted to get in from the driver's side. Of course I agreed. As I got in the truck he told me that he would be right back after he checked with his friends about the plans to stop by the local Dairy Queen. As I sat there alone in the truck I gave myself a quick mirror check and purposely slid over more toward the driver's side so we'd be closer together once he got back in the truck. I know, sneaky right?

We had a great time but it was the ride home that was interesting. I felt God finally talking to me.

"You weren't supposed to fall in love with Kenny. He wasn't the one, but it was necessary for him to be in your life for you to meet Jerry Dale. Jerry Dale is the one you've been praying for. He will be the one you will marry. I have plans for you both."

I was blown away and didn't know how to feel or what to say. Out of no where, Jerry Dale asked a question.

"So, how do you feel about the whole situation with Kenny?"

He wanted to make sure that I wasn't on the rebound or still had feelings for him.

"Well, we're pretty upset with each other right now but I think we'll always be friends. Kenny's a great guy but I think God has other things for me."

"What things do you think God has for you?"

"Oh, just. . . .things. What about you? What do you think God has for you?"

"Things."

He was smiling when he said it, but then, so was I. I think we secretly knew what each other meant without saying a word. I wasn't about to tell him what I felt God telling me just a few minutes before. What I learned later is that God had told Jerry Dale the same thing about us being together. We both wanted to be very careful of how we handled this relationship.

Do you remember me telling you about Jerry Dale's Dad having a strange smile as I talked with him for the first time at their house? God shared with Bro. English that I was going to be his future daughter-in-law. He just sat there and smiled but never said a word to anyone until much later.

We finally arrived at my house and I invited him in. As we walked into the living room where Dad was sitting, I took one look at Dad's face and I knew something was wrong. I think every parent has this look—the look that tells you that you're in trouble without ever saying a word. That was the look I was getting. I wasn't sure why so I asked Jerry Dale to leave earlier than I wanted him to. Jerry Dale didn't understand but he agreed so I wouldn't get in trouble. I walked him to the door and we both said goodbye without a hug, a kiss, or even a hand shake.

As I walked back into the living room Dad asked, "So what grade is this boy in?"

My first thought was he knew very well that he wasn't in school at all since Jerry Dale had a full beard and mustache. They didn't allow those in school. My second thought was that I honestly didn't know how old he was. I hadn't ever thought to ask. I found out later that he had turned twenty that March and I was only days away from turning sixteen.

"He's already graduated."

Without any further questions Dad announced, "Well that's the end of that. You won't be seeing that boy again."

A God Moment

Just when you think that everything starts to work out in your life, sometimes a big wrench is throne in the mix. You can mark it down that whenever God is working out something awesome in your life, the devil doesn't like it and will try to mess it up every time. If your life has been one that really didn't focus on God or being obedient to His Word, then the devil isn't really worried about you much. But the moment you get serious about serving Him and try changing your life for the better, the devil hates the idea of losing his grip on you. Just because things aren't working out the way you planned, doesn't necessarily mean that you're out of His will. Pray for wisdom and stick to the path that you know God has you on.

Chapter 22

Unexpected Roadblock

"Trust in the Lord with all your heart, and lean not on your own understanding; in all your ways acknowledge Him, and He shall direct your paths." Proverbs 3:5-6 (NKJV)

"What? Why?" I asked.

"That boy is too old. He's old enough to be thinking about things that he doesn't need to be doing with you. He's marrying age," Dad explained.

"Actually, he's old enough and more mature to be thinking about other things besides having sex. We're not planning on getting married, Dad. He's a good Christian guy."

"I'm sure he may be a nice guy but if I let you date a guy that much older than you, then I have to let your sisters date guys that may be total jerks that age, too."

I was so upset and began crying as I went to my room to be alone. Mom came to comfort me as she always did and allowed me to talk out my thoughts.

My sisters and I understood but didn't agree with Dad's reasoning about the issue of what was good for one of us, was good for the rest of us. We understood that he was trying to make everything fair between us, but we were all individuals that were very different. If Amy, the oldest, was allowed to do something and she broke the rules, then that privilege was taken from not only her, but Mary and I wouldn't get to do it either when we were old enough. That happened a few times since Amy was more brave about pushing the boundaries than Mary and I were most times.

I knew Dad was just trying to protect me from an older guy possibly hurting me and I loved him for that, but I also felt it wasn't fair to judge Jerry Dale without knowing him and taking such drastic action against a possible relationship between us.

After I poured my heart out to Mom as we sat together on my bed, she said that she would talk with Dad and see what she could do. Mom advised me to just be quiet and pray about it. The next morning, Mom told me that Dad agreed to allow Jerry Dale to call me once a week and we could only talk for five minutes. He would also allow us to write letters to each other. This was all before the time of personal cell phones and texting, so I took what I could get.

Jerry Dale didn't understand why we couldn't see each other but he honored Dad's requests and we began writing letters to each other almost daily. I remember looking forward to checking the mail everyday, hoping to see an envelope addressed to me with Jerry Dale's handwriting. We still have every letter we wrote each other and they're stored away for safe keeping.

With the phone calls, we never talked for only five minutes. Mom understood that we needed more time to talk, and allowed us to stay on the phone a little longer. We both appreciated and treasured those few extra minutes.

The first day back at school of my Junior year, Kenny came up to me and questioned about what had happened with Jerry Dale. I told him that he simply asked me out for ice cream and took me home. Evidently someone came and told him a bunch of stories about us.

For the next several days someone began spreading rumors that Jerry Dale and I had already liked each other; that we had the whole break-up planned so we could be together. When I heard this I laughed at how ridiculous it was.

It wasn't long that Kenny came to me in the school office while I was working and asked to speak with me privately. I agreed to meet with him in the auditorium where we could talk. Kenny began apologizing to me for his behavior and he admitted that he was the reason for the break-up. He couldn't really explain why he acted the way he did but he wanted me to give him another chance.

It broke my heart as he knelt in front of me, crying and apologizing. I respected him for humbling himself the way he was, and the Kenny that I grew to like so much was finally back. I truly didn't want to hurt Kenny but I had to let him know that I knew God was putting me and Jerry Dale together for a reason. I had to not only follow my heart but follow what I knew was God's will for my life at the time. We hugged and agreed to remain good friends, which made me feel better but I knew with him being cousins with Jerry Dale that it was going to be awkward.

It was so hard for me and Jerry Dale not getting to see each other. We were getting to know each other more through our letters and short once-a-week conversations. It took us about three months before either of us mentioned the word "love". Both of us felt it was important to not say it unless we knew we meant it and it was real.

The first time I got to see Jerry Dale in person was at the Logansport graduation. He and his family were there for his cousin Jerry Allen and we were there for Amy. My family and I were sitting one section over from where they were but when everything was over, Dad made sure that he kept us apart where we couldn't talk or be together. That made us both very angry because we didn't know when we would be able to see each other again after that.

I had never felt so strongly for a guy, but then I hadn't really dated much either. I thought about him constantly. We went all summer without seeing each other except once. I found out that he worked at a machine shop in Grand Cane. I managed to talk Mom into stopping there for a couple of minutes on our way to do some shopping in Mansfield. I don't know whether she ever told Dad about that short little detour we took that day but Jerry Dale and I were so grateful. Those couple of minutes together helped us last until school started.

Starting my Junior year in high school was a fresh start for me, and belonging to Jerry Dale made it all that much sweeter. I was still very skinny but I had filled out a little more over the summer. I was looking a little better and I had a new-found confidence. What I loved about Jerry Dale is that he fell in love with me while I was still somewhat in my awkward stage. He fell in love with what was on the inside of me and my love for God, not necessarily my looks, although he always said I was beautiful.

I couldn't wait to see Jerry Dale again but wasn't sure when that time would come. One day on the bus ride home, we realized that Jerry Dale was behind us about ten minutes from being at my driveway. He went home a different way that day and happened to discover that he could catch the last part of my bus route if he went that way. I was so excited that I could hardly contain it and hoped that he would stop and see me.

He did stop after I got off the bus and we talked for a couple of minutes before he had to leave. Since our driveway was so far from the house with woods in between, no one ever knew except my sisters and brother. Jerry Dale made this a routine about once every couple of weeks and it always made my day when he did.

Even though we weren't in the band anymore, my family always went to the football games to support our team and hang out with friends. Dad couldn't keep him from showing up at a public event so Jerry Dale made sure to show up at every one he could, just to be with me. Dad never went to the games and Mom always watched out for us so everything went fine. Going to the games was so much more exciting knowing that I got to spend precious time with Jerry Dale. It was at one of the games that I got my first kiss from him.

The closer that Jerry Dale and I got, the harder it was getting for us to be kept apart. With every decision that Dad made to try to separate us, Jerry Dale and I both got more aggravated and frustrated. Jerry Dale had made good friends with my cousin Scooby, who lived just down the road from us and sometimes hung out with him.

One weekend Scooby came to where we were cutting wood and passed me a note that Jerry Dale had written for me. Once I read it I became angry and very upset. Jerry Dale had basically broken up with me because he didn't think he could take much more of what Dad was putting us through. I think that's what Dad was hoping for. I guess he thought that Jerry Dale would be a phase and he would eventually give up and go away like a bad rash.

I didn't know what to do but I started taking my anger out on the wood I was throwing and yelling what I really wanted to say to Jerry Dale. Since he wasn't there, Scooby would have to do instead.

Scooby shouted, "Don't shoot the messenger! I didn't write the note so save it for Jerry Dale, not me!"

I apologized for snapping at him but I really didn't know what to do since I hadn't done anything to cause the break up.

I got word that Jerry Dale would be at the home football game that coming Friday. I was a little nervous about seeing him face to face after the letter he sent. It was hinted that he was going to apologize. After I arrived at the game I saw him in the distance but acted like I didn't see him. I made him come to me.

He asked if we could sit together and we began to talk. Jerry Dale apologized for his behavior and said that he couldn't break up with me, even through the tough times. He told me he loved me and gave me his senior ring to wear as an outward symbol that I was officially his. I was so excited and forgave him immediately. I was so happy to have him back in my life and we both agreed that we wouldn't give up on each other no matter what, or who, tried to get in between us.

So far Dad still had not allowed Jerry Dale to come over to our house at all but Christmas was coming and we both had gifts that we wanted to exchange. Jerry Dale hinted that I would really like my present and one of his best friends, Ray, told me the same thing at church.

Mom convinced Dad to allow Jerry Dale to come over but somehow the details of how long he could stay got mixed up. I was so excited that Dad was finally allowing him to come over, even if it was just this one time. I figured maybe if he met him and talked with him that Dad may start to like him.

Jerry Dale showed up at the house and I introduced him to Dad. We stayed in the front living room the whole time and were rarely left alone. Dad managed to give us enough time to exchange our gifts and my present almost made me cry.

Jerry Dale had designed a promise ring just for me. It was gold with a diamond in the middle, and our birthstones connected on either side. He said the birthstones represented us but the diamond in the middle stood for our love and God, which held us together. I think I did cry after he explained the meaning and put it on my finger. I was so happy.

Dad came back in the living room, sat down across from us and just kept staring us down. I didn't know why but I just thought he was making sure that we weren't going to do anything. After an awkward time Dad finally got up and left without saying anything. We finally figured that Jerry Dale better go so I walked him to his truck, got my hug and kiss, and he left.

After I got back in the house I showed Mom my ring. We were both excited but Mom suggested that we tell Dad it was a friendship ring. She thought Dad would go ballistic if he really knew it was a promise ring. I'm not sure if he ever really knew exactly what kind of ring it was, but if he knew, he never said anything. Just the fact that I was wearing Jerry Dale's Senior ring wasn't sitting well with him so I didn't think he liked the idea of another ring on my other hand.

I can't remember if it was later that night or the next morning but I discovered why Dad was acting the way he was. He had only given permission for Jerry Dale to come over just long enough for us to exchange gifts. Then he was supposed to leave, but somehow I never got that message. I don't know if Mom forgot to tell me or what, but I knew I had to really kiss up and apologize to Dad. I could tell he was still angry but I think he forgave me.

Not long after that, I guess Dad figured that Jerry Dale wasn't going anywhere so he gave him permission to start coming over to the house to see me but we couldn't go anywhere together. Since football season was over we really didn't have a way to see each other on a weekly basis anymore so we were both thankful to take anything he offered. I didn't care about going anywhere just as long as I got to be with him.

Jerry Dale let me wear his jacket and I loved smelling his cologne all around me. You would think he was there to play with Joey from the way my little brother acted but neither one of us minded. I enjoyed sitting back watching him and Joey wrestle, throw a football, play basketball, or just build crazy stuff with Joey's Lego's. I think Joey was just so thrilled that he had someone like a big brother to spend time with him. All Joey ever had was a bunch of big sisters that mothered him so Jerry Dale was a welcomed change.

After my seventeenth birthday came up in May of 1987, Dad finally thought I was old enough to go out with Jerry Dale. Dad began allowing him to take me out on real dates, away from the house. We had been together a little over a year at this point so I think Dad realized that Jerry Dale was here to stay.

Again, we were so grateful and appreciated every moment we had together. I sat as close to him as I possibly could in his truck and we cuddled the whole way to Shreveport, talking and enjoying every minute we had. It felt like our relationship was made in heaven. Well, it actually was since God put us together but it wasn't always heavenly.

A God Moment

Parents don't always get it right, no matter how hard they try. Most parents genuinely love and care for their children and only want what's best for them, although some of the things they do may make you think otherwise. We don't always understand why our parents do what they do, but we need to trust them. After all, they have already lived more years and have much more experience in the life department. The Bible instructs us to honor and obey our parents if we want to have long life. I've heard kids say that their parents were not worthy of their respect. It doesn't matter if you think they're worthy or not. To be in line with God's Word and stay in His will, we all need to honor, obey, love, and respect our parents. No matter how old you get or how wrong you think they are. Pray for your parents because raising you isn't, or wasn't, the easiest job they've ever had.

Chapter 23

Bringing Up The Past

*"Therefore, if anyone is in Christ, he is a new creation; old things
have passed away; behold, all things have become new."*
2 Corinthians 5:17 (NKJV)

After we had been together for several months, Jerry Dale called
me on the phone and started sharing some personal things that
he had never told anyone. He felt that our relationship had grown
to the point where we needed to take things to the next level. He
wanted us to trust each other and have absolutely no secrets.

Jerry Dale was scared that once he told me about a couple mistakes that he made in his teenage years that I might not want to date
him anymore. I could tell he was very nervous as he poured his out
to me but I told him his mistakes weren't that big of a deal to me and
for him not to worry about it. I thought he was making a mountain
out of a mole hill, but I could tell that it was really bothering him so
I let him know that everything was alright.

Once he was finished, he asked if there was anything that I
wanted to share with him. I told him that there was something that
I did want to share but I didn't know if now was the right time.
Jerry Dale started getting worried, thinking that I may have done
something really bad, something that may damage our relationship.

He started pressing me to talk about it. I really hadn't planned
on telling him about my past yet but I knew I was going to have to

tell him now or he would think I was trying to hide something from him. I didn't want Jerry Dale to have any reason to think he couldn't trust me so I began sharing my past horrors concerning Bill and his family.

I remember Jerry Dale was very quiet as I told him everything. Then I asked him if he was alright, but I could tell he was crying on the other end of the phone.

"Are you crying?" I asked.

"Yeah. What did you think I was going to do?"

"I don't know. I didn't think you would cry."

"I love you, Heather. When I hear of anyone hurting you, it literally breaks me to pieces. I don't want you to ever have to hurt like that again. If I ever meet your father, I can't promise you that I won't hurt that man."

"Well, I don't know if you'll ever meet him. I haven't seen him in a while. I've pretty much decided not to see him or the rest of the family up there after the way they treated me the last time I called. It's hard to forgive them after the things I was told, especially about them not wanting me up there anymore if I couldn't behave myself. All I did was finally tell the truth of what had been happening right under their noses. But I'm scared about the future."

"What do you mean you're scared? Scared of what?"

"I don't know if the statutes of limitations are the same as they used to be but when I turn eighteen, the limits will be up for me to file charges against him if I wanted to. I think he knows this. He also knows that I'll be a legal adult. I'm afraid he'll try to find me again and want to have a relationship with me but I don't want that. I haven't been around him in a while so I don't know what's going on in his life or what's on his mind. I don't know what his intentions are anymore. All the unknown just scares me."

"Heather, I will never let anyone else hurt you, especially your father, so don't worry baby. I will always protect you and take care of you. If we ever get married, I will hide you if necessary so none of that side of your family can find you, to hurt you anymore. If any of them knew where we were, they would just tell your father and I'm not gonna let that happen."

I felt so safe with Jerry Dale. Every time we said our good-byes on my front porch I loved for him to just hold me in his strong arms. I could stand there for hours just being wrapped up with him, laying my head against his chest. Feeling the love and warmth of his body against mine was so comforting to me. I knew I could trust him and I felt safe every time I was with him. I had longed for the loving embrace of a man for a long time but I didn't want to go looking for it in the wrong places, in the wrong ways.

I've known other girls who were abused like me but they thought of themselves as used or damaged goods. They craved that love they weren't getting at home but they chose a dark path. These girls became sexually active at an early age and started creating bad reputations for themselves.

I knew what they wanted, what they needed, but I determined that I wouldn't go that direction. I had more respect for myself and my body to allow any other guy to abuse me like that again. I determined at an early age that I would wait until I got married before I gave up my virginity. I wanted my wedding night to be amazing, giving my gift of purity to the man I loved. A gift designed by God for my husband, and him alone to unwrap. I didn't want my first time to experience sex to be cheap, with me feeling dirty and guilty, during or after.

After Dad started letting me and Jerry Dale go out on dates, Mom sat down and talked with me about the dangers of dating.

"I know you love Jerry Dale but there are going to be times that temptation is going to come up when you're all alone and you need to be prepared for this."

"Mom, don't worry. Both of us are virgins and we've talked about waiting. Neither of us want to have sex until we get married. We both decided this before we ever met and we're determined to stick with the plan no matter what."

"I understand that but this temptation is going to be hard for you both to ignore. When you don't love a guy, it's easy to say, 'Get off of me, you creep!', but when you really love him, it's very hard to say, 'No. Let's wait.' I'm just warning you when the time comes, Jerry Dale will depend on you to tell him when to stop. It's a little easier, physically speaking, for a girl to back off in these situations than it is for a guy, so you need to help him out. Tell him when he needs to back off and I don't think you'll have any problems with Jerry Dale complying with your wishes, especially since he truly wants to wait, too."

On most dates, Jerry Dale and I never put ourselves in a position where we were alone in a place that gave us the opportunity to do anything inappropriate with each other. However, there were a couple of times that we found ourselves in a bad position, making the wrong choice of parking his truck in an area where no one could see us.

We began kissing and things were heating up. Before either of us knew it, Jerry Dale's hand found it's way up my shirt, touching my stomach. At first I got a little nervous but then again, it felt great with him touching me so softly. I still felt safe with him, but then his thumb slowly made it's way under my bra, just far enough that it could touch either of my breasts with the slightest movement.

We stopped kissing and looked at each other. For the first time, I felt uncomfortable with Jerry Dale and he could see it all over my face. He asked me what was wrong but I remained silent. I didn't know what to say. Suddenly, Jerry Dale came to himself, removed his hand from underneath my shirt and got out of the truck. He knew he had to get away from me to cool off, but then he started getting angry with himself. He walked away from the truck but didn't go far. I didn't know what to think at this point. What was he doing?

Jerry Dale finally came back after a couple of minutes and got back in the truck.

"I am so sorry. You trusted me and I betrayed that trust by touching you. I told you I would protect you and not let anyone hurt you but here I am doing it myself. I don't want to ever take advantage of you. I love you, Heather, and I'm sorry."

"It's alright, Jerry Dale. We made a mistake so let's just learn from it and move on from here."

I looked down and noticed that his knuckles on his right hand were slightly bleeding.

"What happened to your hand?"

"I hit a tree. I was so mad at myself."

"Why would you do something like that? All you did was hurt yourself. Are you alright?"

"Yeah, I'm fine. It'll heal, but I'm worried about you. Can you trust me again?"

"Of course I trust you. We just got caught up in the moment, that's all."

"Please don't let me do anything like that again. I don't want to give you any reason to feel anything but love and trust from me. We've got to do something to prevent this from happening again, like put a bible in between us or something."

At that we both laughed and then hugged each other. I looked after his hand as we drove away to look for a place to go where we couldn't be alone like that again. As we were riding around, I started thinking about everything that had just happened.

Mom was right. All it took was one small opportunity for Jerry Dale and I to mess up. I had no idea that things could get out of hand so quickly. I knew we were going to have to be a lot more careful in the future or we were going to end up failing on our quest to stay pure in our relationship. This was going to be a lot harder than I thought it would be.

Jerry Dale hitting the tree was another matter I was concerned about. I never saw anyone hit something just because they were mad. I had heard of people having bad tempers and even boyfriends that abused their girlfriends. Could Jerry Dale ever do that to me? Did he have a bad temper? These thoughts were making me a little concerned but I pushed them back. He loved me too much to hurt me, right?

A God Moment

When you're dating, take the necessary steps to ensure that neither of you will have the opportunity to do anything that you shouldn't. Plan out your date so there will be no surprises. You don't want to go out with no plans because you'll end up parking somewhere, alone, just to have something to do. We all know that's not a good idea. Take a Bible and have it in the vehicle to remind you both of your commitments to each other and to God. Stay in public places, double date, anything to keep you from being alone and having the opportunity to do something you'll later regret. Let your dating relationship be something that is God-honoring and He in turn will bless it.

Chapter 24

Engaged in High School

"Beloved, let us love one another, for love is of God; and everyone who loves is born of God and knows God. He who does not love does not know God, for God is love." 1 John 4:7-8 (NKJV)

Dating Jerry Dale was one of several highlights of high school. I had a steady and serious relationship with a grown man, not an immature boy, and that made me feel special. There were a couple more of my friends that were dating guys around Jerry Dale's age, too. I felt like part of the crowd.

During my Junior and Senior years in high school, I was paying more attention to my looks and started getting more of a figure. The ugly duckling was finally becoming somewhat of a swan.

When guys flirted with me I thought, "Sorry buddy. You had your chance but now a man has my heart. He saw me as God's beautiful creation before I was actually beautiful looking on the outside. He saw me when you couldn't. . . .when you wouldn't."

There is one thing that I can say about my graduating class of 1988 and that is we were all like family. It didn't matter what the color of our skin was, academic levels, or economic backgrounds. We all loved each other, and got along more like brothers and sisters than just good friends. Even now there are very few of us that have not stayed in touch throughout these past twenty-plus years.

I did get picked on a little from them concerning me dating Jerry Dale however.

Jerry Dale and I both made a commitment to staying sexually pure in our relationship. While I didn't walk around announcing my virginity, I didn't hold back from anyone who wanted to ask or talk about it. I wanted to set a good example and prove to my peers that keeping your purity is indeed possible if you really want it bad enough.

During my Senior year, I remember a couple of my fellow classmates asking me if Jerry Dale and I had played "grab butt" yet. When I told them we hadn't, it was really hard for them to believe, even though they knew the kind of girl I was. They just couldn't wrap their minds around us dating for nearly two years and never "doing the dirty." That's the kind of world we live in I guess.

The last two years of high school were the years that I started gaining some respect from others because I pretty much practiced what I preached. After being tested, tried, and having all my buttons pushed in so many different ways, I tried to be the example God wanted me to be. I didn't always get it right, but I did everything I could to remain a Godly young lady in every situation possible.

There were still times that I got picked on for doing the right thing or being a "goodie-goodie." Even teenagers in my own youth group at church picked on me, and it made me feel hurt and alone, but it didn't sway my belief of being a daughter that my Father God could be proud of. I tried very carefully to be a good girl without acting "holier than thou". I had seen other people that were judgmental and unloving to others. That was always such a turn-off for me. That helped me to develop more of an understanding and compassionate heart for others. I never wanted to be a judgmental person. I wanted a heart like Jesus.

It was a little easier for me to be that Christian young lady because it wasn't an act or a mask that I put on everyday. It was really who I was. My thoughts and actions came naturally because deep inside I craved learning about the Bible and truly fell in love with God at a young age. Of course, I was tempted and made mistakes just like everyone else, but I asked for God's help on a daily basis to not make it a habit.

When I look back I can see how God was preparing me for my future roles as an adult, all through my childhood and teenage years. I sometimes thought I was weird because while other teenagers were falling asleep and disinterested in church, I loved listening to my pastor preach. While other teenagers were living the party scene, that never really appealed to me, especially the kind of parties they were. Staying at home and staying out of trouble was perfectly fine with me.

I missed both of my proms but I don't regret it. I got to be part of a small group of my Senior class that missed a whole day of school to go help decorate for our prom. We all had a lot of fun although I knew I wouldn't get to go since Jerry Dale had to work. I didn't want to go without him.

My Junior year, I missed my prom since Dad wasn't allowing us to go out on dates yet. If I couldn't go with Jerry Dale, then I really didn't want to go at all. We came up with a solution where he came over dressed up in his finest suit and I put on the gown I wore in the Homecoming parade my Freshman year. We had our own private prom in my living room at the house and we were both fine with that, just as long as we could be together.

Before prom my Junior year, Jerry Dale invited me, my sisters, and cousin Scooby to come to the youth Valentine party at his church. Dad agreed that we could all go as long as Mom stayed. This was the first time that Jerry Dale and I were allowed to be alone together outside of the house so we cherished every moment.

Before the party began, Jerry Dale asked me to come with him into the sanctuary of the church because he wanted me to try to sing with him. It was a Christian song but the way the lyrics were written, it could have been considered a love song, too. We were both loving that short time singing together and it just felt so natural.

Once the party was over, Mom allowed me and Jerry Dale to have a few minutes alone in his truck to say our good-byes while she and the others were not far away in our car. I'll never forget those precious few minutes. It was then that Jerry Dale unofficially proposed to me.

"Heather, I love you. I want you to be my wife and the mother of my children."

Did I just hear what I thought I heard? I couldn't believe it but my heart was doing cartwheels with excitement. We both teared up.

"There's nothing that I could ever want more."

It was a few months later when we made it more official by shopping for my engagement ring together. Instead of Jerry Dale picking it out and surprising me, he wanted me to be able to get exactly what I wanted. We started out by going to one of the local malls, looking through every high priced jewelry store they had. Things turned a little sour after we reached Zale's.

A salesman approached us at the jewelry counter where the engagement rings were and everything was going fine, or so I thought. After a few minutes, Jerry Dale suggested that we needed to leave. At first I brushed it off as I told him that I wasn't through looking yet, but after looking at his face I could tell he was getting angry. I didn't know what was going on but I knew something was wrong so I reluctantly left with him before I was through looking at the rings. At first I thought he was getting overwhelmed by the high prices of the rings, but after I asked what was wrong, he didn't hold back explaining.

"Didn't you see that guy looking at you?"

"What guy?"

"That sales guy! You didn't see him? He kept staring at your breasts!"

"No, I didn't see him. I was too busy looking at the rings. I wasn't looking at him."

"Well, he couldn't keep his eyes off your chest. You shouldn't have worn that sweater. It shows off your breasts way too much."

At that I looked down to inspect whether my sweater was too tight and it really wasn't. I had never seen Jerry Dale so intensely jealous like that, but that wouldn't be the last time.

He eventually got over it and I finally suggested that we just go to Wal-Mart to look for a ring. Every time I looked at the rings in those jewelry stores all I saw was extremely high prices and a monthly note that would certainly follow. I couldn't see spending that kind of money on a ring. I didn't want to start our first year of marriage with a monthly note on something other than furniture or something we actually needed.

I would have felt really guilty if Jerry Dale had to work hard just to pay off what we owed on a ring on my finger. It didn't matter to me how much he spent on the ring as long as it was something that I thought was pretty and I could be happy wearing for the rest of my life.

At first, Jerry Dale argued about taking me to Wal-Mart to shop for my engagement ring. He was afraid that I wouldn't be satisfied with a ring from there, but I finally convinced him that I was serious and would have no regrets. He finally agreed after I told him that gold and diamonds are the same no matter where you buy them, it's just the prices that are different.

We found a beautiful gold band with a cluster of small diamonds on the top that he could pay for in full. That made us both happy but we had to wait for it since they didn't have my size for my very skinny finger.

Once the ring came in, Jerry Dale picked me up and took me to the Logansport riverfront to officially propose. We sat there by the water with the stars above us as he proposed once again but this time he made it official by placing the ring on my finger. As we sat there in the truck enjoying our amazing moment together we looked up and saw a cop car coming toward us.

How were we going to explain this one? He's going to think that we were "parking". Sure enough, the cop pulled up beside us but Jerry Dale was immediately relieved to see that it was his uncle. To prove that we weren't doing anything other than the proposal, I stuck out my left hand to show him my new ring. We all got a good laugh and his uncle congratulated us as he drove away.

I was so happy when we all came back to school from Christmas break. I could now show off my new engagement ring. Most congratulated me but I got some "I could care less" looks from some of the girls. I wasn't going to let anyone pull me down from the cloud I was floating on.

On the other hand, there were other things that were starting to concern me about Jerry Dale. I was seeing some things in him that I didn't know how to handle. One of them was his temper. He had gotten mad a couple of more times and had hit the dash of his truck. I didn't know what to think since no one in my family ever hit things, or each other, out of anger. Once while we were saying our good-byes on my front porch Jerry Dale could tell there was something bothering me and began to question what it was.

"I'm just concerned about something. I've seen you lose your temper and hit things that were around you. What if one day I make you really mad? What would it take for you to eventually hit me?"

"Heather, I love you. I would never do anything to hurt you. I would never hit you."

I knew he was telling me the truth and I knew he genuinely loved me. As he stood there and held me for the longest time, I still had my doubts, but there was something else that was concerning me. It was his jealousy.

It was like he was scared to death of losing me to someone else. If he even thought that another guy was looking at me, or even worse, that I was looking at another guy, he got so jumpy and angry. Accusations would start flying until I finally convinced him that he had nothing to worry about.

It was because of his past relationships that scarred him for several years. Since all it took was his guy friends flirting with his girlfriends to make them leave Jerry Dale for them, he was so afraid that he would lose me in the same way. I understood why he had a jealous streak but sometimes it was hard for me to deal with.

Because of my past, Jerry Dale was sometimes over-protective of me as well. He was determined to make sure that nobody would ever hurt me again but he didn't realize that he was smothering me all the while he thought he was protecting me. I knew he meant well but he was driving me crazy at times. It wasn't until about three months after we got married that he finally understood that I was going to be alright and he couldn't protect me from everything or everybody. The real question: would he ever have to?

A God Moment

My Mom always said that if we ever had any doubts, especially concerning relationships, then don't do it. It's usually those little clues that others give us, that we seem to ignore but they're there to give us a warning. If you're in a relationship, be mindful of these character flaws and/or habits that could cause major damage if not dealt with correctly. Whatever you carry in your dating relationship will only be amplified after marriage. Deal with these issues by talking them out together, taking it to God in prayer, and then do what you must to change these destructive habits or character flaws.

Chapter 25

A Birthday, A Graduation, and A Wedding

"Love suffers long and is kind; love does not envy; love does not parade itself, is not puffed up; does not behave rudely, does not seek it's own, is not provoked, thinks no evil; bears all things, believes all things, hopes all things, endures all things. Love never fails." 1 Corinthians 13:4-8a (NKJV)

Once Dad started allowing us to actually date after my birthday in May of 1987, Jerry Dale and I thought that the worst was behind us. We enjoyed the whole summer and were together as much as we could be, but I soon found my world tumbling underneath me on one of our dates.

After pastoring at South Oak Grove Assembly of God church in Stanley, LA for over thirteen years, Jerry Dale's parents got a call to try out for the Senior Pastor position at a church in Crossett, Arkansas. They also needed a new Youth Pastor. I found out that not only Bro. and Sis. English were voted in, but Jerry Dale was to be their new Youth Pastor as well.

The news was very exciting for the ministry opportunities opening up for them all but the fact that Jerry Dale had to now move over a couple of hours away was too much to think about. We had just begun to have the freedom to date and now we would be separated again.

Jerry Dale had already been the Youth Pastor under his parents at their church for about a year or so. It was starting to sink in that this was going to be a way of life for not only him, but me as well.

I guess I thought he was just doing the youth ministry thing because there was a vacancy and he happened to be the Pastor's son so they asked him to do it. After talking with Jerry Dale, he shared that his heart was for the youth and he knew that was what God was calling him to do. I always knew that God gave me my voice to sing for Him but it never occurred to me that I would be a minister's wife one day.

Was I ready to be a minister's wife? I started searching my own heart and began praying for God's guiding wisdom in this huge life decision. God started showing me how He had been preparing me for this all along. He had been grooming my heart to have the patience, understanding, and compassion that it would take to be in this difficult, but rewarding role. Then I thought about the issue of me being only eighteen years old when I got married. Jerry Dale would be twenty-two but since I would still be a teenager myself, how would the youth react to my age?

I didn't know what to say when Jerry Dale told me that he was about to move to Arkansas. I felt like all of the air suddenly was let out of my balloon that had been flying so high just moments before. We had just started going out on dates and spending quality time together alone, but now he's telling me that we will be separated once again.

"Really God? What are you doing? I know we're supposed to be together and now that the obstacles have been removed, You want to move him away from me? Why God?"

The next question was when would he have to move. It was sooner than we wanted it to be but he had to leave the same morning that I started my first day of school as a Senior. The day before he left we made sure we had as much time together as possible. Jerry Dale planned an evening that was special and neither of us wanted it to end. It got harder as the night pushed on, knowing that we would have to say good-bye for a while.

I didn't want to let go. We stayed on my front porch holding each other for so long with neither of us wanting to move from that moment. We both cried as we knew we had to say good-bye. I finally managed to let him go and stepped inside the living room but as I looked through the glass of our front door, I locked eyes with Jerry Dale and I broke down crying even harder. That broke his heart and he motioned for me to come back to him so he could comfort me. I immediately swung open the door and ran back into his arms, holding each other so tight and never wanting to let go. He promised to call me the next morning before I left for school and with that, he finally left.

It was so late and I knew I was going to have to wake up at 5:00 A.M. the next morning, but I didn't care. I wanted every moment with Jerry Dale that I could have. The next morning we talked over the phone for only a couple of minutes, right before I was to walk out the door to go to school. We both started crying again so I ruined my make-up for the first day of school. It was so hard to get myself together and stop crying, but every time I thought of him, the tears came flooding back. I didn't want my nose and eyes to be red and puffy for my first day of Senior year so I tried to distract my thoughts with other things, at least until I got back home.

The months went by slow but I kept myself busy planning for our wedding that was scheduled for June 3rd of 1988. That year was so busy since I would turn eighteen on May 18, then graduate from high school on May 23. I had so much to do and plan that sometimes it was a little overwhelming. As I received gifts, I had to keep up with not only what I got and from whom, but also separating them for what occasion they were given. The thank you notes tripled in number but I didn't mind since I was extremely grateful for every gift.

Although my Senior year was hectic, it was my best year. I was an officer in almost every club, including being voted as Student Council Vice President by the entire student body. I involved myself in most extracurricular activities like helping to lead in school assemblies and singing at a majority of them.

I planned on going to college to become a registered nurse or something in business administration. With my grades, I could have gotten scholarships, but I ended up choosing a different path. Since I knew that my life would be consumed in ministry, I started praying about this major decision and knew that God was leading me in another direction. Once I made my decision, I felt good about it and I've never had any regrets.

Once graduation was over, planning the final touches of our wedding kicked up a notch. I wanted my wedding to be perfect since I was only going to have one in my lifetime. Jerry Dale and I had talked about our relationship and decided that no matter what happened in our marriage, divorce would never be an option. We knew as long as we kept God in the forefront of our marriage and we were willing to work through any problem together, we could make it through anything. Our vows would mean more than just words that we repeated on our wedding day.

Jerry Dale and I both decided to write and sing our own songs to each other at our wedding and have his older brother, Dennis, play his twelve-string guitar for us. That was our personal touch to the ceremony and it turned out beautiful.

My dress was gorgeous, with a long train, covered with beads, pearls, sequins and scalloped lace. It had a small opening in the back with five bows going down the train and my veil was equally beautiful. I felt like a princess. Grandma James wanted to make sure that I had the dress that I wanted so she agreed to pay for it as a wedding gift. I was so grateful because we couldn't have afforded the dress that I picked out without her help.

We decided to have our wedding on a Friday night so we could have more time together for our short honeymoon. After moving to Arkansas, Jerry Dale found a job as a salesman at the local Otasco store making just over minimum wage. Since his Youth Pastor position didn't have a salary attached to it, that was our only income. It wasn't much but it was a job and he saved every dime he could.

We only had that weekend together since he had to be back at work that following Monday. Our honeymoon would start in our first little home in Crossett, Arkansas on our wedding night since it would be so late after leaving Longstreet. Then we would get up the next morning and head to Hot Springs, Arkansas for a couple of days. We didn't have much money but we were determined to just enjoy finally being together.

Jerry Dale and his parents were living in the church's parsonage that was right next to the church. They started slowly fixing up an old fellowship hall from the original church building to be our new little house that we would live in. They did a great job designing the layout and decorations and it was perfect for a young couple to start their new lives together in.

Packing to move to my new little house was exciting but scary at the same time. It was hard boxing up everything that I had collected over the years of my life together with my family, only to leave them behind for my new life.

Mom and I decided to go to Crossett with the rest of my things on the Wednesday of the week of our wedding. Mom helped me get settled in and we both spent the night together in the little house. That night, Jerry Dale and I stayed up until around 2:00 in the morning, just talking on our very own little back porch. I remember crying out of happiness and it all felt like a dream coming true, but I was afraid that I might wake up and find it all to be just a fairy tale. Jerry Dale reassured me that what we had was no fairy tale but very real and it was all about to happen in just a couple of days.

When we started sending out the invitations for our wedding, I naturally sent one to my past best friend in Texas, but I really didn't expect Tammy to be able to come. I got the surprise of my life when she and her mother showed up early at the church where Mom and I had been decorating and setting up some last minute finishing touches to the reception hall.

Although we had kept in touch through writing letters, we hadn't seen each other since the fifth grade. Tammy came back to the house and fixed my hair for me while I did my makeup. It was so wonderful to have her there with me on my special day along with my other great friends. We couldn't afford a professional photographer so Tammy's sweet mother ended up taking a bunch of beautiful pictures for us.

We asked Jerry Dale's Dad to marry us and my Pastor to assist. We tried to involve as many of our family and friends in the ceremony or reception so we wouldn't hurt anyone's feelings, but without making the wedding too big. I even invited my grandparents on Bill's side of the family and Aunt Audrey, but Bill wasn't invited. After Jerry Dale and I discussed it, we didn't want anything or anyone to upset our day so I asked Joe to give me away instead. We knew that having Bill there would only upset me and make Jerry Dale very angry at the sight of him so we thought it best that he stayed away.

Everything turned out beautiful and there were no big mishaps, only a couple of small ones. It's a good thing we lived so close to the church because I showed up only ten minutes before the ceremony started. I was ready except for putting my dress on so we had to hurry. Every time someone picked up my train to get me to the front doors of the church, it kept getting twisted. By the time we were ready to open the doors for me to walk down the aisle, we couldn't because they were trying to get it untangled. Although it felt like an eternity it didn't take long to fix it and it all turned out wonderful.

After the wedding, Jerry Dale and I made it clear with Mom that we were not going to give our new Arkansas address to Bill or any of his family. The agreement was that Grandma and Mom could call or write to share about what was going on with us in our new lives since I chose to cut myself off from them.

My anger and bitterness towards Bill seemed to grow like a slow cancer but I didn't know what to do with it or how to get rid of it. I also hadn't forgotten how the family defended him and quickly turned against me. I felt that I was justified by my decision so I stood by it, no matter how it hurt. In my mind, I was starting a brand new life and if they didn't like it, they could just get over it. I had a lot to learn.

A God Moment

Starting something new is always exciting, especially when it's a good thing. Whatever future steps that you are about to take, no matter how big or small, make it a matter of prayer before you do anything or make any final decisions. When God is placed first in your life and everything in it, then it will always turn out fine. He has you in the palm of His hand and won't ever let you go. If you're not feeling as close to God as you once were, guess who moved?

Chapter 26

The Honeymoon

*"Then the rib which the Lord God had taken from man He made
into a woman, and He brought her to the man. And Adam said:
'This is now bone of my bones and flesh of my flesh; she shall be
called Woman, because she was taken out of Man.' Therefore a
man shall leave his father and mother and be joined to his wife,
and they shall become one flesh." Genesis 2:22-24 (NKJV)*

After the wedding and reception were over, Jerry Dale and I
went out to quickly get into the truck as everyone threw bird
seed on us. We soon discovered that several of our family and friends
had really decorated it up. Among the toilet paper and shaving
cream, they had "Just Married" spelled out with masking tape on
the back window.

It wasn't until we were in the truck that Dean knocked on our
window to tell us that we would have visitors on the way to Arkansas.
He had just let 50 crickets loose inside the truck but we were lucky
since they all hid under the seats and never chirped. Later that year, I
had the privilege of singing at Dean's and my friend Mary's wedding.

The two and a half hour ride to our new little house was sweet but
Jerry Dale and I were both anxious and nervous about our wedding
night together. We both wanted it to be super special and didn't want
anything to ruin it. Neither of us had ever been with anyone else
sexually, so as the night progressed we were both getting nervous

but excited at the same time. For so long I had dreamed of this night where the man I loved would wrap me in his strong arms and hold me all night long. To feel safe enough to fall asleep in his arms while cuddling with one another was something I was looking forward to.

That night I wore a beautiful white night gown that Gam made special for me. It was such a special night for us both and we held each other all night long, never letting go for a second.

I remember lying there thinking, "So this is what it's like. This is what I waited for. I'm officially a woman now."

I know that sounds silly but I changed in every way that night. I didn't want anything to change, but everything changed for the both of us in a wonderful way. We were starting our lives together and it was only the beginning.

Since I was introduced to the sexual world in such an awful way, I wanted to finally see what sex was supposed to be like, as God designed it. Let me say that our first night was beautiful and worth waiting for. There was nothing dirty or wrong about it. Nothing to be ashamed of or feel guilty about. We did things the right way as God meant it to be by waiting until we were officially married. People don't realize what damage they do to themselves, not just physically, but mentally and spiritually, when you don't wait for sex until marriage.

God designed our bodies to be sexual but it won't be blessed or a positive experience when it's done outside of His will. When a couple comes together sexually for the first time, there are so many different things that happen to them, binding them together forever. Let me take a side step real quick and give you a God-style sex education for those of you thinking about not waiting for sex. Maybe you have already crossed that forbidden line and are wondering why you feel the way you do. Some of this I found through the years of studying and preaching to teenagers and it's pretty good stuff.

Sex God's Way

We hear a lot about abstinence but what does it really mean? What is the difference between abstinence and purity? Abstinence simply means avoiding certain things while purity means to live according to original design. Abstinence is a habit, or even a rule, but purity is a virtue. It's not just the choice to not have sex, but a commitment to live according to God's design. Purity means waiting for sex so that you're able to experience it within the loving marital relationship that God created and designed it for.

Some people think that God and the Bible are against sex but that's not true. God takes sex very seriously but He gives us a picture of sexuality that's more intense, vibrant, and sexy than what our culture teaches. Actually, sticking to God's plan for sexuality leads to sex that is far more fulfilling than the sexual experiences supported by the world. There are several scriptures that talk about sex being satisfying and intoxicating. The Song of Solomon is full of steamy descriptions of love scenes between two lovers totally immersed in satisfying each other. The Apostle Paul recommends sex between married couples often. There's not a single verse in the Bible that calls sex sinful or dirty. It's not sex that is wrong but the misuse of sex outside of God's design.

God designed sex as a gift to be shared and unwrapped between a husband and wife. He wants us to wait because sex according to this design is so wonderful that it's worth protecting. The Bible gives us three specific reasons for sex. You probably already know the first one and it's called procreation, or making babies. God has given us a very God-like ability to create life through the act of sex. God intended the results of sex to be a blessing. Of course it's possible to make babies outside of marriage, but creating life is one of the most amazing things you will ever do. It deserves to be celebrated without the shame and distractions of bad timing, within the bounds of a God-honoring marriage.

The second reason is unity. As humans, we are hardwired with a deep desire for intimacy. Sex is scientifically proven to create a bond between two people, but the deepest levels of connection and intimacy can only be achieved by pursuing God's plan for sex. The bond between a husband and wife is so strong that they become united into one, or they are so joined together that you can't pull them apart. Researchers have discovered a hormone called oxytocin, or the "cuddle hormone." Oxytocin is a chemical your brain releases during sex and the activity leading up to it. When this chemical is released, it produces feelings of caring, trust, and deep affection. The purpose is to create a deep human bond or attachment. Every time you have sex with another person, your body has a chemical reaction that tells it to attach. Research has also proven that God's design for intimacy is at its best between a husband and wife with no other sexual partners. When we wait until marriage to have sex, we establish a level of intimacy that is unequaled, forming a bond with our spouse that is difficult to break.

The third reason God created sex may surprise you. It was for our enjoyment. Yes, God wants sex to be fun! God intended sex to be exciting and enjoyable. It's true that sex outside of marriage can be fun, but it can't reach the level of enjoyment and pleasure that we find when we stick to God's plan for sex. Studies have shown that people who have sex early and those who have had multiple partners are less satisfied with their sex lives than those who entered marriage with little or no sexual experience. God created sex for our benefit and His glory. When sex is enjoyed according to God's plan, the result is amazing. When we move outside of the boundaries God has established for our sex lives, pleasure is weakened, intimacy is cheapened, and the blessings God intended as the results of our sexual encounters can spoil.

The most powerful sex organ isn't covered by your swimsuit or found between your legs but it's between your ears. When it comes to sex, your brain is where the real magic happens. Though weighing only three pounds, your brain contains 10 billion neurons, 100 billion support cells, and 100 trillion connectors that connect those cells and neurons. Every second one million new connectors are created. Your brain is the most intricate mass in the universe. During sex, the brain sends messages though the body commanding physical function. When it comes to responding to sexual experiences, clearly the brain is calling the shots.

But not all brains are equipped for maximum sex. Without going into a big science lecture, your brain doesn't become hardwired to make fast, wise choices about sex until you are in your twenties. While we're teenagers, our brains aren't fully thinking correctly and are not fully equipped to make choices based on future consequences.

If you ask anyone that was sexually active at an early age, you'll find that the vast majority wished they would have waited.

By God's design, the best rewards for sex happen in your mind, but when you engage in sex outside of marriage, there are physical consequences in your brain. Female brains receive high doses of the "cuddle hormone" oxytocin whenever there is touching and hugging, while vasopressin is a hormone that does the same thing in the male brain. God has designed our bodies to respond physically to long-term intimacy, and that response takes place in the brain. When we continually change partners, oxytocin levels decrease and the brain's oxytocin release function doesn't work as it's supposed to. Promiscuous sexual activity wears down vasopressin production in the male brain, causing men to become desensitized to the risk of short-term relationships. Short-term, noncommital sex can literally change your brain at a chemical level.

Oxytocin and vasopressin aren't the only sexual responses generated in the brain. Sex also triggers a "feel good" chemical called dopamine. Dopamine is released anytime we do something exciting or rewarding. If oxytocin is the chemical that tells us we're in love, dopamine says, "I've got to have more of that!" It's important to understand that dopamine is value-neutral. It can't tell the difference between constructive and destructive behaviors or between good and bad relationships. In many ways, dopamine works like a drug. Our brains need increasing doses in order to achieve the same level of pleasure. Sex outside of marriage causes an increasing craving for dopamine that has serious consequences on our relationships. If the relationship ends, it affects the release of oxytocin, and more and more sexual contact is required to get the same dopamine rush. Every time you move to a new relationship, you have to have a little more sexual contact in order to satisfy your brain's craving for dopamine, and the bonding effect starts to break down. Also, because dopamine triggers intense feelings of pleasure, sexually active couples often substitute that feeling of excitement for feelings of affection. Their relationships quickly deteriorate as they start chasing the dopamine high instead of chasing true intimacy.

When sex is reserved for marriage, our brains still receive doses of the neurochemicals that make sex so exciting, and our brains are then able to process those chemicals in a way that promotes healthy relationships and responses.

Here is something else about your brain. Any time you are in an emotional situation with your five senses involved, your body releases a chemical called norepinephrine, which is called the "memory chemical." When you experience a highly emotional and sensory event, this chemical is released in your brain and it "paper-clips" it to your brain for recall. Every time you have a sexual encounter, it is attached to your mind. When you get married, you will bring those paper-clipped experiences into the relationship with you. Since our sexual encounters are imprinted into our brains on a biological level, you won't be able to shake the memory of your other sex partners.

Hebrews 13:4 tells us, "Marriage should be honored by all, and the marriage bed kept pure." This verse is better translated as "Let sexual intercourse be pure." One definition of purity is "containing no foreign element." When we don't wait until marriage for sex, mentally we are bringing our other sexual partners into the marriage bed because they are permanently imprinted on our minds and affect how we respond at a chemical level.

Hopefully this information will enlighten you on just how important waiting for sex until marriage truly is. I can say from personal experience that waiting for sex was well worth it. One question that I've heard more than once is, "But what if the sex is bad since neither of you have had any experience?"

Well, that's the best part. Neither of us had experience with anyone else so we would have the amazing pleasure of learning together without being compared to someone else. That's all part of the fun, finding out what the other one likes. Every person is different so even if you gain experience with someone from your past, it doesn't mean that your spouse is going to like the same thing. You'll still have to learn with your spouse even if you have past experience so why not wait and save that special gift just for them?

A God Moment

Today we live in a world and society that accepts the belief of whatever feels good is alright as long as it doesn't hurt anyone else. The problem with that theory is that our sin always effects someone else, somehow, eventually. We have come from a society that once frowned upon premarital sex to one that literally celebrates it. Choosing any and all forms of sexual activity outside of God's original design is socially acceptable today and classified as not actually being a sin anymore. How did we get to this point? How did fornication, adultery, sodomy, and homosexuality become a good thing? Very slowly and methodically. Sounds just like the tactics of the devil, doesn't it?

Chapter 27

Marriage and Youth Ministry

"And I thank Christ Jesus our Lord who has enabled me,
because He counted me faithful, putting me into the ministry."
1 Timothy 1:12 (NKJV)

The morning after our wedding, Jerry Dale and I went on to Hot Springs, Arkansas for the remainder of our short honeymoon. As the day progressed on and we were riding in our truck, I remember thinking that Jerry Dale would have to take me home to my parents soon. Then it hit me that I didn't ever have to do that again. I felt so free at that moment. I was a married young woman now with my own life, my own husband, my own house, my own bills. Growing up can be a scary experience sometimes but as long as I had God and Jerry Dale, I knew I could handle anything.

After coming back that Sunday, it was time to start our new routine of me being a house wife and Jerry Dale going back to work. It was also going to be my first week as a new youth pastor's wife. We were both anxious to see how this was going to work and how the teens would accept me.

Everything was pretty busy for the next month as we prepared for the youth group's biggest fundraiser of the year—a fire works stand located in the local Wal-Mart parking lot. I didn't know very much about many of the fireworks so I had to do my homework since I was expected to help out.

Although most of the people liked me, I could tell there were a handful that not only didn't approve of me, but they didn't like Jerry Dale either. There was one particular lady named Debbie that liked to stir up trouble in different areas of the church. She had her sights set on getting rid of us and taking over the youth ministry. I had already seen her in action against my in-laws and how Bro. English and the deacons had to pull her into the office to have private discussions with her. This wasn't how ministry was supposed to be was it?

I thought I knew what to expect in being part of a ministry since I was involved in church for several years, but I was sadly mistaken. There is so much more that goes on behind the scenes that no one really knows about and I found out quickly that I had a lot to learn. There were intense family meetings around the dinner table in the English house concerning the church. We discussed what we all needed to do better, or maybe how to handle difficult situations. I was getting a crash course on how hard things can get in running a church.

I remember one particular day that I learned a hard lesson. After each service, The English's stood in front of the doors on one side while Jerry Dale and I stood on the opposite side, shaking hands and hugging necks as our church people left. We had just recently found out some very hurtful and damaging things that Debbie had done against the English's so as I saw her walking toward my mother-in-law, Sis. English, my first thought was how I would love to slap her lying face.

I wanted to see how Mom English reacted to her as she went by and I was surprised. Mom English kept a smile on her face and hugged her.

"Love you sister. God bless you."

How could Mom English say that to Debbie after all she knows that she's done? I don't know if my face showed it but I was shocked.

After everyone left and the church was locked up, we all went to the English's house to eat lunch together. I had to find out how she did it.

"How did you do that? How can you hug Debbie after what she's said and done against you, our family, and the church? I just want to smack her!"

"Well, Heather, you've got a lot to learn about the ministry. Although people will get on your nerves or hurt you, whether it's intentional or accidental, you've got to forgive and love them anyway. You have to keep your cool and integrity as the leader of the church and be the example that Christ would be proud of. It takes a lot of patience, understanding, and prayer to do what we do. In time you'll learn this for yourself."

I had plenty of opportunities to test my patience during those months we were in Crossett. It eventually got so bad at the church that Jerry Dale made the decision to leave once he knew that he could no longer be an asset there, and his parents resigned shortly after that. We stayed in the area, moving into a rental trailer while my in-laws moved back to their home in Stanley, LA. Jerry Dale's great uncle was the pastor at a church in town so he asked us to help them with their youth program and we agreed.

Things were going alright until Jerry Dale's job called him one morning to tell him that he didn't have to come in to work. We both thought that was suspicious so he got up anyway and headed down to the Otasco store to see what was going on. When he got there, the doors were locked and the store had been officially closed with no warning. That's how we found out that Jerry Dale lost his job, so he immediately began looking for another. The only thing he could find was a night stocking job at the local Safeway grocery store. It didn't pay well but he was willing to work any position to provide for us and I loved him for that.

It wasn't long that we figured out how hard it would be just to make it and pay our bills. After talking with the English's they told us to just come home to Stanley. Since Mom and Dad English were currently pastors at a church in Hornbeck, Louisiana, they told us we could move into their house. It was breaking their hearts knowing how we were struggling with no close family near us. My Mom and Dad were also worried about us and were so happy to hear that we were coming back home. They all came to Arkansas in their vehicles, helped us pack everything, and headed home in a convoy together.

What would happen to us now? Would Jerry Dale find another job in time to pay our bills? What about our ministry? There were so many questions with no real answers. It was now January of 1989 and we were basically starting over. We both started praying for God's will and His direction for us as a couple, as well as young ministers. What would God have in store for us now?

A God Moment

When we say "yes" to Jesus, that means we say "yes" to being ministers of His gospel. Some are called to be teachers, preachers, evangelists, pastors, counselors, prayer warriors, and much more. But there are so many other things that we can do. Just by living your life in front of others as a living testimony of His goodness and love is just as important. God calls us to live the life if we wear the name "Christian". If we say we're a Christian, then that means we carry the label of being "Christ-like" and "follower of Christ". We're all called to serve. What's your calling? What are you doing with it?

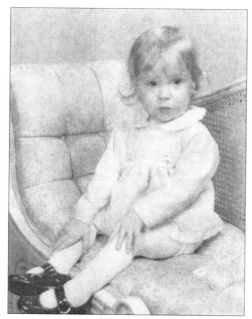

Heather

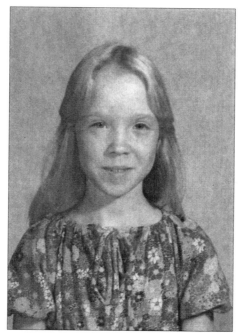

Heather

Heather

Heather

Heather

Heather

Dale & Heather

Dale & Heather - 25th Anniversary

Dale English

Daniel English

Daniel English

Daniel & Stephanie English

Christian English

Christian English

The English Family

Chapter 28

Making Strides

"We are hard-pressed on every side, yet not crushed; we are perplexed, but not in despair; persecuted, but not forsaken; struck down, but not destroyed. 2 Corinthians 4:8-9 (NKJV)

After getting moved into my in-laws' house back in Stanley, Louisiana, Jerry Dale found a job on what they called the "green end" at Louisiana Pacific plywood mill located in Logansport. It didn't pay much but it was a job so we didn't complain, although it was hard seeing Jerry Dale work so hard and come home completely exhausted. I learned quick just how hard-working he would be. I never had to worry about him being lazy, even when it came to getting things done at our house.

The only problem with Jerry Dale working at L.P. was it was literally making him sick. His job consisted of him standing by a conveyer that brought down different sizes of wet, green sheets of plywood, and he had to quickly grab, sort, and stack them on carts behind him. It was an extremely physical and exhausting job.

Jerry Dale's shift started around 6:30pm and ended at 2:30am. Our routine was he would wake me up when he got home early in the morning and collapsed on the bed while I took his boots off. He was so filthy and covered with sweat that he couldn't go to bed without taking a bath first so I let him rest for a few minutes while I ran his bath water. Even in the winter months his socks were saturated in sweat and I would have to peel them off his feet. Once his bath water was ready, I woke him up so he could get clean enough to crawl into bed with me.

Once we were in bed, we always cuddled together but Jerry Dale twitched from the constant motion that his body had been doing at the plant for the last eight hours. I slept on the right side of him, with his right arm around me so I couldn't get back to sleep until the twitching stopped. We eventually switched sides for a while after he accidentally punched me in the face by his arm twitching so hard in his sleep. He apologized for days after that.

A New House

We got a surprise phone call from Jerry Dale's parents saying that they were moving back home soon. That meant we had to start looking for our own place to live. Mom and Dad English had been the pastors at a church in Hornbeck, Louisiana but felt God moving them back home.

The English's had almost twenty acres of land so they offered a portion of it to place our own trailer on if we wanted to. Since we couldn't afford to buy land of our own and we didn't want to waste money on rent, we decided to try looking for a second-hand trailer that we could move onto the property.

We knew we couldn't afford anything pricey but Jerry Dale said that he wasn't paying anything over $5,000 on a trailer. I thought he was crazy and told him that there was no way we would be able to find anything for that price that was worth living in. We went to prayer and asked God to help us find something perfect for us.

We looked for days and ended up at a place about an hour south of us. We found a 14' x 56' used trailer that wasn't in bad shape like most of the others we had found. It was small but really cute and we both liked it. Some of the other trailers we found that were in bad shape were more than we could afford so we were afraid to ask how much this cute little trailer was. After the salesman told us that it was only $4,995, Jerry Dale and I were both amazed and quickly told him we wanted it.

"See, I told you we could find something for the price I wanted."

I knew it had to be a miracle from God based on all the other prices we had been seeing. That same day we got a phone call from the owner of the lot that had our trailer with some interesting information. He explained that he had to leave the lot but left it for a short time in the hands of a family friend. His friend had no idea how much anything was worth, and wasn't supposed to quote any prices without calling him first.

We learned that our little trailer was actually over one thousand dollars higher than what was quoted to us but the owner knew he had to sell it to us for the agreed upon price. Jerry Dale and I both immediately gave praise to God because we knew He answered our prayers and blessed us with this trailer.

It was an amazing feeling moving into our very own home and I really felt like a true house wife. Jerry Dale and I could call this small trailer ours and decorate it any way we wanted, within our budget of course. The trailer was perfect for a young couple and maybe a baby later on since the second bedroom was more like a big walk-in closet. The plan was to have this trailer paid off in three years so we could finally build the house we really wanted on the back side of the property.

My in-laws finally moved back to Stanley not long after we got settled into our own little place right beside them on the other hill. We could tell that they were glad to be back home, especially Dad English since he had his shop to tinker in and his tractor to ride on. Jerry Dale and Dad English loved being outside, especially fishing. Bass fishing was one of Jerry Dale's favorite outdoor hobbies and he was pretty good at it, too. Hunting came in at a close second.

Shortly after we married, Jerry Dale wanted me to go hunting with him that first season but I had to have some shooting lessons since I had never fired a gun on my own. He started me off with a small .410 shotgun and set up some cans for targets in the woods. We were both shocked that I had a pretty good aim so he eventually graduated me up to a .20 gauge shotgun. That would be my weapon of choice every time we went hunting together, whether it was deer or squirrel we were after.

With Jerry Dale's parents living next door and his sister, Lisa, living just on the other side, it made it easy for us to help each other.

They were always willing to help us in any way they could and we ate together as a big family at their house at least once a week. Dennis and his family came as often as they could from Benton, Louisiana.

It also meant that we could help them out with things around the property as well. Jerry Dale loved knowing that he could be there to help his parents and sister when they needed him. I remember one day in particular.

The Fire

I'll never forget the day that I saw Jerry Dale's face with a look of horror that I hope to never see again. Dad English and Jerry Dale had been welding underneath the shed behind the barn. They had been lying down on some flattened out cardboard when some of the sparks ignited a couple of places but they quickly put them out. When they were finished, they both made sure that everything was put up and the cardboard was placed inside the small crappie boat under the shed after checking that it was still out.

Jerry Dale had to get ready to go to work at L.P. so we both laid down for a short nap before he had to go. It was then that we heard it. Suddenly Jerry Dale sat straight up in the bed. He heard something that sounded like a small explosion so he quickly ran out of our trailer to find the shed and barn engulfed in flames.

Jerry Dale ran quickly over to his parents' house to see if they were home. He began running through their house screaming out for his dad, but no answer. Panic started to set in as he ran back outside to find his dad while screaming at me to call 911. As Jerry Dale reached outside he suddenly heard something that sounded like a man screaming from inside the fire. That's when he lost it, running to get a water hose so he could go into the fire.

After I had called 911, I ran back outside to find Jerry Dale with the water hose screaming, "Dad's in that fire! I have to go in after him!"

"Jerry Dale you can't go in the blaze with only a water hose. You'll burn up, too! The fire department is on their way right now. Are you sure your dad is in there?"

"I heard what sounded like a man screaming and I can't find dad anywhere in the house. I'll go back inside one more time just to make sure."

Jerry Dale ran back inside the house, calling out for his dad but this time Dad English finally answered him back. He had been taking a shower the whole time and never heard Jerry Dale calling for him. As soon as Dad English answered him, Jerry Dale sighed in great relief knowing his father was safe. Jerry Dale then realized that he almost risked his life to save an oxygen tank from the welding machine that exploded in the fire and sounded just like a man screaming.

After the fire was put out, it was hard looking at the damage that was left behind. It was a total loss with everything in the barn and under the shed. Their boat, lawn mowers, and Dad English's big tractor were all destroyed. Although their home was insured, the barn wasn't so they had to start all over on their own. That was hard since they had limited income but they never complained and trusted God to help them recover.

A God Moment

It's hard to trust God in the middle of change or a disaster. It's during those times that we need to lean on Him the most. It seems that when things are going great that we rarely have time for God, but the minute our lives are literally falling apart, that's when we run to God on our knees, begging for His help. We need to learn to stay on our knees no matter what's going on, giving God praise through everything, whether good or bad. Don't wait until God has to put you on your knees—volunteer to go there yourself.

Chapter 29

Stepping Up In The World

"I will instruct you and teach you in the way you should go; I will guide you with My eye." Psalm 32:8 (NKJV)

Not long after the fire, we noticed that Jerry Dale was staying sick and completely exhausted so I talked him into going to the doctor. It was then when we found out that he needed to quit his job at L.P. since it was working there that kept him sick. I had just started working as a legal secretary for a lawyer in Mansfield, Louisiana and we realized that my job came just in time.

Jerry Dale wanted to do more to provide for us and our future family so he decided to put himself through training as a medical assistant at Southern Technical College in Shreveport. My salary would carry us while he went to college for those nine months.

Jerry Dale did very well and he finished his month-long internship at a local physical therapy clinic in Bossier City, Louisiana. They were so impressed with his work ethic that they wanted him to come to work for them as soon as he graduated.

While Jerry Dale was going through training, I was loving my job but I was having a difficult time with my boss. The lawyer I worked for treated me well but he had a problem with alcohol and prescription drugs that periodically interfered with his ability to work. When my boss went through difficult times with his family, I felt like I was his counselor or psycho therapist since he constantly wanted to talk about his problems and get my opinion on the issues.

As long as my boss stayed sober, he was an amazing and effective lawyer but when he wasn't, I couldn't get him in the office to take care of his clients. That made me have to shuffle his appointments around and make excuses for him. While working for him, my boss went through a divorce and the tragic loss of his father. Both of these events sent him over the deep end, causing him to fall off the sober wagon once again.

Although she was older than me, Penny was one of my best friends growing up and she used to work as this lawyer's secretary. Now she worked as his bookkeeper part time and I always loved it when she was in the office. We always had so much fun together and she also helped me through the tough times working for the lawyer.

On one such occasion, Penny, Jerry Dale, and I went to the lawyer's house for an intervention. While Penny tried to talk some sense into him, Jerry Dale and I went through his house pouring out all the liquor he had stashed away. He eventually checked himself into a rehab center to dry out and get the help he needed, but that wouldn't be the first, or last, time.

Penny and I decided that after going through this messy routine twice, if our boss did this to us again, we would quit. The problem with the lawyer is that when he tasted alcohol, he couldn't stop. He would stay drunk for weeks, not eating, and missing all of his court dates and appointments.

There were several times that another lawyer friend came over and instructed me to sign my boss's name with his special green pen so he could go file papers on his behalf. That saved my boss's tail more than once. Thankfully none of those papers were major legal documents. With me being an artist I had the ability to sign my boss's name just like he did in times of emergency. This lawyer friend had the same problem as my boss so they took turns covering for each other at their lowest points. I began to think this was an epidemic with all the lawyers of that area.

After Penny and I discovered that our boss was on another drunken stint, we called him at the same time and announced our resignations. I hated that I was losing my job since Jerry Dale had just started working for the physical therapy clinic and we were enjoying the two incomes. For only a month we were a double income household but we both knew that God had sustained us with my job long enough for Jerry Dale to go through college and find a better job, so for that, we were grateful. So what would I do now?

A Touch of Heaven

Mom and I had played around with the idea of us opening a flower and gift shop together since we both loved it so much and we were good at it, but we never really talked about it seriously until after I quit my job. After much discussion, we launched out to open our own business in Logansport and called it "A Touch of Heaven." We offered everything you would expect out of a flower shop plus our own hand-painted ceramics by me and Mom, as well as our own wood crafts that Dad and my brother-in-law, Glenn, made themselves. Mom and I took their wood creations and decorated them, adding our own special touches.

We knew in order to stay competitive that we would have to go apply and pass the state floral exam to sell fresh flowers. What a lot of people don't realize is that in the state of Louisiana, if you want to sell fresh flowers in your shop, you have to pay the state to take a written, as well as an arranging exam, which is extremely hard to pass. You're graded by other florists from how you wire your flowers to how you place the pin in your corsage.

It's more than just making things look pretty. You better know your plants, greenery, and name every flower they place in front of you. If you cut yourself and got one drop of blood on any of your assignments, you failed. If you didn't finish everything on the list in the time they gave you, you failed. If you used the wrong greenery, filler, or flower required for any piece, you failed.

We didn't know what we were up against so Mom and I decided to pay the amount required and drive to Baton Rouge for a trial run through the testing process. Neither of us expected to pass but we wanted to see what was needed to pass. I passed the written test but failed the arranging part because I didn't finish everything in time. I cut my finger on one of the very sharp picks from my pick machine and wasted much time trying to find a band-aid.

After waiting the required three months, I went back to retake the arranging portion of the floral test and passed. Mom didn't go back because the law stated that as long as you had at least one licensed florist working in the shop, the others working there didn't require a license. We were well on our way, expanding wherever we could and making a name for ourselves.

I remember when we became popular with our homecoming corsages and garters because they were so unique and beautiful. Back then, everyone wore a corsage from the little kids to adults. It became a contest between the high school students to see who would have the biggest and best corsage to show off on Homecoming day. We were also known for amazingly huge, hand-made bows that were used for decorating the cars and floats but since Mom said her bows always ended up uneven, I made every bow that walked out of that shop.

Since we were a new business, every dime we made had to go right back into the shop to keep it going and expanding. Although we weren't making a salary, Mom and I enjoyed coming to work everyday and building up our business to where we would one day afford to bring home a paycheck. Valentine's Day and Christmas were a lot of work but we loved every minute of it. It made us happy to put a smile on someone's face and tried to spend time getting to know our customers.

Youth Pastors Again

Not long after the English's moved back home to Stanley, they informed us that God had been dealing with them for some time to open a new church in Logansport. There were no Assembly of God churches in that immediate area and they felt led to open one, so they started looking for property for their new church.

They found an old two story church that was built in 1924 by the First Baptist Church of Logansport that had been vacant for about ten years or more. When the Baptist church moved and rebuilt down the street, the Assemblies of God bought the property and kept it for many years after that. Somehow the Word of Faith got the property but then rebuilt across the river in Joaquin, Texas when they outgrew the facilities as well.

The church building was in poor shape. The downstairs had around two feet of water with old rummage sale stuff floating all in it, but the English's knew they found their place to build the church. They knew it would take a lot of work and used their own retirement money to get everything ready. The English's were determined to be obedient to what they knew God was telling them to do. Although they had friends, and even family, that told them they were crazy for doing it, they never stopped pushing ahead to get the church's doors opened.

While the English's were making their plans, they approached their daughter, Lisa to help them. They also asked Jerry Dale and me to help by becoming their youth pastors. Jerry Dale told them that he would help them for a while to get things going but he wanted them to be looking for someone else to eventually take his place.

The target date for our first service at First Assembly of God/ Family Worship Center was in June of 1989 and we were getting excited to see what God was going to do.

Everyone had an important part and at first, every position was filled by our family. Of course Dad English preached, Mom or Dad English led singing, Mom English or Lisa played the piano, Jerry Dale played the bass guitar, I played the drums, Jerry Dale and I were the youth pastors, Lisa was the women's ministry director, Mom English was the secretary/bookkeeper, and all of us were Sunday School teachers. Since we started the church with just our family, we all had to do practically everything but we were praying for God to send more qualified people to take over some of these positions.

Over time, God brought us some amazing people but it wasn't without some struggles. It was definitely an uphill climb the entire time we were there but everything you go through is worth the fight when you're in the service of the Lord. I've always heard that any-thing worth having is worth fighting for. This statement would also prove to be true in my marriage. We went through some tough trials that almost pushed us both over the edge.

A God Moment

For most of us, there have been at least a moment or two where we had an epiphany concerning our lives. You know those moments where you finally understood why something happened in your past that you questioned, but now it was suddenly made very clear? God is always lining out, ordering our steps, for our good, not our hurt or destruction. It is often our reluctance and disobedience that brings great pain and suffering along the way. Trust God as He directs your path and try not to question Him as He is working things out. Never forget how much our Heavenly Father loves you!

Chapter 30

Trouble In Paradise

"Let all bitterness, wrath, anger, clamor, and evil speaking be put away from you, with all malice. And be kind to one another, tenderhearted, forgiving one another, even as God in Christ forgave you." Ephesians 4:31-32 (NKJV)

Being a very young, newly married couple has it's wonderful moments but it's also not without a few bumps in the road along the way. We've seen several couples divorce before they passed the five year mark in their marriage which is unfortunate because it generally takes at least that long to work out all the kinks. Bringing two very different individuals together to now try to live as one unit, with all their habits and stubbornness, is a major challenge but worth the effort. Divorce was never a word that ever came out of our mouths but there was a time that Jerry Dale and I almost separated.

Before I get into that let me share a different kind of struggle we had that was all my doing. There was something else that I brought into our marriage with me that could have damaged our relationship if I hadn't eventually allowed God to heal me. It was my past.

Although I enjoyed being physically close to Jerry Dale and feeling his gentle touch, it was also certain things that made me terrified and uncomfortable. If Jerry Dale did anything that reminded me of what my father had done to me, even a simple touch that was eerily familiar, I made him immediately stop while I took the time to collect myself and my thoughts.

I remember one time in the darkness of our bedroom, a dim light shined on Jerry Dale's face that made him look just like my father for a moment. That was enough to make me scream out, "Get away from me! Get away!"

Jerry Dale knew about my past but had no clue what to say or do when I had these flashbacks. He was so patient with me but I knew these sudden outbursts and crying binges were getting to him. I had to convince him that it wasn't anything that he was doing wrong. It was so hard for him to fully understand what was going on with me on the inside. He was getting afraid to touch me in fear that he would set off one of my downward spirals.

All it generally took was a television show or movie that had a scene in it containing some sort of sexual abuse to send me back to my past, making me cry and depressed for a few hours. Meanwhile, Jerry Dale is trying to console me, not knowing exactly what to say or how to handle it. He grew up in a very sheltered and loving household so he really didn't know how to deal with someone going through an abusive past.

"Heather, I don't know what to say."

"You don't have to say anything, just hold me. There are really no words right now that's going to change how I feel so just be here for me. I need you to help me past this bad moment. Just hold me please."

I felt so safe in Jerry Dale's arms and it helped me move on to a better, happier place in my mind. My past became my greatest enemy that I fought against until I got help. That wouldn't be the only thing that I would fight against.

Temper, Temper

It's funny how we have issues and think we have them under control but all along, they really have control of us. We say, "I don't have a problem," but we know deep inside we really do. It's hard to look at ourselves—who we are when no one's looking. Who we really are in the inner most part of our heart, mind, and soul.

We pick up our masks on a daily basis, hoping that no one will figure out what's really behind the mask. Praying that they'll never find out the hidden truth. It's not a pretty sight to look at ourselves in the mirror, seeing the reflection of what's past the outside, but what's on the inside. We may look like we have it all together on the outside, but the inside tells a much darker story. We all have a story. We all have a past. We all have secrets or things we're ashamed of. So what's your story?

I'm about to share something that may surprise you but that's the beauty of what God can do. No matter what habits or character flaws we have, and problems we create for ourselves, we can always trust God to be there to help us through it all. The only difference between failure and success with all of these things is if we actually let go and let God.

There are some things that we can't fix ourselves. Some things are much bigger than us and we're not physically capable of changing completely without a touch from God. This requires us to surrender every part of us, confessing our need for God to help change us for the better.

It is not for us to judge others once we recognize their weaknesses or failures either, but to lift them up in prayer instead. We rarely know the whole story behind what goes on in other people's lives and when we start assuming things, it usually gets us in trouble as we believe things that aren't so. We should be a support system, someone that others can trust and lean on in their times of struggle. Why do we take pleasure in the pain and destruction of others? Why is juicy gossip more enjoyable than understanding and helping those that need our help and prayer support?

Throughout our time in ministry, we've seen the warning signs. Not just through our own experience but through counseling with so many other people with the same problems. For example, there is generally a pattern of development when it comes to someone with an explosive temper. The signs usually start at a young age, coming out in the teenage years with full force. If they're not dealt with, anger issues will continually get worse as we don't know how to control it. People with temper problems don't just hurt those they love around them, but they hurt themselves from damaging the relationships they have with those that are the closest to them.

What I am about to share is only for God to get the glory and to help others that may be going through the same issues that Jerry Dale and I did. Let this testimony be a lesson of what to do and what not to do. I pray that our experience will help you in your relationship, whether you're in one now or any future relationships you may have. I pray that what we went through, you can avoid.

Jerry Dale had a problem with his temper and had very little patience, which only set off his temper more often. His parents really didn't realize how big of a temper he had until things came to light after we got married. Thinking back, Mom English remembered a couple of things that happened when he was a teenager but didn't think much of it. While watching through the kitchen window, she saw him throw a wrench across the yard after getting aggravated with his dirt bike he was working on. On another occasion, she noticed a hole in the door of their shed outside. She questioned Jerry Dale about it but he just brushed it off.

Jerry Dale and I were married a few weeks before I made him mad for the first time. We had gotten into an argument and since I wouldn't listen to him, he pushed me onto the bed. He didn't hurt me but I was shocked that he was so physical with me. I suddenly remembered what he promised on my front porch. He promised he would never hurt me. Those same questions that I had asked before started coming back. Would he ever hit me?

It didn't take long to figure out that Jerry Dale had a short fuse, but as quick as he lost his temper, he was just as quick to get over it. That aggravated me because when I got mad, I stayed mad for a while. That reminds me of a clip in a movie I saw once where the woman said, "I'm mad and I don't want to lose it!"

He got over whatever we argued about so quickly and wanted to go on with our normal life but I wasn't over it yet. I hung on to my anger much longer than he did which made him get impatient with me. Most of the time he went his own way, giving me my space so I could work through my anger by myself.

At first it was just an occasional push or shove but then things started getting a little scary. In the middle of arguments I looked into

Jerry Dale's eyes and the man I loved wasn't in there anymore. The look on his face was so unpredictable and unfamiliar. I was beginning to become afraid of him whenever he lost control of his temper. He instantly transformed into another man that I didn't know. He said things that were so out of his normal character, things that were hurtful and I knew he really didn't mean.

Jerry Dale's temper was beginning to become expensive since he threw and broke whatever was close and within his reach. He didn't throw the objects at me but it made me angry that he was being so out of control to where he was breaking what little possessions we had in the house. After he had time to calm down and cool off, the Jerry Dale I knew and loved soon returned and he immediately became remorseful.

"What did I say? What did I do? Oh my God! Please forgive me!"

Every time Jerry Dale lost his temper, he immediately apologized to me through his tears, making sure that I knew he was deeply sorry for his actions. Then he went to find a place to pray for forgiveness from God, pouring his heart out, asking God for His help with his anger issues. I knew he loved me and didn't mean to do or say everything that he had, but the fact still remained that he had a problem and it was getting old quick.

I was getting tired of being afraid of him and after some time, I began to get angry and fight back. The fear was slowly leaving and a boldness grew in me to stand up to him, daring him to touch me. I was getting where I pushed his buttons, which was definitely the wrong thing to do. Instead of backing off, shutting up and allowing him to cool off, I continued to argue my point to prove that I was right. Things sometimes got physical between us, but he hadn't actually hit me—not yet anyway.

I remember the first time Jerry Dale slapped me. We were arguing and I could tell he was getting to his boiling point so I tried to get away from him by hiding in the bathroom, but he followed me. I sat down on the toilet while he squatted in front of me, still arguing. I can't remember exactly what he said but I rolled my eyes at him and that was enough for him to lose it.

I never saw it coming. Jerry Dale slapped me hard enough to knock me off the toilet and it took me a couple of seconds to collect myself to realize what had just happened. I was so shocked. He had never actually hit me before but now he had crossed that line.

All I wanted to do was get away from him before something else happened. If he was mad enough to slap me, what else would he do before he calmed down? I managed to get past him out of the bathroom and ran to get the car keys. Jerry Dale knew what I was doing and wasn't going to allow me to leave so he tried to get the keys away from me. I shoved my hand in my pants pocket with the keys tightly clinched inside to keep him from prying the keys out of my hand, but that didn't last long. He eventually pulled hard enough where the pocket of my khaki pants ripped and he got the keys.

I managed to walk out of the house without him following me and I started running toward my sister-in-law's house across the pasture. For the first time in a while I was truly afraid of Jerry Dale again and I hated that feeling. I was crying as I knocked on Lisa's back door and she immediately took me to her bedroom so we could talk privately. As she listened I could tell she was having a hard time believing what I was telling her. Jerry Dale hid his temper from his family through the years so for me to tell Lisa what her little brother had just said and done, it was all very hard to take in all at once.

Jerry Dale called Lisa's house looking for me and I went back home after I knew he had cooled down from his explosive temper. Once again we talked through it and he apologized for his behavior and so did I. It was very hard for me to admit I was wrong but I knew the arguments weren't completely his fault. I played a part in it, too, but I wasn't going to put up with Jerry Dale getting physical with his anger toward me. I had heard about battered women in relationships but now I had found myself in a similar situation. I didn't know how to handle it so I went to my in-laws for advice.

How do you deal with this? I loved Jerry Dale with all my heart and I knew he loved me but his temper was starting to damage our marriage. He knew he had a problem and prayed about it continually but it just seemed to get worse instead of better. Mom and Dad English sat us down and counseled with us on the dangers of losing your temper. They had similar problems during their earlier years of marriage so they knew from experience what it can do to a relationship. I appreciated that they didn't automatically take their son's side like some parents do, but they talked to him about where he was wrong and he needed to do better.

I could tell that Jerry Dale was trying very hard to keep his temper under control but he still lost it from time to time. There were only two more times that things got out of hand. I had told Jerry Dale that if he ever got physical with me again that I would hit him right back. I wasn't going to just sit back and take it.

"You can't hurt me," Jerry Dale laughed.

"I don't care if I hurt you or not but I'm taking my stand."

In the back of my mind I knew that wasn't the smartest thing to do because it would only fuel him to go further in his rage, but I felt I had to take up for myself somehow.

One day right after church we were in our mini van going home. I remember that we were arguing over something very insignificant concerning one of our youth. I could tell Jerry Dale's temper was rising and I couldn't understand why since what we were arguing about was pretty stupid in my mind. I learned to never try to predict his temper because you never knew what was going to set him off.

Jerry Dale suddenly reached over while driving and back-handed my arm while telling me to shut-up. It really didn't hurt since he didn't hit me hard but the fact remained that he had hit me and that was enough. I hit him back in his arm.

"I told you if you ever hit me again that I was going to hit you back."

"You can't hurt me."

Jerry Dale then back-handed me on my arm a little harder so I hit him back again. That morning, he decided to wear his class ring on his right hand as he would do sometimes, but today was a bad day to wear it. After I hit him back, Jerry Dale was still driving and wasn't looking when he swung to hit me back on my upper arm, but he missed. This time he swung a little too high. The back of his hand just caught the left side of my face. His class ring hit the side of my nose hard enough to give me my first bloody nose. It caught me by surprise and it hurt so I grabbed my face with both hands and kept them there until we reached the house.

Jerry Dale didn't realize the extent of what just happened and thought I was really milking the situation. I kept my hands around my face because I felt something wet other than my tears so I knew my nose must have been bleeding and I didn't want blood to get all over my clothes. I just sat there in the van and didn't say a word until I got out to go into the house. After I went straight to the bathroom to clean myself up and survey the damage, it was then that Jerry Dale realized what he had done. He had no idea that he had hit me in the face that hard and immediately began apologizing.

I knew it was an accident and instead of getting mad at him, I felt numb. In a way, I felt sorry for him and that felt strange for me. I was supposed to be furious with him but I wasn't. It was like I was internally shutting down and my love meter dropped a notch. Jerry Dale knew he had crossed a line farther than he had ever expected he was capable of so he left me alone—withdrawing himself to the living room to cry and pray for about an hour.

Jerry Dale never wanted to hurt me and desperately wanted to be rid of this temper problem once and for all but he didn't know how. He kept praying about it but he just couldn't seem to get it under control. My Mom knew something was up because when I showed up for work the next day I had a slightly swollen eye and make-up couldn't cover up the bruise completely around my eye and nose. She already knew about Jerry Dale's temper from me confiding in her before, but for some reason I just couldn't tell her the truth. I didn't want her to form a bad opinion about my husband so I lied with a story that I fell and hit my face on the edge of my coffee table.

I could tell by the look on Mom's face that she didn't believe me but she never said a word and neither did I. I appreciated her not pushing me about the issue. Later that day I had to go make a deposit at the bank where Lisa worked and I saw the look on her face as she was looking at mine. She knew what happened without even asking but I talked to her privately about it later. News spread to my in-laws and they immediately had a strong conversation with Jerry Dale.

I told Jerry Dale that if he ever hit me again that I wouldn't divorce him but I would leave him for a while until he could get his temper under control. By this time we had our first child and I feared for him. I had grown up with abuse and I was not about to allow anyone, including my own husband, to lay a hand on my children other than the normal punishment routine. I swore to myself that

I would always protect my children with my life and I meant it. I didn't want my kids to have to go through anything remotely close to what I had. Jerry Dale had to do something before that happened, even by accident.

A couple of years passed with no big temper explosions and we both thought we were on our way to a much better marriage. We were slowly growing closer and maturing as a couple. One Saturday night we started arguing about something while we were settling into bed for the night. I turned my back toward him as we laid there in the bed. Since I wouldn't agree with him and shut-up, Jerry Dale first lightly punched me in my back and then reached around and popped me in my mouth. He didn't rare back and smack me hard but his fingers just happened to hit my lip in such a way that it cut against my front teeth and started bleeding.

We laid there and remained quiet as we both were thinking that our two-year record was now broken. My hopes that this was all behind us was now gone and I knew Jerry Dale was thinking about what I had told him a couple of years earlier.

We both had a hard time sleeping that night. As we got up to get ready for church the next morning, my mind was spinning about what to do. I decided to take a walk up to my in-laws' house for some wisdom. As I walked out the door, Jerry Dale asked me where I was going and I could see the fear all over his face. I told him that I just needed to take a walk to clear my head but I think he knew where I was going and he didn't stop me.

I had never seen him quite so humble after one of our fights but I still needed some help deciding what to do. After speaking with Mom English she told me that I needed to follow through with my promise and she would help me do it. She advised me to say nothing and she would give me the keys to her car after we were all at the church. She then told me to wait until Dad English's sermon was about half way over, then quietly slip out the back door to leave for my parents' house.

I did everything as Mom English advised and showed up at Mom and Dad's house just as they were getting home themselves. They knew something was up and we all went inside to talk. I expected a phone call once Jerry Dale realized that I had left but he waited a while since his Mom advised him to give me my space.

Jerry Dale was pretty upset with his Mom for interfering with our relationship and helping me leave, but he also understood why she did it. He already felt bad enough and planned for us to talk after church but now I had left and he was afraid he had lost me forever. After he waited a while, Jerry Dale finally called.

"Heather, I'm very sorry for everything that has happened and I wanted to talk to you today about it. Are you planning on coming back home so we can talk?"

"I don't know if I'm coming home or not yet."

"I understand but I would really like the chance to talk this out before you make your final decision. I know you're scared so my parents said that they would stay after church tonight with us and we can all talk together. That's all I'm asking is for you to come to church tonight so we can talk. After we talk, if you still want to leave, then I won't stop you. I promise I won't hurt you."

"You've promised that many times but I'll think about your offer. If I show up for church then you'll know that I'll stay to talk and we'll go from there."

"I'll take what I can get. I love you very much and hope to see you this evening."

As I hung up the phone I really didn't know what to do but my heart was leaning toward giving him a chance to talk things out. The last thing I wanted to do was break up the wonderful thing we had. Our marriage as a whole was a great thing but we just had this one issue of getting along when we were both angry. We both had to change our way of existing as a couple if we were going to survive.

I appreciated how my parents didn't immediately hate or judge Jerry Dale, but were very understanding and ready to forgive. Although they didn't approve of his actions, they still loved him as their son-in-law and were willing to help however they could. That gave me the strength to make the decision to go that night, to hear what he had to say.

I was pretty restless during the church service that night in anticipation of what was about to happen after it was over. After we said good-bye to everyone, it was just me, Jerry Dale, and his parents at the church. I remember us gathering around the platform with me sitting in the front pew as a spectator.

It was hard sitting back, listening to Mom English talk so hard to Jerry Dale but everything she said was exactly what he needed to hear. As she shared her own experience of hard times dealing with Dad English's temper in their earlier years, I found myself relating to everything she was saying. I was already crying but there was one thing that really got to me.

Mom English explained to Jerry Dale that every time his Dad lost his temper, she felt her love for him decrease, little by little. After the Lord healed him of his temper, the damage had already been done so he had to prove his love for her until her heart was healed. She felt like Dad English took advantage of the love she had for him, that it would always be there but he gradually pushed it away with his temper until she felt like she started to hate him.

As soon as she said that she felt her love decreasing, I got scared and started crying even harder. I realized that I had begun to feel the same way. Through my tears I looked up and saw Jerry Dale looking down at me. I saw total fear across his face as he began to cry with me. He knew why I was crying harder and it was devastating for him to realize what he was doing to me and our relationship. At that moment we both recognized the trouble our marriage was in and we were at a crossroads. Could our relationship be healed?

With God's help, time, a lot of prayer, and some simple adjustments, we managed to come out victorious . Jerry Dale had to surrender his temper to the Lord while I had to learn that I wasn't always right. Jerry Dale learned what triggered his anger and I learned to stop pushing his buttons.

We also learned how to genuinely talk through our problems. When I tried to walk away to escape his wrath, Jerry Dale would get mad because he thought I was trying to get the last word or just didn't want to listen to him. Now he knew that allowing us to be apart for about ten minutes would help him have time to cool down and both of us to think things over before we spoke. It gave us time to reflect and use wisdom with our words instead of blurting out the first thing that came to our minds in anger.

Once we learned how to prevent our arguments from becoming heated and blown out of proportion, our marriage began to grow stronger. Jerry Dale knew he had to prove himself before I could learn to trust him again. To know that I was safe in his arms and his hands weren't anything I feared anymore. It was a feeling I longed for, and eventually found.

We both had to let go of the past, forgiving and forgetting so we could start fresh. Although it took a little time, with God's help we made it victoriously on the other side. We both realized that there are some things that we can't do on our own, that are beyond us, but we need God's help to overcome. Without God we would have never succeeded.

We will need Him again but with an entirely different matter.

A God Moment

One of the many reasons I chose "Beyond Myself" as the title of this book was because of this chapter. We all have things in our lives that are beyond our control, beyond our capability of fixing. We have to learn to fully trust in the Holy Spirit to heal us, guide us, deliver us from those things that are totally out of our reach. It is against our human nature to fully trust and surrender ourselves to God but with faith and humbleness, it is possible. What is that one thing in your life that you haven't trusted God with? Talk to Him about it today and take the steps toward surrendering it to Him fully.

Chapter 31

Weddings and Babies

"Be anxious for nothing, but in everything by prayer and supplication, with thanksgiving, let your requests be made known to God; and the peace of God, which surpasses all understanding, will guard your hearts and minds through Christ Jesus."
Philippians 4:6-7 (NKJV)

After Jerry Dale and I got married in 1988, later that year Mary found a great guy named Glenn that she met at Sears, where they had worked together. With Mary being shy and not really wanting to go through the expense of a big wedding, she and Glenn decided to elope right before the new year.

Not long after that, Amy met a great guy named Ronnie and it wasn't long before they were planning for their wedding as well. I missed being able to be a part of Mary's wedding but I was about to dive in head first into Amy's.

I was honored to be one of Amy's bridesmaids and she asked if I would sing one of the songs in her wedding, too. To save her and my parents some money, Gam altered my wedding dress to fit Amy and she looked absolutely beautiful in it. I had also been playing around with cake decorating for a while so I volunteered to make her wedding cake.

On Amy's wedding day I started off in the kitchen making her cake. Then for pictures I changed into my maid dress where I rode in the back of Dad's suburban, unladylike, trying to hold on to the cake so it would make it to the church all in one piece. Thankfully the church wasn't far away.

I chose a cute dress that had buttons all the way down the front to sing in. Then as soon as I got through with my song, I quickly went to the back to change in the nursery where our neighboring friend, Brenda, was waiting for me with my maid dress. I unbuttoned the first dress then stepped into the other dress, grabbing my bouquet while Brenda zipped me up. Finally, I quickly ran around the outside of the church to meet up with the rest of the maids to walk down the aisle.

It was funny when it was my turn to walk because I heard a couple of people say, "Wait. Didn't she just sing a couple of minutes ago?" It was a great trick and the wedding went beautifully.

As the three oldest sisters were all getting married, the next obvious question was who was going to have the first baby. Jerry Dale and I had talked about it and we definitely wanted kids but we decided to wait until we had some time alone first and maybe a little more financially stable. Although I really wanted a baby, I knew it would be better for us to wait a little while and it would be a wise decision. Jerry Dale and I had the time we wanted and needed to grow together as a married couple because once children are a part of the household, it's never the same.

Mary ended up getting pregnant first and although I was very excited and happy for her, I was secretly a little jealous. The first grand baby was a beautiful girl and they named her Mary Faith, but called her Faith. I loved getting to hold her and longed to have a baby of my own.

About a year later, Jerry Dale and I decided to go ahead and try for our first baby. I know this sounds unlikely but I knew I was pregnant the morning after conception. I literally felt different in my body, like everything in my stomach area was kicking in gear for the first time. I started getting excited about the possibility but I didn't want to really believe it, only to be disappointed, so I patiently waited until I was far enough along to take a pregnancy test.

The anticipation was killing me but I remember the morning that I took the test and it was positive. I don't recall being that happy too many other times in my life but it was an amazing moment for me. I started dreaming immediately of how I would reveal the news to everyone else and my mind started racing about what the next nine months would bring us.

To help with money, Jerry Dale's boss at the physical therapy clinic agreed to hire me to come in and clean their house once a week. His wife and I became friends quickly and I enjoyed her being there at the house with me when I cleaned. They just had a baby themselves so when I got pregnant, she had plenty of advice and maternity clothes to pass on to me. I couldn't wait until I started showing so I could reveal to the world that I was pregnant.

A Miscarriage

I was in my third month of pregnancy when something happened that changed everything. I was cleaning at Jerry Dale's boss's house when I had to use the restroom. I discovered a small amount of blood on the tissue so I got a little worried. I asked my friend if that was normal so she asked if the blood looked old or fresh. I couldn't really tell so she said to wait a little while and go check again to see for sure. I felt a little reassured when she explained that some women spot bleed during their pregnancy so I was hoping that was all this was.

After going back to the bathroom to check, I discovered even more blood and it looked fresh so I started worrying. My friend told me to sit down and rest with my feet up for a while and see if that helped but I started cramping soon after that. I quickly drove myself back to Jerry Dale's work place to tell him what was going on and I could tell he was worried as well. After going back to the restroom I discovered a lot more blood. I had already been crying but now I was losing it. We called my OB/GYN and they told me to come in immediately.

My mind was racing as I was crying and praying out loud for God to help me. As Jerry Dale was driving he was also praying and worried about me. When we arrived at the doctor's office they immediately let me go straight to the back where my doctor tended to me. After a couple of tests they confirmed my greatest fear—I had lost the baby.

My doctor explained that many young women miscarry their first pregnancy and some, not knowing that they were ever pregnant, miscarry but just thought they were having a bad period. That comforted me a little since I thought there might be something wrong with me or I may have done something to cause the miscarriage.

Although the doctor reassured me that I was physically alright, I was devastated and worried that I may have problems with future pregnancies. My good friend Penny kept trying to have a second child with her husband but she kept miscarrying. She had five miscarriages before they finally had their second child, a beautiful baby girl. As it turned out, heavy stress in her life was a major factor. As I remembered what Penny went through, I couldn't bare the thought of losing another baby, much less five. I desperately wanted a baby but I didn't want to get pregnant again if it meant I was just going to lose it.

That same evening, Mom and I were scheduled to coordinate a wedding rehearsal and Penny was the photographer so I collected myself and went to work. It kept my mind off of my emotional pain so it was a welcomed task. After it was all over, Penny volunteered to ride back to the shop with me so we could talk.

Penny shared her miscarriage experiences with me and gave me hope, praying that something she said might make a difference or help in some way. After putting on my mask for several hours, I let myself back into my reality and began to cry. At first Penny thought that she made me cry and began apologizing for hurting me but I reassured her that she was helping, not hurting. I just needed that time to cry and I appreciated her being there for me.

Well-meaning friends and family tried to reassure or comfort me but they couldn't make it better. Sometimes they said things that hurt me but I knew they didn't mean it.

Right after the miscarriage, we all gathered at Gam and Papa's house one day and Uncle Jerry said, "There's ole 'false alarm.'"

I stood there in shock at first to what I had heard and eventually muttered, "What?"

He said it again and that's when I figured out that he must have been told that I was never pregnant instead of me miscarrying. I didn't correct him but just put on a quick, fake smile as I agreed and sat down with everyone. I was still mourning over my loss as I sat there watching Mary play with her baby, Faith. My emotions were overwhelming as I watched them and before I lost it in front of everyone I quickly ran to the bathroom to quietly cry alone.

On another occasion I was walking with my sister Mary and our friend Mary into the LHS football stadium for a game as they started talking about their babies. Our friend Mary had her first baby, too, so as they talked together, I felt very left out.

"When you have your own baby then you'll understand."

It cut like a knife and I had to fight back the tears quickly before they saw my pain. I knew they didn't mean any harm and I never said anything to them. My emotions and hormones were going crazy and I knew it, so I didn't blame them, but myself.

Not long after that, Mom and I were working at our flower shop when she noticed that I looked depressed. We started talking and it was like a flood gate had opened and I couldn't stop. I knew I could be open and real with Mom so I started crying and pouring my heart out to her. She could tell how much agony I was in and she cried right along with me. She hurt for me and tried to console me but she knew there wasn't much that would help besides being there for me.

I've always been an optimistic person so to feel myself slowly slipping into a depression was a scary moment for me. I knew that God didn't take my baby so I never blamed God or was angry with Him. I had to go to God for help so I started praying, asking God to heal me of this pain. God knew about my worries and soon sent me the remedy.

A God Moment

The Bible says that it rains on the just and the unjust. If you've paid attention, you've probably noticed that bad things happen to everyone, no matter who you are. Although there are times in our lives that we cause our own circumstances through poor decisions, there are many more times that we've done nothing to deserve what life dishes out. Difficult times can often bring clarity, and most times closer to God. Let these times be your moment to reflect on what God can do through you, or the situation itself as a possible miracle moment or testimony for others. There's always a reason for everything. Ask God how your current trial or storm can bring Him glory and you victory!

Chapter 32

A Prophetic Dream

"And it shall come to pass in the last days, says God, that I will pour out my Spirit on all flesh; your sons and your daughters shall prophesy, your young men shall see visions, your old men shall dream dreams." Acts 2:17 (NKJV)

Coming out of a medicated sleep I began to collect myself, looking around, trying to figure out exactly what's going on and where I am. It looks like I'm in a hospital room and there are several people all around me, standing shoulder to shoulder. Then I noticed that they were slowly admiring and passing a baby down the line of people.

Just as I was about to fully sit up in my bed to see more of what was going on, Mom came to me, leaned over to look at me closely and asked, "How are you feeling?"

"I don't know really. Where am I? What's going on?"

"You just had a baby!"

"No, Mom. I lost my baby, remember?"

"No, sweetheart. You had a healthy baby. Everything went fine."

"Well, let me see it!"

Mom brought the baby over to me as I tried to sit up in my hospital bed. I put my knees up as I held my baby up against my legs to get a better look. I noticed that it's a boy and he's beautiful.

Suddenly the scene quickly changes, only lasting a few seconds per glance, at this little boy growing up. Then I wake up.

If you're like me, I can have some pretty crazy dreams sometimes and I know they're just dreams but this one was different. Right after I woke up and got my thoughts together, I felt the Holy Spirit prompting me, speaking to my soul.

"Pay attention. I'm trying to show you something important here."

I immediately thought about the dream and it was like the Holy Spirit hit the rewind button, showing me every clip while narrating what everything meant. He interpreted what the dream meant.

God knew my heart and heard my prayer concerning wanting a child but He also knew that I was worried and scared to get pregnant again. God showed me in my dream that I would not only get pregnant and have a baby, but that it would be a boy and what he would look like. Finally God shared short clips of this little boy growing up.

Then I felt God speak to my heart again saying, "You don't have to worry anymore daughter. You will have a healthy baby boy, he will grow up and be fine. Trust Me."

I started smiling with such a wonderful peace that came over me as I lay there in the darkness of our bedroom. I was so excited that I immediately woke Jerry Dale up to tell him everything that just happened. Jerry Dale was happy to hear about the dream and we both cried together as we held each other until we fell back to sleep.

Two months later I became pregnant again, but this time would be different in a special kind of way. I didn't have any fear and fully trusted God concerning the dream He had given me just a couple of months earlier.

Since we didn't have any insurance and couldn't sign up for Medicaid yet, I had to go through LSU hospital in Shreveport. They didn't allow ultrasounds unless something was wrong so I never had the privilege of finding out the sex of the baby like most do, but then again, I really didn't need to. I already knew it was a boy since God showed me the sex of the baby in my dream.

I got a lot of funny looks when people asked, "Do you know what you're having?"

"Yes. We're having a boy."

"Oh, you've had your ultrasound already?"

"No. God told me."

Yeah, that always went over well. I knew it sounded strange and I didn't get upset over their doubting looks. I was confident in what I knew and no one was going to make me feel anything less.

About half way into my pregnancy, I noticed that I was starting to have trouble with my heart. I was born with a heart murmur and the pediatrician told Mom that I shouldn't have much trouble out of it until I got pregnant. My heart would start racing for no reason, skip, jump, or beat hard in my chest. It was pretty scary so the doctors kept a close watch on it.

I stayed busy working in the church, singing on the road with our family group, and working at our flower shop. Jerry Dale and I often said that this little boy was going to have to come out loving music as much as he constantly heard it.

It was getting close to my delivery date and I enjoyed getting everything ready for the baby. Penny told me when I felt like cleaning everything in the house as well as having to use the bathroom really bad, like cleaning out your colon, then I was about to go into labor. I just laughed at her but she was serious and knew from experience with her own pregnancies.

One particular day when I was cleaning, I started getting sharp pains in my stomach so I went to lay down in the bed to see what kind of pains they were. I started timing the pains and they seemed to come around every five minutes. Was I in labor or was this just a bad case of gas? I wasn't sure but I knew it hurt. Suddenly the phone rang and I made myself get up to go answer it.

It was Mom and she could tell I sounded funny, like I was out of breath so she asked, "Are you alright? Why are you breathing funny?"

"Yeah, I think I've got a bad case of gas. I may have to go use the bathroom in a minute."

"No, Heather, you're in labor!"

"I don't think so. It really feels more like my stomach is messed up."

"Have you been timing these pains? How far apart are they?"

"I timed them at first and they were around five minutes apart, but I really think it's just tummy trouble, not labor pains."

Of course Mom wasn't going to believe me. She made an excuse to get off the phone so she could immediately call Mom English next door to come check on me. Sure enough, it wasn't five minutes before Mom English and Jerry Dale arrived at my back door to see if I was indeed in labor or not. They were all nervous, preparing to possibly make a trip to the hospital when I suddenly jumped up from the bed to run to the bathroom. Let's just say that I was right, or maybe I should say that Penny was right. I felt so embarrassed that everyone was excited over my gas pains, thinking I was actually in labor.

Around 2:00 AM, I woke up with a pain that I had never felt before. I laid there for a few minutes trying to make sure if I was really going into labor this time. It was my due date so I finally woke Jerry Dale up to tell him what was going on. I didn't want to go to the hospital until I timed these pains and made sure they weren't going to suddenly stop. I went to the kitchen to time my pains while I ate a bowl of cereal. I didn't want to go to the hospital hungry.

After I determined that the pains were steady and increasing, I alerted Jerry Dale and called both sets of parents. It happened to be a Sunday so the English's had to take care of the church before they could come to the hospital. They thought they had plenty of time since it usually took a long time with the first baby. Mom, Dad, Stacey and Joey came on to the hospital and Penny followed right behind them. The nurses determined that I wasn't dilated enough to admit me but I wasn't about to drive all the way back home to only come right back, so Jerry Dale and I walked around LSU hospital.

Since we arrived at the hospital so early, no one had time to eat breakfast so everyone decided to walk across the street to eat something at McDonald's. I knew I really didn't need to be eating a big breakfast right before delivering a baby but I didn't care. I was hungry and in pain. I ate pancakes and sausage while everyone else laughed at me, but I was happy. I concentrated on finally seeing my baby boy that I had already met in my dream.

Eventually I progressed far enough for them to admit me. I was excited but nervous at the same time. How bad was this going to hurt? Would my delivery go alright? The dream showed me that my baby would be fine but it didn't show me how my delivery would go. I opted for the epidural and it worked like a charm and just in time. Just as I was feeling the full brunt of my labor pains, my lower half was numbed and I could relax.

When the young doctor told me it was time to push, it wasn't long before he made me stop. They noticed with every contraction, my baby's heart rate was plummeting. They determined that the chord was wrapped around him somewhere, possibly his neck, chest, or both. That didn't surprise me at all since my baby boy was constantly kicking and moving during the entire pregnancy. I was alright until I saw the young doctor sitting at the foot of my bed with his head in his hands, trying to figure out what to do. That wasn't much of a confidence booster for me.

They decided to go ahead and take me into delivery but I was having trouble pushing so they tried several different things to help me. Suddenly they made Jerry Dale leave the room without telling either of us why or what they were about to do. We both immediately began to worry and got angry about making him leave. I desperately wanted Jerry Dale there with me for our son's birth but now I didn't know if they were going to let him back in.

I heard them say something about using forceps, again without asking or informing me or Jerry Dale about anything. They tried pulling our baby out several times with no progress, but then I heard them say, "We'll try one more pull and if the baby doesn't come, then we'll have to take her to have an emergency C-section."

Now I'm worried and they're still not conversing with me. They pulled once more but this time it felt like they were literally pulling me in half. They were trying to force our baby out so they wouldn't have to do a C-section. Finally his head was about half way out and they brought Jerry Dale back in the room so he could see our son being born the rest of the way.

Daniel Dale English was born healthy, more than 8 lb., but his poor little head was bruised and severely cone shaped from the difficult birth. We were all pretty upset with the doctors on how they handled everything, including how negligent they were with my care during the delivery. It took them over an hour to stitch me up and even longer for me to heal, but the joy of holding Daniel in my arms over-shadowed any pain or discomfort I was going through.

A couple of weeks later, Daniel's swelling and bruises went away and his true cuteness was coming through. As I held him in my arms I remembered the baby in my dream. It was truly Daniel's face that I saw and he was absolutely beautiful.

A week before, Jerry Dale and I took him to church for the first time so we could dedicate our son to God. We wanted to give him back to God, asking Him to bless Daniel with something that he could bless God back with when he got older. We had no idea what that something might be but we left it in God's hands and couldn't wait to see what God was going to accomplish through our son's life.

The Hangover Dream

After another great church service, I looked around and noticed that Sister "X" wasn't there. After inquiring where she was, someone gave an explanation for her absence.

"She's home with a hangover!"

Then I woke up.

I've had several dreams and visions since the first one God gave me about Daniel. I normally dream a lot and most of them are pretty crazy, but there was just something different about this one.

As soon as I wake up from a prophetic dream, the Holy Spirit immediately gets my attention. This particular dream was my second one, so I wasn't accustomed to how God was speaking to me through them yet. I guess I thought the dream I had concerning Daniel was a one-time event.

While I was sitting on the edge of my bed, I was trying to make sense of what I just dreamed. I knew Sister "X" very well but why was the Lord showing me something very private about her? She was very active in the church but I wouldn't have pegged her as someone missing church because of a hangover from the night before. I didn't know what to do with this information so I called Mom English.

"I know this is going to sound crazy, but does Sister "X" drink?"

"Yeah, she's been known to. Why do you ask?"

I explained my dream to Mom English in detail and she thought it was definitely interesting that God would show that to me.

Sunday finally came around but I had forgotten about the dream. After service, I noticed that three of my youth girls weren't in church. I found another girl that would know about where they were and if they were all okay.

"Do you know where the girls are?"

"Oh, they had to babysit for Sister "X" this morning. She had a really bad migraine and couldn't get out of the bed."

I immediately remembered my dream and was blown away by the accuracy of it. I never said anything and kept the information to myself until the next day.

Two of my youth girls that missed church to babysit for Sister "X" showed up at my work to visit with me.

"We really missed you girls yesterday at church."

"We're sorry but we had to babysit for Sister "X" because she had a bad migraine."

"Don't you mean a hangover?"

They both immediately looked at each other in shock.

"Who told you that?"

"The Holy Spirit."

"No, really. . . .who told you?"

"Well, you both just confirmed it by the way y'all are acting, but I was serious when I said the Holy Spirit told me."

I explained the dream to the girls and could tell they were getting a little freaked out. I think they were scared that the Holy Spirit might show me something about them.

To this day I have not told Sister "X" or anyone else about the dream. I assume that God gave me the dream to help me see that He was giving me another gift, and maybe to help those girls understand the power of the Holy Spirit.

The Breast Cancer Dream

As I walked down the hall, I finally came to the elevators of the hospital. While I'm waiting for the elevator doors to open, I looked back to see my doctor still standing there, with his clipboard, just looking at me. I thought it was strange for him to be lingering outside of his office.

Just as I was about to get on the elevator, I looked back and saw that he was still standing there. He had a worried look on his face but I didn't know why. Suddenly, he calls out to me.

"Wait! I can't let you leave like this. I have to tell you something. We found something abnormal on your right breast so I need you to come back so we can run a few more tests."

Then I woke up.

This dream occurred only a couple of years ago so Dale has had plenty of time to know about my dreams. It's early and we were both getting ready for work when Dale noticed that I had been sitting on the edge of the bed for a while, like I had something on my mind.

"What's wrong?"

"I had another dream."

"Oh, Lord! What was this one about?"

Dale sat down beside me on the bed as I explained the dream to him. He instantly became concerned.

"Well, I guess you need to make an appointment with the doctor."

"Yeah, I guess so. It's past time for my mammogram anyway."

I went to have my mammogram done, so all we had to do was wait for the results. I finally received a letter in the mail and it said that I needed to come back for further testing. They found something on my right breast.

Dale and I asked for the church to pray but I took it a step further. The next Thursday I explained the situation to my youth and asked if they would pray over me. All fifty-plus teens crowded around me, anointed me with oil, laid their hands on me, and prayed the prayer of faith for my healing. I felt so much love and peace that night.

I went back to the doctor for further testing but I knew in my heart that it was going to come back clear. Just as I expected, the results came back negative. God is so good!

A God Moment

God has given me more dreams, as well as visions while I'm awake, but I'll just leave you with the three examples that I've given. I love how the Holy Spirit moves in each of us if we only allow Him to. It's in those quiet moments with God that He is allowed to speak to us in our hearts and spirits. When was the last time you stayed quiet and allowed Him to speak to your heart? He wants to use us in a powerful way, not for our gain or glory, but for His. Draw close to God, develop that loving relationship with Him. That way when He speaks to you, you'll already be very familiar with His voice. You won't ever have to ask, "Is that You, God?" You'll know.

Chapter 33

The English Version

"Praise the Lord! For it is good to sing praises to our God; for it is pleasant, and praise is beautiful." Psalm 147:1 (NKJV)

The busyness of my daily life as a teenager still remained true in my twenties. I didn't know any other speed than wide open on most days, staying busy with mostly ministry duties. Jerry Dale and I were progressing in our marriage as we were also pushing ourselves to impact the youth of our area as young Youth Pastors at Family Worship Center in Logansport. If we weren't busy enough with everything we were already involved in, we were about to take on a whole new adventure.

When I married into the English family it didn't take me long to notice that the entire family had singing and/or musical talent that also extended into nearly the entire side belonging to Mom English. Before Jerry Dale and I got married I had the opportunity to spend some time at one of the Neal/Nunley Christmas family gatherings. After everyone was full from eating, they all got out their musical instruments and began singing hymns and good ole gospel songs they grew up with. They welcomed me with open arms and loved having me join in with the family group singing.

Before we married, Jerry Dale and I knew that we would sing together and we loved that bond we had with our music. On one of our first dates at the house, Jerry Dale brought his guitar and started showing me some of the songs he had written. He asked if I would sing harmony with him but I didn't know how. With me being a soprano I always sang the melody, not the harmony, so I had to train my ear to start listening for the other notes that were there.

Jerry Dale already knew how to hear the harmony since he sang it with his family but when he tried to show me how to do it, I couldn't do it immediately. I started listening to his guitar and what notes he was playing blended well with the notes he was singing so I started singing with the guitar. After working hard it didn't take me long before I could pick out both harmony parts.

Jerry Dale and I loved singing together and our voices blended great. We both still sung solos from time to time but we mostly sang duets. Later on his sister, Lisa, sometimes joined in and we'd get three-part harmony going, which I absolutely loved.

The three of us were asked to sing at the local River City Fest in Logansport one year and we really enjoyed it. We received so many compliments after that day and many said we should sing together more often. The three of us really didn't think much about it but Mom English saw an opportunity and went to work. It wasn't long that the four of us together would make up the singing group called "The English Version."

We started off singing mostly songs that other groups sang with a mix of a little southern gospel and some contemporary. Then Jerry Dale and I started writing a few songs of our own. Our first few singing engagements were at different churches but then we started branching out to festivals, revivals, and then prison ministry.

Although we loved what we were doing, it could get really tiring. We tried to not book anything on Sunday mornings since we all held important ministry positions at the church, so the majority of our concerts were Saturdays and Sunday nights. There were times that we traveled to minister somewhere on a Saturday night, tore down and packed everything, loaded up on the bus, and didn't get home until 2:00 AM Sunday morning. Even though we were all exhausted, we still got up and went to church, leading the worship and teaching our classes.

The group started getting busier so we started buying more equipment, which meant we needed a bigger vehicle, so we purchased a small motor home to haul all of us and our equipment together. It wasn't long that we traded that one in for a much bigger motor home, especially since we had a baby traveling with us everywhere. I remember singing and traveling all the way up to two weeks before my deliver date with Daniel and I was miserable. I did the same thing with my other pregnancy later.

Since I breast-fed Daniel, we had to take him everywhere we went but it just became a routine in our lives. As Daniel grew, traveling with us on the road became normal and we never lacked in someone volunteering to watch over him as we sang on stage.

On one particular night at a church we were singing at, a nice lady was watching our now three-year-old Daniel on the front pew in front of us. Right in the middle of a song, Daniel quietly got up from the pew and started walking up the steps toward us. The lady didn't catch him in time but we quickly gave her a small gesture that it was alright. With us still singing, Jerry Dale reached out for Daniel's hand and held it until we finished our song. He then quietly sat Daniel down on a small pew that was right beside him on the platform. Daniel remained still and quiet beside his Daddy for the remainder of the concert. He had never done that before, or after that night, and we still don't know why but it was a sweet moment.

After ministering at several places we began to get more requests for tapes and CDs so we made out a plan of action to get in a recording studio. We found a guy that we respected in Shreveport to cut our first album and it was an amazing and fun experience. It was also scary listening to ourselves in headphones or playback with nothing to cover up our mistakes, but it made us push ourselves to be even better. We eventually went back into a different studio to make another album a couple of years later and it was just as fun as the first time. This ministry lasted close to ten years before we had to move on to different ministry opportunities and we cherished every moment.

A God Moment

God has blessed everyone with a gift—something that you can turn around and bless Him with, as well as others. It may be pretty obvious for some as to what their gift, or gifts, may be, but for others, it can be challenging to figure out. I urge you today that if you know what God has gifted you with, to begin praying what exactly He wants you to be doing with it. If you're not quite sure, then begin seeking God's will for your life and ask Him to reveal what He has gifted you with. Ever heard the term, "If you don't use it, you'll lose it?" It's true, so don't let your talents and gifts go to waste. Time is running out so start using what God has blessed you with today.

Chapter 34

A Moment With God

"The Spirit of the Lord God is upon Me, because the Lord has anointed Me to preach good tidings to the poor; He has sent Me to heal the brokenhearted, to proclaim liberty to the captives, and the opening of the prison to those who are bound."
Isaiah 61:1 (NKJV)

With our lives centered around ministry and music, I felt compelled to use my past to help others somehow. Jerry Dale had written several great songs already and it inspired me to try to write one of my own. I decided to write about the very thing that weighed the heaviest on my heart and that was children being abused. They say to write what you know and that was something I definitely knew about. I wanted it to touch a wide range of people, not just those who were abused by their fathers. I named the song "Daddy's Home" and it turned out pretty good considering it was my first song.

Here are the lyrics:

Verse 1
I've always heard that anyone can be a father
But it takes someone special to be a Dad
The story is yet to be told for sons and daughters
They're wishing for the daddy they never had

Daddy's home but there's no laughter in the air
For abuse is in the hearts that live here
They're just searching for someone to show they care
And help their pain as they fight the tears

　Chorus
Jesus is the Daddy that you never had
He's waiting to hold you in His tender-loving hands
He'll never hurt you or make you feel sad
His love for you is as endless as the sands
He wants to heal the pain you feel inside
And let you know that you're never alone
You can call on Him at any time
Because in your heart. . .your Daddy's home

　Verse 2
Too often children are neglected or abused
Parents thinking that's an alright attitude
A stranger, or a person next of kin
No matter who the offender, it hurts deep within
A couple on a date thinking everything's alright
Until someone starts to push for what's not right
One thing leads to another, the hurt will soon begin
They're not thinking of the other person; only of their selfish sin

　　I sung this at our concerts, as well as in the prisons we ministered in, but it was sometimes hard at first. I gave a short testimony before singing it and that made it hard for me to make it through the song without crying. I still hadn't really healed yet. I wanted it but just didn't know what to do, but that soon changed.

　　I spoke in an earlier chapter of how my past would creep up and take over, making me step inside an emotional roller coaster that I felt I was forced to ride. I so desperately wanted off. All it would take was something to remind me: a picture, a spoken word, a moment, a movie clip, etc.

　　Jerry Dale and I were enjoying some down time together as we cuddled on the couch, watching a movie that we heard was supposed to be good. Suddenly a rape scene appeared in the middle of it unexpectedly. Although it was brief and didn't show anything, the agony of knowing what was transpiring through the characters in the film was enough to send me over the edge. Most times I got upset and cried when I saw anything that brought up my bad memories, but then I was alright shortly after and went on with life as usual. That night was different.

I ran to the bedroom and began crying uncontrollably as Jerry Dale followed to try to console me. This time I was angry. I was angry with God and I didn't like that feeling. I began ranting about how I couldn't take it anymore and how I was tired. I wanted to know why I had to go through all I had.

After I had time to calm down, I told Jerry Dale that I needed time alone to think and pray. I knew I better spend some time talking with God since I could feel emotions toward God that weren't right. Contempt and bitterness were beginning to creep in my heart toward God and I had to correct that quickly before it took hold permanently. I didn't want to even play around with the idea of turning against God.

Alone in my bedroom I began to search for God's help but I wasn't prepared for the encounter I had with Him. Have you ever known that God Himself was "talking" to you? It may not be a literal, audible voice, booming at you but instead that definite, but small, still voice inside your inner-most being. Your heart knows without a doubt what the Holy Spirit is speaking to you so you stop and listen. This is the conversation that God and I had in my bedroom:

"God, why did You allow this to happen to me? I know it's not Your fault and You didn't cause all of this, but You could at least take this pain from me! Your Word says that You won't allow us to be tempted beyond what we're able to bear. Well this really isn't a temptation but this burden is too heavy and I can't handle it anymore! You said that Your burden is light. Why won't you take this from me?"

"Daughter, I can't take away what you won't let me have."

"What? That doesn't make any sense! Why wouldn't I allow You to take it? I don't want it!"

"Your past has become your crutch, your security blanket of sorts, and you use it to your advantage when it might get you a little attention. You're also afraid of the unknown. . .since this is all you've known for so long. How will your life be without this being a big part of it? You also know what you have to do but you're not willing to do it."

I knew exactly what God was referring to. For years I told others and myself that I had forgiven my father. It was the right thing to do, especially since I was a Christian. The Bible explains that God will not forgive us of our sins if we can't forgive those who have sinned against us. As a Christian we can't hold grudges and it's good to let things go. I convinced myself that I had forgiven him as far as I could. I had justified my actions based on my father doing things that were way beyond being forgivable in my mind.

As I sat there with my thoughts, I felt God dealing with my heart about this.

"But God, I've tried to forgive him but it's just too hard!"

"You know you haven't forgiven him and you haven't really tried. You've been putting it off so you wouldn't have to deal with it."

"But God, you know what he did to me. He doesn't deserve my forgiveness!"

"Well, if you want to put it that way. . .neither do you. Through the years you've made plenty of your own mistakes and bad choices. All have sinned, including you." [Ouch!]

"That's not fair, God."

"Let Me remind you of something that wasn't fair. Giving My Son up to be tortured and killed for your redemption and healing, when He was perfect in every way and did nothing wrong. That's not fair. That's grace, mercy, and love beyond your comprehension."

"I know what you're saying. I know I need to forgive but I just don't know if I can do that. Its hard to let go. I don't know how to forgive and let go of something that big."

"I want you to hold out your hand and make a fist."

"Alright God. I don't know what You're doing here, but okay."

As awkward as it was, although I was alone, I held out my fist, waiting for God's next instruction.

"This is your life, in your own hands. You've got such a type grip on your life that not even I can help you. You've got to learn how to open up that hand (your life) and let me come and guide it, while healing you."

"Well, that's the part I don't know how to do. How do I open my hand—my life?"

"That's where forgiveness comes in."

"Like I said before, I don't think I can do that."

"You're right. There are some things that are just too big for you. You're only human and can only go so far with some matters in this life. Those are the times when you have to lean on my Holy Spirit to help you, to strengthen you. I give the ability when you give Me the chance to accomplish what I need to do in you. Just have faith. All you have to do is ask."

"Okay God. I'm not sure how we're going to do this, but I'm going to trust You."

I knew what I had to do. I went into our living room and asked Jerry Dale to watch Daniel while I spent time with God in our bedroom.

"No matter what you hear, don't interfere or come in the bedroom. This is just something I have to do alone with God."

I really didn't know what was going to happen, or what I was going to do, but I just let God lead me however He wanted to. I felt like God was telling me that I had to let go of all the hate, bitterness, and anger that I had allowed to build up inside of me. How was I going to get rid of it? I felt prompted to do a physical act, something outward to help the inward part of me.

I got on my bed, grabbed my pillow and began hitting and screaming into it. I started saying everything that I had always wanted to say to my father's face if I ever had the chance to. I was jumping on my knees on the bed and getting physical with my pillow by throwing it, hitting it, slinging it. My heart started slowly breaking into a million pieces as I poured my inner-most fears and emotions out like a river. It felt so good, like a release, unlike anything that I had ever felt before.

After a while, I started feeling empty, like I had nothing left. I had given everything to God. At this point I really didn't know what to do next so I just laid down on my bed and start praying. Laying face down across my bed, all I could do was cry. It was a cleansing type of cry. I didn't feel sad, or even mad, but more like an in between "lost and found" moment. A moment with God that kept getting stronger. I felt God there with me in that bedroom and started praying for His help.

"God, I feel like I'm broken and this is where I need Your help. Please put me back together the way You want me. Use my life to be an effective witness for You. I don't know how this is going to happen but I'm asking You to help me forgive my father and others that have deeply hurt me. I don't understand how You're going to help me with this but I trust You. I'm willing to forgive if You'll help me and show me how."

At that moment, I literally felt like God's hand touched me, physically lifting my burden of anger, bitterness, unforgiveness, and hate off of me. I physically felt lighter, like I could have floated. I was finally free, and it felt absolutely amazing. I had never felt such peace and joy in my entire life, other than the day I received Christ as my Savior.

As I laid there, I began to cry again, but now it was tears of joy and happiness. I started thanking God for healing me and wondered why I hadn't done this sooner. Why did I hold on to my past for so long? This was the most amazing feeling and I never wanted it to end.

As God waited for me to process what had just happened, He broke His silence.

"My daughter, there are so many more who are hurting out in the world, just like you. They have locked themselves up in their own prison like you did and they don't know how to get out. They're searching for the keys but don't know where to find them. I have given you the keys today so now it's your turn to share them with others who are locked up. Go let them out, Heather. This will be part of your ministry from now on: to help those who are hurting, broken, abused, neglected. . .to give them hope. You can relate and understand where they are, what they're thinking on a level that others cannot. I'll help you through this, maturing you one step at a time."

I felt so much love and peace. While trying to take in everything, I began to get excited, thinking about all the possibilities of how I could help people. People like me, but how would I do it? I had talked to different teens and women about my past before, trying to help them as best as I could, but I really couldn't help them fully since I was still struggling with my own issues.

Now I had been given the final pieces of the puzzle to fill the gaping hole in the portrait of my life. It was now all coming together and fitting nicely. This was a new thing for me and I couldn't wait to see how my life would change.

I wasn't prepared what God had in store for me next. Although an amazing change had taken place in my life, I had no idea that God had so much more for me. God had just gotten started.

A God Moment

We all go through bad stuff that life tends to chunk at us like a fast ball but it's what we do with that stuff and how we handle it that determines the outcome. Do you like to hang on to everything, never letting go? Do you enjoy staying mad and having leverage over someone who may have hurt you by holding on to the past? I have another proposition for you: do you want to finally be rid of your past and feel the peace that surpasses all understanding? Then go to God and allow Him to heal you, fully restoring your life further than you could possibly imagine. Only then will you truly be living the life that God intended for you—shackle free.

Chapter 35

God Wasn't Finished

*"Blessed be the God and Father of our Lord Jesus Christ, the
Father of mercies and God of all comfort, who comforts us in
all our tribulation, that we may be able to comfort those who
are in any trouble, with the comfort with which we ourselves are
comforted by God." 2 Corinthians 1:3-4 (NKJV)*

I was enjoying this new-found freedom God had given me. I began
to realize that more opportunities were presenting themselves to
minister to others concerning physical, emotional, and/or sexual
abuse situations. It had to be a God thing how women, teen girls,
and even boys, were crossing paths with mine, who were searching
so desperately for someone to listen to them, believe them, and
possibly help them. I knew I didn't have all the answers but I felt the
Holy Spirit giving me insight into their lives, while giving the right
words to say, at the right time. I couldn't have made it without the
guiding wisdom of the Holy Spirit.

God lovingly gave me a grace period with my new life, but He
now had another step for me to take that would completely heal me.
I thought it was all over, but I didn't understand that it wasn't quite
finished for me or my family.

One day I felt God speak to my heart again, but this time I really
didn't like what He said.

"You need to find and contact your father."

At first, I questioned if I heard Him right. Did God really just say that? I began arguing with God.

"God, I'm fine just like I am. I don't need to open that can of worms! I don't think I can handle talking to him right now. No, I'm good."

I ignored God and pushed what He asked me to do aside, thinking that would be the end of it. God waited about a month before he came to me once again with the same words.

"You need to find and contact your father."

Again I pushed it aside. Another month later God came to me once again with the same words.

"God, You're not going to let this go, are You? I don't understand why this is so important. Why do I need to contact him? I'm doing great and I don't want to mess that up. What good can come from me contacting him?"

"I have a plan in motion to not only finish healing you but to heal your father and the rest of the family as well. I can't make all of this happen until you obey Me. You have to trust Me in this."

"I still don't understand what this will accomplish. I don't know if I'm ready to talk to him."

"I know you have reservations but you're now strong enough and ready for the next phase of your healing. This is going to accomplish even more for your father. There are things going on in his life that you don't know about. He needs you just as much as you need him. He's also carrying a burden concerning the past that no longer exists considering you have forgiven him. He doesn't know that you're healed and have found peace while forgiving him of his mistakes and actions toward you. He needs to know this."

"Okay, God. I understand but this is going to be really hard. I don't know what to say and I'm afraid of what he might say."

"Just obey and trust Me. I'll handle everything so have faith in Me to finish what I've started."

Even after that conversation with God, I still had my doubts and fears of this awkward step so I decided to see if I could get a couple of confirmations about it. Naturally, I went to the two people that had every reason to tell me not to do it, based on their own feelings toward Bill.

Surely Mom and Jerry Dale would tell me that it was a bad idea. I asked them both if I should seek Bill out and they both gave me the exact same answer after I explained everything God had told me.

"If God told you to do it, then that's exactly what you need to do. We will back you up on whatever you decide to do. We support you and love you no matter what."

That's not what I was expecting at all but that affirmed what I needed to do. I really didn't know where to find Bill so I decided to contact Grandma through a letter requesting his address. After all, God didn't say how He wanted me to contact Bill. I decided to take my time, write down my thoughts, mail it to him, and let him handle it however he wanted or needed to.

Since I hadn't had any contact with that entire side of the family, I asked Mom for Grandma's address. Mom had been corresponding with her, letting her know everything that had been going on in our lives, including the birth of Daniel.

I really didn't know where to start or what to say but I began writing my letter to Grandma, requesting how I could get in touch with Bill and why. After explaining why I hadn't contacted anyone and asked for forgiveness I gave her my in-laws' phone number. That was where we were temporarily staying in between moving out of our trailer and into our new house, but that's for another chapter.

Grandma got the letter and then invited Bill to come down for lunch soon after. She gave the letter to him which was something I never thought was a possibility. I figured she'd read it and just simply write back or call, giving me his address. Things don't always go as we plan. Instead, now he had my address and a phone number.

Jerry Dale and I had been out shopping for supplies for our new house but when we got back to the English's house, we were met outside by Mom English.

"Some guy called for you earlier, Heather. I didn't recognize his voice but he said he would call back tomorrow."

My stomach immediately felt like it was in my throat. Something inside of me knew who the mystery man was.

"What did his voice sound like?" I asked.

Mom English explained that it sounded proper and calm. That was enough for me to know that it was Bill. My heart started racing inside my chest.

This was not happening. It wasn't supposed to happen this way. I didn't want to talk to him. My plan to write my feelings down on paper and send it was much better and safer. I was not prepared to talk to him after all these years but now I knew that this conversation was going to happen some time the next day. How do you prepare for a phone call that will probably change the lives of both people on each end of the line?

Just as he promised, Bill called back the next late afternoon as Jerry Dale and I drove up after shopping for supplies for the new house again. Mom English quickly met us outside as we were getting out of the car.

"That guy is on the phone again! He's waiting for you."

My stomach immediately had thousands of butterflies and my heart started pumping so fast in my chest. Suddenly any preparation that I may have had left me. I had no idea what I was going to say. I carefully reached for the phone, slowly placing it to my ear.

"Hello?"

"Hi, Heather. This is your father."

"I know."

"I'm sorry for calling and I know this is awkward but Grandma showed me the letter you sent and I just wanted to know why you were wanting to find me."

"Well, I just wanted to let you know that I'm doing well and I'm moving on with my life. I wanted you to know that I have forgiven you so you can move on with your life, too. God has healed my heart and I didn't want you going on thinking that I still hated you or held the past against you."

"You don't know how long I've waited for this conversation. For years I wanted to call you but Carol told me that it wasn't a good idea, that I had to wait for you to call me. It was hard to know that you didn't want any part of me but I understood why. I asked her how long I would have to wait and she told me it could be years but that you would contact me one day."

At this point I'm crying uncontrollably, hardly able to speak at all. It was a moment of cleansing and healing for me. It was the release I had needed for a long time, like a dam of emotions that finally broke free and nothing could stop it. Bill knew it was going to be hard for us to really talk with my current emotional state.

"I really can't talk for much longer because I have to leave for work, but I promise I'll call you back in the morning, Heather, if that's alright. We can talk as long as you want and I'll pay the long distance phone bill. Can I call you in the morning?"

I barely could get out, "Yes."

After I hung up the phone, I was still crying but it felt good and I couldn't stop. It was time to eat supper and I could barely collect myself long enough to eat. God was finishing what he started in my healing and everything was coming full circle. I was curious what tomorrow would bring but I was enjoying my time of healing that night.

The next morning, Bill called just as he said he would but this time it was a little less awkward. We were both more relaxed and talked for over two hours, sharing and catching up with what had happened in our lives in the past few years.

Bill talked about getting another divorce and the struggles it brought between him and his son, my brother, Jared. He felt alone but he found God to be very real in his life, got saved, and started faithfully going to church. When God told me to find Bill, it was the very time that he needed me back in his life the most. He needed to be healed just as much as I did.

That conversation started something new for both of us but there was a portion that was more important than anything else that he could have ever said. Those words that I had longed to hear from my father for years.

"I'm sorry. It wasn't your fault, it was mine. I'm truly sorry."

I knew in my heart that he truly meant it. It felt good talking to the father that I once knew, at least the parts of him that were good anyway.

We decided that seeing each other was the next step but we wanted to include the rest of the family, too. It would be like a small family reunion. That side of the family had never met Daniel and

Bill had never met Jerry Dale either so we arranged a day together at Grandpa and Grandma's house in Arkansas. For the first time I was getting excited about seeing everyone again, but on the way up there I started feeling nervous.

The closer we got, the more nervous I became. Jerry Dale finally broke the silence.

"How do you feel? Are you alright?"

"I'm not really sure how to feel. I mean, when I see Bill, do I hug him? Do I shake his hand? What am I supposed to do?"

"You'll do whatever feels comfortable to you at the moment."

As we pulled into their driveway, all the old memories of that place came flooding back all at once. My heart leaped in my chest as I glanced over and saw what appeared to be my father checking the food on the grill. My heart was racing as I saw him coming to meet us at the car. We both naturally reached out to hug each other at the same time and for the first time in years, it truly felt good to have my father hold me. I knew my past was truly behind me at that moment. There were no uncomfortable feelings about him touching me. The loving embrace of a father toward his daughter is something every girl longs for and needs.

It was a great day seeing my Aunt Audrey and her boys along with my grandparents. Watching Daniel play with his cousins and meeting his Grandpa for the first time was priceless.

After lunch, I took Bill aside and allowed him to listen to the song "Daddy's Home" on the tape we recorded and gave him a copy to keep. He quietly listened. I watched his face, looking for any sign of disappointment or approval from him. Tears started welling up in both his and my eyes and then we embraced each other. It was like that last phase of the healing between us.

Things were different from then on and we all couldn't wait to start our new relationships with one another. God knew what He was doing. Why didn't I obey Him sooner? Why did I ever question Him? God always wants nothing but the best for us. It's we who stand in the way of His will, wanting to do things our own way. This was a lesson in life that I never forgot. I determined that I would listen to His voice more carefully and step out by faith to do His will in the future. But what would my future hold for me now? Was the worst part of my life over?

A God Moment

How often has God has tried to speak to you, lead you into His will and you refused to listen? If we would only obey His guiding hand and His word, our lives would be so much better. Now, God never said that everything would go perfectly our way, but He did say He would bless us for our obedience. God wants to start something brand new in you, so why not let Him finish what He already started when He died on the cross for you. It was YOUR cross that he carried—not His. Jesus is your everything; all you have to do is accept Him and allow Him to be Lord over your life. It's your move.

Chapter 36

More Blessings

"And God is able to make all grace abound toward you, that you, always having all sufficiency in all things, may have an abundance for every good work." 2 Corinthians 9:8 (NKJV)

Our little trailer that God blessed us with was getting too small as Daniel was slowly getting bigger, making us look for bigger furniture. We found him a cute bunk bed but it nearly took up the whole bedroom. We knew this day would come and had already thought about our next move, but now we had to put our plans in motion.

We thought about possibly getting a double-wide trailer but then we thought about trying the same route Mom and Dad did with remodeling a house that needed to be moved. They're generally much cheaper but you just have to keep searching until you find the one you want that's still in good shape.

We finally found a three-bedroom wood frame house just off North Market Street in Shreveport that a widow woman used to live in. The family had to put her in a nursing home but didn't want the house, so they wanted to move it off the property.

When I saw the house for the first time it looked like it was stuck in a time zone that looked similar to the sixties or seventies, but it seemed structurally sound. I looked at it like a blank canvas, just waiting for a good coat of paint and tender loving care. Jerry Dale and I felt like God blessed us by how we even found this house, especially after looking at so many other houses that were literally trashed or falling apart. The price was right so we bought it.

It was exciting starting over with our first real house. We couldn't wait to get started on slowly remodeling it as we had the extra money, which wasn't much. Daniel had plenty of room in his new big bedroom and loved playing in there. It wasn't long after we got settled that we started discussing the possibility of a second baby.

We didn't want our kids too far apart in age where they wouldn't be able to play together, but we wanted them far enough apart where we wouldn't have two in diapers at the same time. After careful thought and prayer, Jerry Dale and I decided to start trying for another baby. I was so excited about the thought of another little one in the house and a playmate for Daniel.

It wasn't long before we found out that we were expecting our next baby and we couldn't wait to see if it was going to be a boy or girl. Since we already had a boy, I was hoping for a girl but we would be happy with whatever God saw fit to give us. My pregnancy was pretty normal except for my heart giving me trouble again, but we were expecting that from what I experienced carrying Daniel.

Now that we had insurance, we would have this baby at Willis Knighton South Hospital. For my first ultrasound we were hoping to find out the sex of the baby so we could plan ahead, but our little one had different plans. The baby had one of its feet stuck right in the way and wouldn't move it no matter how much the nurse poked at it, so we had to wait. The second time we took a look, my Mom and Grandma James came with me. They were both allowed to be in the room as we found out.

The nurse said, "Oh, there it is!"

"What? What is it?" I asked.

We're all glaring at the screen, trying to figure out what we were looking at when the nurse finally said, "It's a boy!"

Suddenly, without thinking, Grandma hollered out, "No!"

Mom scolded her for the outburst and reassured me that they were both happy with whatever the baby was. I didn't get upset but laughed a little on the inside, knowing my Grandma the way I did. She loved sewing frilly, lace-lined, little dresses and outfits for me when I was little and she had already been looking forward to spoiling my baby just like that again if it was a girl.

At first I was a little disappointed by the announcement but that quickly left with the idea of God giving us another boy, the perfect playmate for Daniel.

It took us a little longer to figure out what we were going to name him. We knew very early on what we would name Daniel and I had already picked out a girl name, but now we had to come up with another boy name. The name had to be perfect so we prayed and searched for the right one. Jerry Dale and I came up with Christian Nathaniel. Christian meaning "servant of Christ" and Nathaniel meaning "gift of God." It seemed to be the perfect combination for our little boy who we hadn't met yet.

Christian's due date was the fourth of July, only a week away from Daniel's birthday, so we figured we'd make the most of having their birthdays so close together. The fact that their birthdays were at least several months away from Christmas also helped when it came to buying presents. Bill was hoping that I'd have the baby on his due date since he would be off work and had arranged for him and my brother, Jared, to come down to be with us for a couple of days.

On the evening of July 3rd, we were all sitting down to a nice dinner together with Bill and Jared when Mom English called.

"How would you like to have that baby tonight?" she asked.

"I would love to have him tonight, but how would we do that?"

"I know you're miserable and ready to have him and I don't know why I didn't think of this before now."

"Think of what?"

Immediately I began to think back of all the strange remedies Mom English would come up with for helping or healing different things. She came up during an era where they didn't always have conventional medicine and different methods were used that sometimes can seem ridiculous to us that aren't familiar with some of these methods. Sometimes they worked, sometimes they didn't, but I trusted her opinion.

"There's something my Mom taught us that was used to induce labor back in the day. If you mix a half cup of castor oil with a glass of orange juice and drink it, you should go into labor tonight."

I had heard of castor oil but never took any so I asked, "If I drink this, what side effects should I expect?"

"Well, it's going to clean you out pretty good, making you go to the bathroom."

"I'm not too fond of that part but at least they won't have to give me an enema!"

"I don't have any castor oil here at the house but if I run to town to get some, will you take it?"

"You don't have to do that but if you do, I'll drink it. I guess it won't hurt to try it."

It didn't take Mom English long before she showed up at our house with the castor oil. She quickly mixed up the cocktail and I can tell you that it didn't look very tasty. Every time I took a drink, I had to stir it up since the juice and oil didn't want to mix. I thought it would taste nasty and although it felt greasy going down, it really didn't taste that bad. I mostly tasted the orange juice.

After drinking only around half of the glass, it was making me feel full and I couldn't eat any more of my supper. I figured if this was going to put me in labor then I better go ahead and take my bath, getting cleaned up for the major event.

After soaking in a warm bath, I was soon feeling the effects of the castor oil. I wasn't enjoying the frequent trips to the bathroom but I held on to the excitement of possibly going into labor.

I finally relaxed with my feet up while we all sat around watching a little television together, waiting to see what the night would bring. Suddenly I felt a pain. Could this be it? I had already had a couple of false alarms earlier in the month so I wanted to make sure this was the real thing before we drove all the way to Shreveport again. I decided to go lay down in the bed for a little while to see if the pains were steady and progressive.

I was going to wait until around 11:00 PM but by the time 10:30 PM came around, I couldn't stand it anymore. The pains were steadily coming every two minutes apart so we made the calls to everyone, including Lisa, who had already agreed to watch Daniel for us when the time came. I was amazed how fast and hard the contractions were coming. My labor with Daniel was much slower than this so I didn't know what to think and I began to get a little concerned. Would I make it to the hospital?

While Jerry Dale was driving, Bill was sitting directly behind me in our minivan, rubbing my shoulders and trying to comfort me as each contraction hit, becoming closer together as we traveled. Jared sat quietly in the third row seat, not really knowing how to take everything in.

The closer we got to Shreveport, I asked Jerry Dale how fast he was going and after he told me, I screamed for him to go faster. I began hearing Jerry Dale mumbling so I asked him what he was saying.

"I'm praying that you don't have this baby in the van! I don't know how to deliver a baby!"

Bill reassured us that he knew what to do if that became an issue but we all hoped and prayed that we'd make it to the hospital. The good thing was that it was almost midnight and there was very little traffic so we carefully ran red lights as we approached closer to the hospital. I'm happy to say that we did make it there, all in one piece, with only less than two hours to spare.

By the time we drove around to the emergency room, my contractions were only one minute apart. Every time I met a nurse, it was pretty obvious as to why I was there, but they all asked if I was in labor?

"Yes! Stick around for another minute and you'll see a contraction."

"How far apart are your contractions?"

When I told them they were only one minute apart, you would have thought I just screamed "bomb!" the way everyone started moving, making things happen quickly, almost in a panic.

I knew how well my epidural worked when I had Daniel so when they asked if I wanted one with this baby, I quickly agreed. I was in full blown labor and wanted relief any way I could get it. Not long after they gave me the epidural, I realized that it was only working on one side of my body so they called to get the anesthesiologist back in there.

The only problem was that a nurse who was checking my progression hollered out, "Cancel that order! This baby is coming now!"

I was immediately scared, knowing that I was about to feel every bit of this delivery. I remember Jerry Dale coming around to my right, grabbing my hand to prepare for his role, and he looked at the sheer terror on my face. I knew he wanted to do something to help me but he knew there wasn't anything he could do except be there for me, comforting me with his love and support.

Christian made his debut shortly after 1:30 AM on July 4th, 1995. The delivery wasn't as bad as I thought it would be because he came so quickly. My mind was so focused on my little man that I tried not to think about the pain. Before Jerry Dale cut the chord, they handed Christian to me, to hold for a couple of moments before they took him away to be cleaned up and make sure he was healthy. That was such an amazing moment for me.

Christian was beautiful and healthy. While the doctor and nurses tended to me, Jerry Dale got time to bond with him a little while before they allowed family and friends to come visit with us in our room. Since neither of us got much sleep, Jerry Dale crawled into my bed and we tried to get a little rest. It was cute how we snuggled and carefully fit on that hospital bed together but we didn't get much sleep because of the nurses constantly coming in.

Jerry Dale left later that morning since all the English family were meeting for a big fourth of July lunch. I was so jealous that I was missing out on some amazing Bar-B-Que but getting to spend some quality time with Christian more than made up for it.

Any time you have a child, your first prayer is that it's healthy and usually we assume it will be. But what do you do when things don't turn out quite as you planned?

A God Moment

It's always nice to reflect on the good things in life. If we truly take a glimpse back, we can see the hand of God everywhere, blessing us over and over. Even in the storms of life, we can find His grace. It's during the difficult times that help us gain wisdom, build character, and sometimes humble us, bringing us closer to God. Then God graciously allows us those calm, beautiful days where we can sit back and rest in His presence—gaining strength for the next battle that comes our way. Try not to focus on all the negativity around you, but rather on the positive. He's worthy to be praised either way!

Chapter 37

Then Comes A Trial

"Beloved, do not think it strange concerning the fiery trial which is to try you, as though some strange thing happened to you; but rejoice to the extent that you partake of Christ's sufferings, that when His glory is revealed, you may also be glad with exceeding joy." 1 Peter 4:12-13 (NKJV)

After having Christian, our busy lives soon returned back to normal. We were still very active in our roles in the church as well as traveling with The English Version, ministering everywhere we could. Just like I did with Daniel, I sang up to two weeks before I delivered Christian and went right back to traveling on the bus with now two babies in tow. We also dedicated Christian to God when he was about a week old, praying that God would bless him in some way that was unique to minister to others.

We were concerned how Daniel would react to having this new baby in the house, competing for his attention, but he handled it very well. Early in the mornings we sometimes heard sounds coming from Christian's room so when we went to check on him, we found Daniel in the baby bed with him. Daniel figured out how to crawl up in the bed and lay beside Christian, gently touching him, spending quality brother time with him. We knew then that Daniel would be a great big brother.

Christian was growing and learning as a normal one year old and we quickly got him into his routine at the house. He was developing a small, but expanding, vocabulary and knew that before lunch we picked up his toys together, then nap time was after lunch. We did all the normal things that parents do to make sure our children are happy and healthy, including getting them vaccinated and eating healthy, but something suddenly changed with Christian when he was about eighteen months old.

I remember the day very clearly when I noticed something wasn't quite right with Christian. He was playing with a few of his toys that were laid out all around him but he didn't move much. He seemed to be fascinated by just one toy, fixated almost, but I didn't see anything wrong with that. I figured he was just really focused, maybe analyzing and thinking things through. Could Christian be a really smart little boy, looking at the world like he's trying to figure everything out around him?

Christian had been very quiet, content playing by himself and I welcomed the chance to clean up a little bit before lunch, but now it was time to put his toys away so we could eat. I told Christian that it was time to pick up his toys but I noticed that he didn't budge from what he was doing. I tried again to tell him but it was as if he didn't hear a word I said. I suddenly got concerned. I had a cousin on my father's side that was born deaf and since Christian had his back to me, could it be that he couldn't hear me?

I tried making loud noises while calling out his name but I made sure not to make any movement so he wouldn't turn around due to the vibrations he was feeling. This time Christian turned around to see what I was doing, which made me feel a little better. At least he was hearing me. I knelt down beside him to talk to him but I noticed that he didn't look at me unless I made a point to get him to. He only briefly looked at me in the eyes before he drew his attention back to his other focus point.

When I told Christian to pick up his toys, he briefly looked at me like he didn't understand a word I was saying. He even looked at me strange like he was trying to figure out who I was. This was all bizarre but just in case he really didn't understand, I took his hand and placed it over one of the toys.

"Alright Christian, let's pick up the toy."

When I lifted his hand, the toy remained. He wouldn't grasp the toy, again while having this lost look in his eyes. Was he already starting the rebellious phase? Was he testing his boundaries?

I scolded him for not obeying and instructed him once again to pick up his toys, while taking his hand to show him what I wanted him to do. Christian cried for just a moment after I scolded him but then quickly faded back to his quiet and confused state.

How could he forget something that we've done everyday for weeks? It was hard for me to grasp what was happening. Do I continue to punish him for his disobedience? What about his strange behavior and the lost look in his eyes? Was he doing this on purpose? I had so many questions but no answers. Until I could figure out what was going on with my baby boy, I determined to watch him more closely.

Things with Christian only got worse, with us discovering more things that weren't quite right. Christian didn't want to talk anymore and became more withdrawn. He seemed to be in his own little world and you weren't invited. The vocabulary he once had reduced to mostly just two words which were "Momma," and "no." Neither of these words meant what they used to anymore. "Momma" could simply mean "hey, you." "No" could easily mean "yes."

Any other "talking" Christian did would simply be echoing what someone else had just said. I found out later that it was called "echolalia." If I told him, "It's time to eat," then he would just repeat, "It's time to eat."

Christian didn't like surprises or changes to his routine but preferred things to stay the same and remain familiar. If something was introduced to his day that he didn't expect or understand, he would have what we'd call a "melt down." It wasn't like a kid throwing a fit because they couldn't get their way. It's more like they're panicking out of fear and the only way they can cope is by "losing it."

Once they get this way it's extremely difficult to get them to refocus on anything else. You can't just distract them with a toy, treat, or whatever you can think of. They're in it for the long haul and you have to hang on for the ride with patience and understanding.

Now don't get me wrong. If Christian misbehaved or disobeyed and we knew that he completely understood what he was doing, then he got a spanking just like Daniel did. Just because Christian was "different" or "special" didn't mean that we couldn't teach him and discipline him as he grew.

Christian was actually easier to teach than Daniel because he desperately wanted to please us. Christian became so upset if he even thought we were mad or disappointed with him. He threw himself down at our feet, wrapping his arms around our legs, screaming, "Pwease! Pwease! I sowwy! I sowwy!"

If you just asked, "Do you want a spanking?" he quickly replied, "No!" Christian then got up and did as he was told.

Daniel was more stubborn and needed constant, never wavering, discipline. We told him that he wouldn't get in trouble or get a spanking if he just did what Mommy and Daddy told him to do. Finally around the age of three and a half years old, Daniel got it. After receiving at least one spanking a day, every day, he finally understood that if he just obeyed, things would be much easier for all of us.

I'm proud to say that we rarely had to spank Daniel much through the years after that. It was hard on Jerry Dale and I to stick with it but we knew we had to for Daniel's sake as we tried to mold his character as a young boy.

If you teach them when they're young, you won't have much trouble out of them when they're older. You're laying the foundation before the age of five, and then building on that for the rest of their lives. We've always disciplined them both with love, explaining why they were in trouble, making sure they understood why they were being punished. With Christian, it took a little more.

On some nights, Christian wouldn't sleep well and cried a lot for no apparent reason. We heard that if you start letting them sleep with you in your bed then you can't get them out, so we tried to do everything else to soothe him. Jerry Dale and I even moved a bed in his room so he could see us, maybe calming him down. We tried that for about a week but nothing helped.

There was no logical explanation for him to scream and cry as much as he did. It was so hard to know that there wasn't anything really wrong with Christian that we could see but he would just scream in terror for hours if we didn't intervene.

We noticed that Christian's food choices started changing and he began craving wheat products like rolls, bread, anything with a crust. Of course he wanted the sweet foods, too, so we had to start hiding anything classified as junk food. If we didn't he would continually raid the pantry or refrigerator until it was all eventually missing. Anything that looked strange or felt weird in his mouth he instantly rejected. I had to bribe him to at least try new foods.

There were other things that we started noticing that were different with Christian. His hearing seemed to be more sensitive and he could hear things that we couldn't. Chaotic noise and many people talking at once only aggravated him. His sense of touch changed. Things that would normally hurt another child, didn't phase him. He preferred tight hugs as apposed to a light touch. When he tried to show physical affection to others he could sometimes be too aggressive and hurt them unintentionally.

Life in general completely changed in our house and Christian slowly withdrew more with each passing day. Jerry Dale and I didn't know what was going on or what to do, which made us ask ourselves if there was something that we had done, or not done, to cause this.

Because he wasn't actually classified as "sick", we didn't know who to ask or where to go. In a way, we were embarrassed to ask anyone for fear of what people might say or think. We were also afraid of what we might hear.

Jerry Dale and I simply adjusted to the new normal and tried to keep going as we always had, making changes as needed. When we were around other people, we made excuses for Christian's odd behavior, trying to explain why he was "different."

As a mother, all I wanted was to understand what was going on with my son so I could fix it. I didn't have easy access to the internet back then but even if I did, I didn't know where to start or how to look for the answers I needed. We had asked for the De Soto Parish school system to test him but they told us that Christian was too young and that boys were sometimes slow in their development. They told me to just give him time and he would most likely catch up to where he needed to be developmentally, but we were getting tired of waiting.

Through some persistence we managed to get an appointment with the De Soto Parish Special Education department but only after Christian had turned three years old. After a multitude of tests we were told that they would get back with us with their findings. We were later presented with a thick report that really didn't give us a clear answer as to what was wrong with our son, but on the good side, they were now willing to allow Christian to start going to what they called a Non-Cat Pre-K class at the Logansport Elementary School. We didn't have the answers we were looking for but it was a start in the right direction.

A God Moment

We never know what life is going to throw at us. I often feel sorry for those people that don't have their hope and trust in Jesus Christ. I don't know how they can go through this life and all of it's disappointments without Him. He is our strength—our very reason for living. No matter what we may go through, He is always there to lift us up. God didn't say that we would never go through the fire, but He did promise He would go through it right along with us, watching over us through it all. Read the story of the three Hebrew children in the book of Daniel if you don't understand my "fire" reference. What an amazing story of God's love and protection when we fully trust in Him!

Chapter 38

The Unexpected

"And all these blessings shall come upon you and overtake you,
because you obey the voice of the Lord your God."
Deuteronomy 28:2 (NKJV)

At this time I had been working at the local Stage store in Mansfield and made a good name for myself as a good worker. Sales went up in every department they set me in charge over. I really liked my job but then out of no where, I got an offer for another one.

While sitting in the stands at a Logansport football game several months earlier, I had several of my youth sitting around me, watching the band march on the field. I remember cringing with embarrassment for those kids, thinking of how much better they could be if they just had someone to teach them. I didn't know the current band director at that time but I had heard several of the kids talk about him. It made me think of my band days.

"If I were a band director, I would do things much differently."

Of course I knew that would never happen because I didn't have the degree to do it. Funny how we say things when we know that we won't ever have to back those words up.

One night at the house I got a phone call from one of my youth saying that Logansport High School was interested in talking with me about coming on as the permanent substitute band director for the remainder of the school year.

"They want me to do what?" I asked.

"Remember that night in the stands when you said that you would do things differently if you were ever a band director? Well we never forgot about that and the band wants you. We boycotted against our band director and now he's quitting. We went to the principal and asked him to hire you since you had experience in band, music, and leading teenagers."

"But how can they hire me when I don't have a teaching certificate or degree to teach? Why did the band director quit? Didn't they just hire a new one this year?"

She explained that they did have a new, and much older, band director but he couldn't get any of the kids to do what he wanted. According to her, he was making them do embarrassing things with their marching and the kids didn't respect his vision for the band. I was surprised when I was told that the entire high school band agreed before practice one day to sit down in the football field stands in protest, refusing to march for him. The band director didn't know what to do so he went and sat down in the middle of the field for the rest of the class period.

After talking to Jerry Dale about the possibility of changing jobs, we both felt that it wouldn't hurt to check it out and see what the job would pay, as well as what they expected out of me.

I had a great meeting with the principal and discovered that I could legally take over teaching as a permanent substitute as long as it was after the first of October in the school year. He explained that the band director wanted to leave before then but they legally couldn't let him. I would also be making more money working for the school than at Stage.

I would start almost immediately as the new band director of fifth grade, sixth grade, seventh grade, and high school band classes. I was a little nervous on my first day. How would the kids accept me, especially since they boycotted their last director? It did help that I already knew several of the kids on campus from us being in youth ministry for several years in the area and they all made sure they came and gave me a big hug.

The fifth grade band class was the first to arrive that morning as I sat in the office of the band hall getting some notes together.

They were all informed that their new band director was starting that day so they were running in the band hall, eager to see who they were getting.

"Our new band director is a chick!"

I had to laugh at the boy's comment. After introducing myself and sharing my vision with my first class, it didn't take long to see that they hadn't been taught much. I basically had to start from scratch with them.

The rest of my classes went pretty smooth, but it was the high school band that the principal was the most concerned about. He had already arranged for me to meet and talk with both the drum major and assistant drum major during my free hour. The band respected their leadership and the principal knew that it was crucial for us to be able to merge our leadership skills to make the rest of the school year work out smoothly. The meeting went well and it ended with the three of us excited about the possibilities to come.

It was finally time to meet the high school band. It consisted of eighth through twelfth grades and the band hall was full of students. After the principal introduced me, I shared my vision of what I wanted to accomplish with them for the rest of the year. I told them of my past experience with band, some of my ideas, and the fact that we were going to have fun while working hard to be a great band together. They all got excited and started cheering so that made me feel more at ease.

I took over right in the heat of football and marching season. I quickly found out that about half of the band members really didn't know how to march. I had to pick out music and figure out new marching routines to perform during half times and get them parade ready as well. I went to every football game and it brought back many memories of when I was in band so many years ago.

The rest of the school year consisted of getting ready for different competitions and concerts that we performed. I had a great time making wonderful relationships with all the students as well as other teachers on campus.

Once the school year was over, Stage offered my old position back so I went back to work for them. I found out that the school hired a great band director to come in for the next school year so it made me feel better about not being able to come back, even though the kids were begging for me.

Since it was hard finding a substitute that would agree to take on the band classes, I went back a few times on my days off. The first day I came back as a substitute in the band hall, the kids screamed in excitement, running to the podium to hug me. They all asked if I was coming back as their band director and I had to tell them I wasn't.

There were a couple of other times that the school called me to come substitute for other teachers. As soon as students found out that I was somewhere on campus, they tried to find out who I was subbing for. The kids got a hall pass from their teacher to go to the bathroom, only to come to my class to hang out with me. I told them I was flattered that they wanted to visit with me but they were going to get us all in trouble if they didn't get back to their classes. I have to admit that it made me feel good that they loved my company. They honestly energized my day just listening to them and visiting with them.

Being around the teens at school, and especially our youth at the church, was a nice distraction away from a lot of the struggles we were having everywhere else. It was easier to help them all with their many problems because that meant we could temporarily take our mind off of our own. Jerry Dale and I found ourselves dealing with so many trials all at once that it was beginning to become too much for both of us. We prayed for God to intervene on our behalf in every area and it wasn't long that He did just that.

A God Moment

Isn't it wonderful how God can come along and help things to happen for our good in a way that we never saw coming? That's how powerful and loving our God is. If we remain faithful with our tithes and offerings, as well as a good steward over what God has given us, He promises to bless us to overflowing and rebuking the devourer for our sake. Are you being a good steward with everything God has blessed you with? If you're not sure, I urge you to seek God for wisdom as to what you can do that could help your situation be better financially, physically, mentally, and above all spiritually.

Chapter 39

New Opportunities

"And we know that all things work together for good to those who love God, to those who are the called according to His purpose."
Romans 8:28 (NKJV)

Being the youth pastors at Family Worship Center in Logansport was a great learning experience and God kept giving Jerry Dale amazing ideas and huge visions on where to take that ministry. For the most part, we had the support of his parents, our pastors, and they allowed us to try new things to help make the youth department grow. There were just a couple of things that stood in our way at times: small church mentality and budget, and a clash of the vision for the ministry.

We were just a small church in a small town with limited funds so we had to get creative on how to reach the teens of our area. Sometimes Jerry Dale wanted to do something that required a little money, and even if the youth had the money in their account, we were always asked, "Is that really necessary?"

We knew that they were only trying to watch out for the limited budget but it always upset Jerry Dale that no one seemed to want to let go of a little money for the youth department. The other frustration was that Jerry Dale would get so fired up and excited about an idea or a vision that God gave him concerning his ministry but because his parents couldn't see it, they often played it down or dismissed it.

They didn't mean to hurt me or Jerry Dale, they just simply didn't have the same vision we did. They thought they were protecting us but they were actually only frustrating us both spiritually.

Jerry Dale knew he was called to this ministry and he desperately wanted to see it grow so he made things work as far as he was allowed and the youth group started slowly growing. For a church as small as ours, we had a pretty large youth group and it was getting more exciting as it grew. We could feel the momentum in the move of God but we were still getting spiritually frustrated because we knew we could be doing more. Through listening to God, studying, and always being open to new things, Jerry Dale and I both had so many great ideas and wanted to use them.

Jerry Dale and I discussed many times about moving our ministry somewhere else where we could really stretch our abilities and apply our vision. We started praying for God to open another door for us. Our original plan was to help at Family Worship Center temporarily until they found someone else, but that didn't happen. Sometimes when you have too much family involved in a ministry, or even a business, it can get sticky or stressful and that's something we never wanted since we all loved each other very much.

Jerry Dale and I soon got word that a church in Lubbock, Texas was looking for a full-time youth minister. We were invited to drive there to see if we felt God leading us to fill that position. We both thought that this could possibly be the answer to our prayers but wasn't quite sure. That weekend everyone at the Lubbock church treated us very well but by the end of our visit, we knew that wasn't where we were supposed to be.

Although we had reservations about moving there since it was so far away from both of our families, we had hoped that this was our next move, our next step up in the world. We had been serving under Jerry Dale's parents' leadership for the majority of our time in the ministry so we desired to get out from under their wings so we could spread our own and fly solo. It wasn't that we didn't love and appreciate everything they had done for us, it was just time for us to grow up and move on.

Other things started happening within the ministry that was really upsetting both Jerry Dale and me to the point that we didn't even want to go to church anymore. The thought of showing up and facing what we knew would be there put knots in both of our stomachs. We knew it was just the devil trying to tear the church apart so we pushed our feelings aside and continued on with what we knew God had called us to do. We both prayed for God to help us in the middle of this trial but it only seemed to be getting worse instead of better.

After one particular bad week, Jerry Dale came to me in tears.

"I just prayed a pretty bold prayer. I told God that if He doesn't put me in a full-time position in another church somewhere—where I can do what I know I have in my heart to do, then I'm going to quit the ministry to just work full-time for my family. I can't keep doing this. I'm starting to hate the ministry. I need God to move me!"

"You prayed what?"

I didn't want God to strike us both down with lightening for his bold move, but then again, I found myself feeling relieved at the same time. I hated the fact that for the first time in my life, I didn't look forward to going to church anymore. I felt guilty that I didn't enjoy being there and counted the minutes until it was over. Something had to change and we both knew it.

Jerry Dale asked me to agree with him in prayer about God moving us so I gladly agreed. One night after church services, we came home to notice that we had a message on our answering machine. It was Jerry Dale's previous youth pastor at South Oak Grove Church in Stanley, LA, who had moved to the Conroe, Texas area a few years earlier to be an associate pastor. The message blew us both away. As soon as I heard his voice and knew who it was, the Holy Spirit engaged inside of me before we heard what he had to say. I already knew what the message was going to be about before I listened to it.

"Hey, Jerry Dale! I know you probably think it's strange for me to be calling you since we haven't been able to talk for such a long time but I have something important to share with you. I was having lunch with another pastor friend of mine yesterday, Bro. Parker, and we had a great visit. In the middle of our conversation, Bro. Parker said that his church is looking for a guy that can be an associate pastor, as well as a full-time youth pastor. He asked if I knew of anyone that I would recommend. I normally don't ever put myself in the position of recommending anybody because it may come back negatively on me, but I felt the Holy Spirit prompting me to talk about you, Jerry Dale. Your name kept coming up in my spirit so I obeyed and brought you into our conversation. Bro. Parker seemed interested and wants to call you so whenever you can, call me back and we'll talk more about the details."

The whole time we're both listening to this, I'm literally jumping up and down in the living room with excitement. Jerry Dale was standing there with a shocked look on his face. I'm beside myself with joy as I knew this was the answer to our prayers but Jerry Dale was very cautious and scared to get excited. I think he was in shock that God had answered so quickly and was almost ready to give up on everything. We were standing there listening to what we both knew was our next move and I'm screaming with excitement.

"Call him! Call him now!"

It was only around 9:00 PM but Jerry Dale said he wanted to wait until the next day to call, which made me frustrated. It's like someone calling to say that you just won a million dollars but you can't come get it until the next day.

Jerry Dale is the type to take his time before he talks or responds about anything of importance so he can have the time to pray and think about it first. I couldn't wait to see what was going to happen and I could see the shock gradually change to excitement with Jerry Dale, too. Neither of us could hardly sleep that night in anticipation for what the next day would bring us. Was our lives about to change?

Both of us had the opportunity to talk with Bro. Parker within the next couple of days. Arrangements were made for us to come to Splendora, Texas to visit with them and attend services that coming weekend at Plum Grove Assembly of God Church. Bro. and Sis. Parker wanted us to meet their people and see what we thought without actually announcing the reason why we were there. They wanted the visit to be laid back and relaxed. We couldn't wait to get there to see what God may be leading us into.

When we arrived at the church to meet with Bro. and Sis. Parker, we were already excited by what we saw on the outside of the property. There was a nice octagon shaped sanctuary built in front with a long, rectangular building attached behind it. You could tell that the church was well taken care of from outward appearances so we couldn't wait to see how everything looked on the inside.

Bro. and Sis. Parker drove up shortly after we did and it didn't take long for us all to become friends. We visited outside in the parking lot for a few minutes before we were invited to come inside the church.

As soon as Jerry Dale and I walked through the front doors, we looked at each other. The Spirit of God hit us at the same time and a peace flooded our souls, letting us know that we were being called to move there. Jerry Dale and I smiled at each other and we knew what we were thinking and feeling without either of us saying a word. We felt God saying, "This is your new home."

A quick tour of the church facilities made us excited about all the future possibilities. They had a big stage for their band and Bro. Parker wanted us to meet their praise team and possibly play and sing with them that weekend. Bro. Parker knew of our musical abilities and couldn't wait to see how we might fit in and add to their worship experience.

We were excited to find out that they played the same style of music we really enjoyed. We liked the old hymns and made them our own creation by changing up the music a little but we really loved the contemporary praise and worship music that was becoming more popular. Hymns talk more *about* God where the new praise and worship music is more talking straight *to* God. That alone can change the dynamic of any worship service, preparing the hearts of the congregation for the presentation of God's Word.

After visiting in the Pastor's office for a while together, Bro. and Sis. Parker took us out to a restaurant in Cleveland, Texas where we could continue our visit. After a great meal together, we later went back to the church to meet those who were on the praise and worship team. They were there for a quick practice and we all became friends in no time. Bro. Parker urged us to play and sing with them so we did and had a great time.

It wasn't long that the worship leader, Karen, said, "Y'all need to come back."

We remembered Bro. Parker wanting us to keep the reason for our visit a secret so I replied, "Oh, we might come back."

Jerry Dale and I were excited to get to be a part of their Sunday services so we could meet everyone and get a feel for how things were done at their church. Everyone was very friendly and we really enjoyed the worship and preaching. It was different than back home but it felt refreshing being a part of something so close to our own vision. They were a larger church, with a vision of growing even further, especially with the younger crowd. That's where we came in. They wanted their youth ministry to explode and they were hoping we could get the job done.

We had learned that a young man in his very early twenties came on board as Youth Pastor a year or two before us and did very well. He was able to capture the attention of the teenagers by his extravagantly laid out sermons, using props or whatever he could to keep them interested. Numbers grew between sixty to seventy teens weekly until one day he resigned.

The youth department quickly fell very low in number. One of the youth leaders that helped the Youth Pastor tried to keep the youth ministry together by holding bible studies but only a few showed up. The problem with both of these leaders was they were too focused on only one aspect of their ministry instead of equally balancing them.

There was a lot of fluff and excitement with the first young man but not enough stability and discipline in the Word, grounding them for the future. The youth were more attached to this young Youth Pastor than they were with God. When the fun left, so did the teens.

The second leader attempted to give them that stability in the Word but failed to bring it in a way that a teenager would enjoy and stick with it. Sitting in a circle with bibles in hand may be good enough to a teen that already has a relationship with God but it won't work with those that don't know about God or didn't grow up in church.

There has to be a delicate balance to reach your "church" kids as well as the "lost and searching" ones at the same time. Our job was to maintain the few teens that still went there, bring back those teens that had left, and find ways to attract new teens to the church. It was a tall order but we were up for the challenge.

After a great service Sunday morning, several people of the church wanted to take us out to a nice lunch. Everything went great until we went back to our car. We had an older model Audi car and never had any issues out of it, but when we put the standard transmission in reverse, something went wrong. The transmission totally went out right there in the parking lot, which was very embarrassing for us both. So now what do we do?

Everyone was so nice and offered for us to spend the afternoon with one of the deacons and his family at their home. Dad English and nephew Josh were going to come pick us up and load the car up on the trailer to haul it back home. Unfortunately, with it being a Sunday, they couldn't come get us until later that evening so we joined the Plum Grove church family once again for their evening services. Dad English and Josh finally arrived with the trailer when church was almost over so they slipped quietly in the back and joined us for the rest of the service.

After service was over, we were pleased to introduce Dad English and Josh to everyone. We wanted them to see where we were feeling God calling us to and the people that made us feel so welcome. I could tell they were excited for us but it was getting obvious that they were getting worried about losing us to Texas. Josh started getting curious if we were going to move or not but we simply told him that we didn't know yet.

As Dad English drove us to where the car had broken down, a couple of guys from the church came with us to lend a hand loading it up on the trailer. We couldn't get over how wonderful everyone had been to us that weekend. It was like a breath of fresh air to us and we loved it. The congregation had just taken up a love offering to help pay for the transmission to be fixed once we returned home, and it was a blessing since we didn't have the money to fix it. It was a total shock that they offered to help us with the expense of fixing our car but we were very thankful.

Since Dad English had to come in his single-cab truck, the men rode in the front of the truck while me and the boys cuddled together in the bed of the truck. Mom English sent along plenty of blankets and pillows for us and we had the camper shell over us. It was pretty late so I was thankful that the boys and I could get some sleep on the way home.

The next day Jerry Dale and I talked about our weekend in Splendora. We already started working on a possible game plan before we even knew we had the job. Bro. Parker set up another weekend for us to come back to officially try out for the Associate Pastor/Youth Pastor position that they needed filled and we couldn't wait to see how God was going to work things out for all of us.

Changing Names

When I met Jerry Dale, I learned that he answered to many names. Sometimes people shortened his name by calling him Jerry while others shortened it even further to simply J.D. His family later told me that his nickname as a child was "Peanut" because he was so small for so long. I was so used to calling him Jerry Dale that I couldn't imagine myself calling him anything else.

After he took the job in Bossier City as a physical therapy technician, he went by the name that he really preferred—Dale. I knew he went by Dale at work but it was hard to remember. One day I called his work and asked the secretary if I could speak to Jerry Dale.

"Who?" she asked.

"Jerry Dale."

"We don't have anyone working here by that name."

"You better have someone working there by that name! Wait a minute. I mean Dale."

"Dale? Yes, we have one of those. Wait. What did you call him?"

"Jerry Dale."

"I didn't know that was his name!"

We both had a good laugh and it stayed an inside joke between us from then on. When he was home and around his family he remained Jerry Dale to everyone but at work he preferred Dale.

When we decided to try out for the church in Splendora, he wanted to be known as Dale so I had to try to remember not to call him Jerry Dale in front of others, since it would probably confuse them all. He now goes by Dale just about everywhere so I'll refer to him as Dale for the rest of this book.

A God Moment

How often do we pray and when God actually answers, we're shocked that He answered us? Why don't we pray with the expectancy that He will answer? Maybe we say, "I know He can, but it's a matter of if He will." Why not have the faith to believe He will? I challenge you to look at your prayer life and see if there may be room for improvement. If you're like most of the population, there's always room for that. What about possible obstacles in your life that may be hindering your prayers according to God's Word? God wants a relationship with us, so how's your communication with Him?

Chapter 40

Health Issues

"Heal me, O Lord, and I shall be healed; save me, and I shall be saved, for You are my praise." Jeremiah 17:14 (NKJV)

In the middle of everything going on in my life, I've had to deal with a couple of "thorns in my flesh" but I praise God that my burden has been very light compared to some. This chapter is not giving praise and attention to the areas where I lack complete health but to give God the glory for keeping me humble and helping me through it all. I realize that things could be so much worse than they are and for that I give Him praise.

As I've mentioned previously, I was born with a heart defect where my valves don't close all the way when beating, causing blood leakage back into the heart. Most of the time I feel fine, but there are times that it acts up. Sometimes bad enough to put me in the bed. It's only been around the past ten years that it has gotten worse.

I recently had to have my first surgery ever—a heart catheterization. They were checking to see if I had any artery issues. Thankfully they found nothing wrong and the doctor said that I had the arteries of an eighteen-year-old.

I've been told that my heart problem won't kill me but it sure will make me feel bad at times and slow me down. Maybe God is trying to tell me that I need to pace myself and slow down sometimes. If He is, I wouldn't doubt it a bit. I was recently placed on a daily dose of medicine that is supposed to help with my irregular heart beats and patterns. We'll see that how goes.

Diabetes runs in my family on my mother's side pretty bad so I've had to watch and guard myself from possibly inheriting this awful disease. I've had the unfortunate experience of witnessing first hand what diabetes can do. My grandmother had to go through dialysis, daily insulin shots, and many more struggles before she passed away a few years ago. Mom has diabetes but she controls it through medicine and diet.

I thankfully don't have diabetes but I was diagnosed as hypoglycemic, which means I have an issue of my blood sugar getting too low instead of too high. I got checked after I passed out at work one day and went into a mild seizure. An ambulance picked me up and took me to the hospital in Center, Texas but that was a joke. My body was still stiff due to the seizure but the nurses kept yelling at me to relax. Not once did they take a blood or urine sample, or check anything else. After just a few questions the doctor finally came in and gave me a diagnosis of stress.

Mom and I looked at each other and we agreed that as soon as they let me out of there, she was taking me to LSU hospital. After we finally got admitted into the emergency room at LSU, a nurse came to me and asked, "What are you here for again?"

"I'm here to check my blood sugar because of what happened to me at work today and to make sure that I haven't inherited diabetes."

"Well, I don't think you have to worry about diabetes at the moment because your blood sugar level checked out at only sixty. Your blood sugar is way too low. That's why you had a seizure."

"Wow. After all this time, even after the ambulance people gave me glucose, if it's registering at sixty now, I wonder how low it was before."

"That's what we're concerned about so we're going to make an appointment for you to get tested."

I was so glad that we were finally getting answers and I was very happy to know that I didn't have diabetes. Although they did say I would still have to watch how I eat and take care of myself. To make sure that my sugar level doesn't bottom out, I try to eat three small meals a day with snacks in between, and I'm supposed to stay away from sugar. That's the hard part!

When Christian was about two or three years old, I couldn't remember when I had my last "monthly." After a quick calendar check I realized that it had been at least a couple of months so I got nervous. Was I pregnant again? I didn't feel pregnant, but I know that not all pregnancies are the same so I took a test and it came out negative. So what was going on?

While visiting with the English's one day, I began telling Mom English about my hair falling out and having hot flashes. She started laughing and said that I was going through "the change," but she was just joking. I didn't think that was my problem but I knew something wasn't right so I made an appointment to get myself checked out.

I've always had an issue with my female stuff. Nothing has ever worked right, was never on time, and the pain was always unbearable. What could be the problem this time? I was only twenty-eight years old at the time so I wasn't expecting to hear what the doctor told me.

After I explained my symptoms and answered all of his questions my doctor kept asking me how old I was. He was having a hard time grasping what my symptoms sounded like, so after a quick blood test, it was confirmed: I had premature ovarian failure, or in other words, I was going through early menopause. It's rare for someone in their thirties and even more rare for someone in their twenties so I felt like a freak of nature.

My doctor started running all sorts of tests and I felt like a guinea pig. I've tried different hormone replacement options but after I started gaining weight, I decided to stop taking anything and see what happened. To this day I'm thankful that I don't have to take medications or hormones and I seem to be just fine.

I was initially a little disappointed that I couldn't have any more children but I'm looking at this as a blessing, especially since I don't have a "monthly" anymore. God already gave me two beautiful sons and maybe God knew that we weren't going to be able to handle another one.

After all, I have had so many wonderful "babies" that I feel I've helped raise through our youth ministries all these years, so I feel blessed. It's not like we don't have a house full of teenagers at any given time and we've been privileged to help a couple of young men in the past by allowing them to live with us for about a year each. Our home has always been a place of love and refuge for those who needed it. We're just glad that we were able to help these boys when they needed us.

I'm happy to say that I've never had a broken bone but I came close of doing some major damage to my knee early last year. I was standing up in a chair in my dining room, painting the ceiling with a roller. I had just filled my roller with paint when I realized that I needed to move over. I was already standing in one chair so I stepped to the next chair, not far from me, when they both decided they didn't like each other anymore. The chairs quickly separated, sliding on the floor and I quickly came down hard. My back hit on the dining table and my left knee twisted in mid-air as I fell. Paint was slung everywhere so after I felt that I was alright, I got up and quickly cleaned up the paint before it dried and then climbed back up in the chair to finish the ceiling.

Later on I figured that I better put that knee up instead of walking around on it. I remembered how after an injury your body can be in shock for a while and not feel the extent of the damage you've done. It's a good thing I did because I had ripped some tissue and caused damaged underneath my knee cap. Thankfully I had a great surgeon and my knee has healed well enough that I can't tell that I ever had the accident. Praise God for that!

A God Moment

How do you handle the struggles of life when you get that diagnosis, live with daily pain, or any other physical problem? You take it to God and have faith in Him and His Word. Sometimes God heals us and sometimes He doesn't. Our imperfections can help keep us humble and remind us of our need of a loving and powerful God. There's always a reason behind why God chooses to heal someone and why He chooses to take them on home to be with Him instead. God knows a whole lot more than we do and He can see into the future. His infinite wisdom far surpasses ours so why question Him? He loves you so pray and believe for your healing and watch Him work in and through your life however He chooses.

Chapter 41

The Tryout

"But those who wait on the Lord shall renew their strength; they shall mount up with wings like eagles, they shall run and not be weary, they shall walk and not faint." Isaiah 40:31 (NKJV)

Shortly after we returned back home from Splendora, we got a phone call back from Bro. Parker. Our first weekend there was not only great for us but everyone seemed to want us to come back for an actual interview, as well as show the congregation and youth what we could do. They wanted us to take over their Sunday evening service as if it were a youth service, with the entire church present, watching our techniques and ideas on how to attract more teens.

We were so excited about going back and couldn't wait to spend more time with some of the people we had met the first time we visited. Everyone was so nice and welcoming to us so it helped us feel more at ease about coming back, maybe even permanently. The church set us up in a nice hotel that Saturday evening as we awaited for the important day to arrive. We could hardly wait to see if everyone approved of us becoming part of their paid staff and church family.

If my memory is correct, I think Dale and I got to play and sing with the worship band that Sunday morning. Dale played the bass guitar and I played my keyboard along side the piano player, Gwenette, while singing back-up harmony with the other singers.

We coordinated our playing where Gwenette played more of the lead while I filled in, or played something that complimented what she was playing. Since everyone accepted us so well, Dale and I playing and singing with the band was an easy transition. It looked like everyone got along great, which made practices and ministry times flow much easier.

After a great service, a big lunch was prepared for us at the church and everyone who held a position of any kind, along with their spouses, were invited to come. The purpose for this special lunch was to allow the leadership of the church to get to know us on a more personal level.

The awkward part came after the meal where anyone could ask us any question they chose and we had to answer it in front of the entire group that consisted of around fifty people. Dale and I were positioned to sit at a head table with Bro. and Sis. Parker, front and center. We were both a little nervous but we knew it would be alright if we just answered everything honestly from our hearts and God would do the rest.

There were many great questions that were asked, some that Dale and I would have asked ourselves if we were in their shoes, and the Holy Spirit led us both in answering every one. There was one question that stood out and made an impression on me a little more than the others.

It was from an older lady that reminded me of my grandmother. I remember she looked and sounded just like her so I felt at ease with her sweet spirit and familiar ways.

"If you move here to be our associate pastors and youth pastors, how far away will you be from your parents and the boys' grandparents? How often would you be able to go back to visit?"

I understood immediately where she was coming from. As a grandmother herself, she was concerned if they would be putting a hardship on our immediate family, as well as both sets of grandparents back in Louisiana, by voting us in. She didn't want to see our children suffer because of our ministry and that meant a lot to me that she was thinking of our boys and their relationship with their grandparents. We quickly reassured her that the travel was only two and a half hours and we planned to take trips back to visit as often as possible. That put a smile on her face as well as on mine.

We enjoyed the chance for everyone to finally get to know who we were and what our vision was for our ministry together, whether it was back home or there in Texas. We both knew what God was calling us to do and how to do it. The only question left to be answered was where, but we had a feeling in our spirit that it was at Plum Grove Church.

After a great afternoon of visiting, it was time for Dale and I to get ready to take charge of the evening service. It was our turn to show the youth and adults what our idea of a true youth service consisted of. Our version of a youth service didn't resemble anything like most would think. It was more like a full church service geared directly to teens. Every aspect was carefully thought out to attract and keep the attention of your average teen off the street, not just your normal church-raised teen.

The youth that were still attending sat up front while the majority of the adults sat toward the back. This allowed the adults to observe but give the youth some space to interact with us without intruding. Word had gotten out that a new young couple was trying out for the new youth pastor position so a few more teens showed up to see who we were and how we were going to run things if voted in. We all had a lot of fun and the teens seemed to love Dale's genuine care and humor in his preaching.

After our youth service was over, we had several that said they really enjoyed it and looked forward to seeing what else we could accomplish for their youth ministry. We quickly learned the church had voted us in as their full time Youth Pastors and Associate Pastors. Needless to say, we were jumping for joy on the inside and began praying for God's direction in this new step that our little family was taking.

This was all so very exciting but this meant another move for us and uprooting the boys from familiar territory. It would mean a fresh start for all of us. What would God have for us in Splendora, Texas? Only time would tell and December 1, 1999 was day-one on the job.

A God Moment

Isn't it amazing to sit back and watch God work on our behalf? He just asks us to remain faithful and trust in Him. He's our Heavenly Father, so wouldn't He provide for us and care for us just like our earthly fathers should? He knows our past, our present, and also our future so sit back and enjoy the ride as He orders the steps of your life to accomplish some pretty amazing things for His glory!

Chapter 42

Let's Move

"For we have become partakers of Christ if we hold the beginning of our confidence steadfast to the end." Hebrews 3:14 (NKJV)

Dale and I could hardly contain our excitement about the move but now we had to face telling his parents, the church, and our youth group that we were resigning all positions at Family Worship Center in a matter of about a month. Everybody, especially our youth, were scared of losing us when we tried out for the position in Lubbock, Texas and they knew we were trying out for Splendora.

I think everyone just assumed we would always be there, that we would never leave. Maybe they even thought we weren't good enough for a bigger church to hire us since we were just a couple from a small church, small town. Now we were about to tell them it was for real this time.

Some of our youth started blaming each other for the reason we were leaving, promising to listen more and act better during youth services. We tried to reassure them that our move had absolutely nothing to do with them or their behavior, but it was still hard for all of us. Our youth had become our babies, our family, so it was harder than we expected to say goodbye to a family we had given our everything to for the past ten years.

Telling Mom and Dad English wasn't much easier either. Not only would we be leaving the church. but our singing group, The

English Version, would have to go on without us, too. We knew it would be hard on them because as parents, they were very proud of us, but as ministers, they were very upset about losing us. We knew they were going to miss us as family and as fellow ministers but we reassured them that we would come back home to visit as often as possible.

You get into a routine, a groove of sorts, and when one nut and bolt is missing out of the works, it throws everything else out of rhythm. We knew it wasn't going to be an easy adjustment for any of them, just as it wasn't for us. We felt bad about leaving them but we knew that this move was God's will for us. We knew if God wanted us in Splendora then He had another plan for the English's and Family Worship Center, with or without us.

Now we just had to get the boys transferred to another school and find a place to stay that we could actually afford. We didn't want to sell our house in Stanley so we needed something within our new salary budget that would support basically two house notes, since you can't depend on renters. We heard that everything was so much more expensive around the Houston area than it was in ours so that made us a little nervous, but we took the matter to prayer knowing that God would provide.

Finding A New Home

Dale was still working so we made arrangements with Bro. and Sis. Parker for me and the boys to come and stay a couple of days at their house while helping us try to find a house to rent. Our niece, Christina, volunteered to come with me to help with the boys and keep me company. Several from the Plum Grove church had been looking through local papers trying to find something and the music director, Karen, took the time to drive us around looking at some of the houses they found.

I was getting pretty discouraged at first because most of the houses that were even close to being affordable ended up being a dump. I remember one particular home that was asking $800 a month for rent. We didn't have to go into the home to make up our mind since the entire yard and outside of the house was trashed.

You'd think with that amount of money it would be more livable and a lot bigger.

After a day with no luck, the Parker's heard of a tiny house that was local to Splendora and hadn't been advertised as being available. An older couple used to live in it but built a nice brick home right beside it. We figured it couldn't hurt to go check it out so we made arrangements to meet with the owners. I could tell that they were reluctant to rent it out because they didn't want their original little house torn up. After they met me and the boys, understanding why we were looking for a house, they changed their minds.

When we pulled onto the street the house was on, we noticed that it was a quiet road lined with nice houses and surrounded by trees. The homes weren't stacked on top of each other like a suburb but had some property in between them, which we liked since we're used to living in the country with no immediate neighbors. When we arrived at the house my first thought was how tiny the house was, especially compared to most of the places on that road. Other than it's size, it looked well kept and had a big fenced in yard for the boys to safely play in.

After a quick walk-through we knew we were going to have to leave some furniture behind. We could live there but it was going to be tight. Not only was it small but the place to put our washer and dryer was in a shed several feet behind the house. It wasn't exactly what we would have wanted but the owners were very nice, the house was clean, and the price was the most reasonable we had found anywhere. We were also told that the Splendora school system was among the best in the area so that was very appealing.

We couldn't move everything at once so Dale and I took a load of our bedroom furniture and the majority of our clothes while Mom and Dad English watched the boys. It was exciting for the both of us to spend the night in our new little home. When we moved the rest of our stuff, we had both of our vehicles loaded, as well as the English's, and their trailer. Everything was fine until it started pouring down rain about half way there.

Several couples from Plum Grove church knew about what time we would be arriving so we were happy to see several of them waiting for us in the rain to help us unload quickly before our stuff ruined.

I've never seen so much furniture and appliances being unloaded so quickly. While the men were bringing in everything, us women were wiping them down before they were permanently damaged.

It impressed us how willing and helpful the church people were toward us and they really didn't even know us yet. Before we were able to form any relationships with any of our new church family, they were already showing Christ's love toward us and our boys. That made us fall in love with the idea of becoming part of their ministry team even more.

A God Moment

One thing we have heard over and over through the years as to why someone chooses not to return to a church is that the people were cold and unfriendly. They didn't feel welcome, felt out of place, or unwanted. That should never be the case in any church, no matter who walks through the doors. The church is not a club for saints, it's a spiritual hospital for sinners. If you're a church member somewhere, make sure you are welcoming everyone who walks through your church doors, no matter what they look like, smell like, dress like, who they're kin to, or what their past is. Jesus welcomes them just as they are and we are to do the same. The Holy Spirit can work on them from the inside and help them to really discover God and start a personal relationship with Him. We "catch" them, He cleans them.

Chapter 43

The Diagnosis

"Let us hold fast the confession of our hope without wavering, for He who promised is faithful." Hebrews 10:23 (NKJV)

Once we got settled into our new little home, it was time to get the boys enrolled in the local Splendora school system. We really didn't know what to expect as we arrived at the Elementary building. Their school was much larger than what we were used to. The entire Elementary section was just Pre-K through second grades, which was about the same size as the entire Stanley school back home.

We brought the boys with us as the principal asked us to meet with her and a few others in a conference room. Dale and I were impressed as we were introduced to the assistant principal, the speech therapist, the school counselor, and a couple of teachers. They had actually assembled a panel to hear about how they could better know and serve our boys. We had never seen or heard of any school doing that, but we were so grateful for their hospitality and genuine concern for the education of our boys.

"Tell us about your children so we can fit them with a teacher that will be a perfect match for their learning styles and abilities. Let's start with your oldest child."

"Daniel is our oldest and he's pretty shy and quiet. He started talking late and sometimes needs a little extra time or explaining to fully understand things, but once he's got it, he's got it. He doesn't respond well to someone that's loud or extremely aggressive because he'll just retract into himself out of fear and shut down. He'll do better with a more soft-spoken teacher that's patient and understanding. Daniel is very well behaved so you shouldn't have any issues with him in that area."

"I think we have the perfect teacher in mind for Daniel. He should do well in her class and we'll let y'all meet her after our meeting. Now tell us about your younger son."

"Well, Christian is different."

"What do you mean by different?"

I began telling them how Christian was born normal but something drastically happened to him around eighteen months of age that changed everything. We explained all the struggles and changes that we'd been dealing with, including us having him tested but still not having any clear answers.

I noticed that the more I explained Christian's behavior and setbacks, the more everyone at the table were looking at each other as if they were all saying, "Are you thinking what I'm thinking?"

I eventually stopped and asked, "Wait a minute. You know what's wrong with our son, don't you?"

"Let us observe Christian for two weeks in the classroom ourselves and we'll read the report that your previous special education department gave you. After that, we'll be going into our Christmas break but we'll talk with you as soon as school starts up again in January. Is that alright?"

We agreed and for the first time Dale and I were hopeful that we might finally have some answers as to how we could help Christian. In the mean time, we had to remain patient as we were not only getting into the new routine of our new life in Texas, but also getting ready for the Christmas holiday that was right around the corner.

Our first three weeks in Splendora flew by and before we knew it, it was time to go back home to Louisiana for Christmas with our families. Since Dale and I were the first to get married out of my family, the tradition of how we compromised the time between our family and the in-laws during holiday gatherings were set by us. Since the English family already had their big Christmas dinner around noon on Christmas Eve, and then opened presents right after, the West family decided to have our big Christmas feast on Christmas night, while we kept our tradition of coming together to open presents on Christmas Eve.

It was good getting to see everyone again and naturally they were all asking how things were going for us so far in Texas. We enjoyed being able to talk about the positive things and how God was blessing us in so many ways, instead of concentrating on the negative struggles that we'd been dealing with. One particular conversation, however, stood out from the rest.

While opening presents on Christmas Eve at the English home, Dale's brother, Dennis and his wife, Patsy, were talking with us about how the boys were transitioning to their new school. Patsy was an experienced elementary educator in Bossier City, Louisiana and studied in areas of special needs concerning young children. As I was sharing with Patsy the meeting with the Splendora Elementary school and what they said they would do for us, she felt comfortable enough to ask a question that she had been keeping to herself for a while.

"Would you like for me to tell you what I think is going on with Christian?" Patsy asked.

I quickly looked at her, remembering that she was an elementary teacher, thinking she might actually have an answer for me. I answered, "Absolutely!"

"I think he has autism."

"What is autism?"

Patsy began explaining how it's a neurological disorder that effects how they interact with others, their social behaviors, their learning abilities, their speech, how they see the world around them. That it usually affects most of their senses, either by making them more or less sensitive than normal.

"It's under the Pervasive Developmental Disorder (PDD) umbrella just like Asperger Syndrome, which is a high functioning form of autism," she explained.

The more I listened to Patsy explain autism, the more I kept saying, "That's Christian!" I finally asked her, "If you could see this in Christian, why didn't you say anything to us before?"

"I was afraid you might get angry and accuse me of improperly diagnosing him," she explained.

"We have been searching for answers for so long, we wouldn't have gotten angry with you. I'm going to get on the internet and start reading up on this so I can better understand it."

"With me being a teacher, you wouldn't believe how angry some parents will get if you try to explain to them that their child may need special consideration or that something may not be completely normal with their learning abilities. I just wasn't sure how you might react if I told you that I thought Christian may have autism."

I understood where she was coming from since I've seen parents act the same way when dealing with their teenagers at church. They come to you wanting you to help them with their troubled teen but when you give them the Godly advice they need concerning their teen, they sometimes turn on you.

We've actually had parents come to us with their teen saying, "Here, you fix him/her!"

Of course we had to respond with something like, "We can do all we can through counseling as well as what we can give them at church services twice a week, but we can't undo in just a couple of hours a week what's been done all their life."

Nearly every parent with this attitude had never made church a priority but suddenly their teen starts coming to our youth services and they want us to make their teen miraculously behave now.

After talking with Patsy about this new word "autism", I decided that when we went to my Mom and Dad's house later that evening, I would ask Dad to do some research on the internet for me. The English's didn't have a computer or internet access but Dad West did. I had never heard of autism but I was certainly going to quickly become an expert on it for my son's sake. As a mother, all I wanted was answers so I could help my son and now I finally had a direction, a starting point.

I waited until after family time and opening all the gifts was over before going to Dad with my request. He readily agreed so we went into their bedroom where his computer was. Dad found a few sites explaining autism so I asked if he could print several of them out in order for us to take them home and read them.

When we were on our way home I started devouring the pages of information. I started sharing it with Dale but he remained quiet for a while. The more I read, the more I could see that Christian resembled everything the articles where describing. On one hand I was terrified, but on the other I felt relieved. It was difficult to read that my son had a neurological disorder called autism, something I had never heard of before, but a comfort to finally have an answer to our many questions.

As I was reading and sharing with Dale, I could tell he was getting upset.

He finally spoke up and said, "My son is not retarded! My son doesn't have some kind of disease or disability!"

Dale was in denial and refused to accept what was clearly right in front of him. I learned later that most men and fathers react this way, with anger and denial. As a man, he should be able to fix it or control what effects his family. Most blame themselves, thinking that they must have done something to cause this, or at least could have done something to prevent it.

Dale admitted to me later that he was thinking, "Why, God? You know we don't have time for a special needs child. We're in the ministry, doing Your work and we can't handle having a child with a disability. We can't do it God! Why?"

I actually thought the same thing but I knew we would just have to do what was necessary to make it all work, but while leaning on God's strength to endure.

It took a while for me to convince Dale that we needed to accept the trial that was placed across our path and take it to God in prayer. I knew I couldn't do this alone so I just had to be patient with Dale coming to fully understand what was going on with Christian and what would be our next steps to help him.

Autism wasn't really known and there were a lot of early speculations as to what causes it and what treatments may, or may not, help with some of the symptoms. We needed to talk with the school to see what their findings were and go from there.

I had a meeting at the school right after Christmas break was over and they shared what they observed from watching Christian. They could not officially diagnose him but they could lead us in the right direction as to what their professional opinions were concerning him as educators. Before they gave me their official position on Christian, they asked if we had a great holiday and that's when I explained what I found out about autism. The special education director looked at me with an understanding smile and I knew what she was about to say. She confirmed our fears as she shared that they, too, felt he was autistic.

"So what do we do now?" I asked.

"Since we can't officially diagnose him, the state will pay to send Christian to one of the best psychologists in Houston to do that for us. After he meets with y'all, he will write up a report for you as his parents, as well as one for us as his educators, helping all of us with some ideas of the best ways to help Christian learn and grow. From there, we will include you and your husband in every decision as to how we can help Christian while we have him here at the school. We'll also look into every avenue available to get you the assistance you may need at home, like private tutoring or therapy."

This was all so much to take in at once but I felt relieved to know that we were going to get the help we wanted and needed. I thought back to the struggle I had with the special education department back in Louisiana. Why couldn't they have told me any of this? After all, they did a full spectrum of testing on him. All the Splendora school leaders had to do was listen to me talk about Christian and they knew immediately what it was.

I even asked them, "How is it that y'all knew what was wrong but Louisiana couldn't figure it out?"

"Maybe because Texas schools have better funding?"

"Better funding shouldn't have anything to do as to whether you can effectively do your job as a special education administrator. If you've been trained to do your job, money or not, you should be able to do your job."

I know that sounds harsh but I was a mother in need of help for her child. I was like a mother bear with a cub and you didn't want to mess with me.

I quickly fell in love with all the Pre-K teachers and Christian's child-specific aide that was assigned to him. They loved on him and cared for Christian as if he was their own child.

Soon after the diagnosis, his teacher told me of a trip that the school was going to send her and me on, totally free of charge, to Corpus Christi, Texas. It was an Autism Conference where educators, therapists, and parents could go for a couple of days. It offered many different sessions you could participate in, depending on who you were and what interested you more. Again, I was blown away at the generosity of the school and made arrangements for me to go.

With more children becoming diagnosed with autism and Asperger Syndrome, an information boom started spreading everywhere. I wanted to absorb everything I could to help our family better understand the road that we had in front of us. We never thought we would be parents of a special needs child. That's not something you usually think about when you start planning on a family and raising children together.

I learned so much at that conference and couldn't wait to share it all with Dale when I got home, but there was something that was said in one of the sessions that blew me away.

"Have you grieved yet parents? There is a process to help you all get through this new world you've been shoved into. Part of this process is to grieve over the child you have lost to the PDD spectrum. Most of you had your child and they were completely normal until something happened between one to two years of age. The child you grew to know and love was suddenly snatched away from you. Now you have another child in front of you that you have to get to know all over again. You need to go ahead and grieve over your loss so you can move on to be a better parent to the new child you have now."

I had never thought of that before but it did make sense. I hadn't let go of the fact that we lost the Christian we knew. I hadn't admitted it but I was still angry over losing him to autism. Being angry or bitter wasn't going to help my son, or me, so I needed to let go of what was, and concentrate on what is.

When I got home and shared everything with Dale, we both broke down and cried together for the first time while holding each other. It was a healing time for the both of us and we knew that we needed to lean on each other, and especially God, during these difficult times.

We prayed for God to help us find the blessing in all of this but it was so hard to see past all the negative. We prayed for Christian's healing, but no miraculous answer came. We asked all the "why" questions but no reply. Was there something that we were supposed to learn from all of this? Maybe to be more sensitive to those with disabilities? We definitely had a new perspective on that now, but what would we do with it? Would this become part of our ministry in the future? God always has a plan.

A God Moment

We all have storms in life that we have to go through, and they're all different. Some of our storms may feel more like a category four hurricane or an F5 tornado, but rest assured that God is still there. Sometimes we get jealous that someone else's storm looks a whole lot calmer than ours, and we even ask God, "Why do they get it so easy? How come their life looks smoother, calmer than mine? That's not fair God." We never truly know the extent of the damage others' storms can produce in their lives, and it's really not our place to compare. Just trust in God while you ask Him all the "why" and "how" questions, allowing Him to guide you safely to shore from your own storms of life. There's always a lesson in the storm, so have you found out the lesson in yours yet?

Chapter 44

Coping With Autism

"For I will restore health to you and heal you of your wounds,"
says the Lord. Jeremiah 30:17 (NKJV)

Soon after we took the positions at Plum Grove and got into the groove of things, Bro. and Sis. Parker felt comfortable enough to leave on vacation for a few days. They hadn't had the chance to get away and rest for a while and they knew Dale and I would be alright handling things until they got back. We soon learned that Bro. Parker wasn't feeling well and they feared it may be his heart so they took him to the hospital to get checked out.

It was his heart and we were told that Dale would have to take care of that coming Sunday's service in Bro. Parker's place. At first Dale was a little nervous but then he felt a peace knowing that this was all part of God's timing, not just for us, but for the Parker's as well. God knew that Bro. Parker was going to have trouble with his heart and would need some much needed down time. God also knew that we needed a fresh start and help with Christian at the same time. There's always a plan.

Now that we had the diagnosis for Christian, the psychologist gave us an idea to help everyone at the church better understand what was going on with Christian and what to expect. Christian looked normal but if you were around him long enough, you'd see that he was different. That sometimes made people uncomfortable, mostly because they couldn't understand what was wrong. We didn't want our new church family to feel uncomfortable around us, wanting to ask what was wrong with our son but not quite knowing how to do that without offending us.

We wanted everyone to understand just as much as they wanted to, so we took the doctor's advice by writing a letter explaining everything about Christian and what autism is. We also helped any of his teachers at the church on how to handle him and what to do, or not do, in certain situations.

One Sunday I started passing the letters out to every family and at first I was getting some strange looks, but once they had the chance to read it, they later thanked me.

"We really appreciate the letter. We knew something was wrong but had no idea. We wanted to understand but felt uncomfortable coming up and asking, 'What's wrong with your son?' This information will really help us out a lot."

Several of our youth girls volunteered to watch our boys if we ever had a ministry meeting we had to go to, where we couldn't take the boys. We never lacked in babysitters, although we didn't need one most of the time. Unless you knew Christian's routine, it was hard watching him, especially since he still wasn't fully potty trained and didn't talk. Daniel would step in to help out a lot and Christian learned to follow his lead.

Daniel was like another little momma hen around Christian and that made Dale and I feel a lot better knowing that he was a good big brother. We had seen other siblings of special needs children that felt weird around their brother or sister. They really didn't want much to do with them so to see our boys be as close as they were was a huge relief.

That first Christmas in Texas, Daniel got a new Nintendo 64 gaming system from Grandpa Bill and fell in love with it, becoming real good at it pretty quick. Christian had absolutely no interest playing the game, although Daniel would give him a controller and tried to teach him how. Christian just wanted to watch Daniel do it. Christian moved and jumped just like Mario did in the game, mimicking the sounds that Mario made. The funny thing is that Christian paid attention to where Daniel went in the game and if he thought

Daniel was going the wrong way, he screamed at Daniel to go the other way until he did.

The first time we needed a babysitter was when Dale and I had to attend a ministry banquet out of town and we couldn't bring the boys. One of our youth, named Sarah, was the first to volunteer to watch the boys and we accepted since we had watched them interact with her in a positive way. Sarah played like Daniel was her little boyfriend and Christian seemed to like her as well so that made us feel good about leaving them both with her. After explaining how to take care of Christian and the instructions for the evening, we left for the banquet but I'll have to admit that I was a little nervous.

I planned on calling about half way through the banquet to check on how things were going but Sarah beat me to it by calling first. Sarah was having one of the worst nights of babysitting that she probably ever had, or will have. Christian had a "#2" accident but it ended up all over him so she decided to go ahead and give him his bath for the evening to get him cleaned up. Then suddenly Daniel vomited everywhere so she decided to put both of them in the tub, while then having to clean up all the vomit.

I could tell she was on the edge of crying as she was asking what she should do next. I felt so sorry for her but she handled everything like a trooper. I was sure she would never volunteer to babysit the boys again but fortunately she did.

While we were doing our best to help Christian, the school was doing the same on their end. They were constantly researching on what they could do to help him while they had him in class. Christian was in the Pre-K class along with the rest of the other students but with his child-specific aide to help him at times, they tried to include him in everything they could. Sometimes they would have to pull him aside to teach him on his level or give him a break from the all the noise of the classroom activities.

His teachers used what they called a snuggle vest that was made of light, stretchy material and velcro to put on Christian to keep him calm. It was made to resemble a light, constant hug and made him feel more at ease. Since Christian didn't like to sit down for very long, they placed this long, rectangular pouch filled with sand or rice across his lap to make him stay seated longer. They usually did this when he sat at the computer and it didn't take long for Christian to fall in love with the learning games on it.

True to their word, the school arranged for one of their teacher's aides to come to our house a couple of times a week after school to work with Christian in his own environment. She gave us a lot of ideas that would help Christian as well as things that he might like for his play time.

Since Christian liked to pace back and forth a lot, she suggested getting him a trampoline, helping to cut down on the pacing. We did buy a trampoline for both of the boys' birthdays and they loved it. Instead of just jumping like you'd normally do, Christian preferred to bounce and walk around the perimeter of the trampoline. He would do this for well over an hour at a time but it cut down on his need to pace once he was inside the house.

Another thing the teacher's aide suggested was an under bed box filled with rice for him to run his hands and arms through. I noticed in their classroom at school that they had a hands-on play table that looked like a sandbox but it had rice in it instead. They explained that rice was less messy and much easier to clean up. The rice box was meant as a calming agent and it wasn't expensive to put together.

I bought an under bed box with a lid and went to a discount grocery store to buy several large bags of rice to fill it. Christian already had some beach toys and cars so I made a place in the dining room area where he could easily get the box, remove the lid, and play any time he wanted.

To show him what we made for him, I got down on the floor with him and began running my hands and arms through the rice. I'll have to admit that it really did feel good—therapeutic even, and Christian loved it.

Dale and I loved to go four-wheeler riding so it wasn't long before we bought one and both of the boys loved for Dale to take them riding. Not far from the house we were renting was a wooded area down the hill, where no houses were, and it was a great place to go for a quick ride after work and before dark.

One day while I was cooking supper, Dale decided to take a ride but didn't say anything to the boys. Once Christian heard the four-wheeler crank up, he ran passed me to the back door to try to catch Dale but he was too late. Before I could catch him, Christian was already half way down the driveway, running straight to the black top after Dale, screaming for him to stop in his own way but Dale couldn't hear him over the engine.

I knew I had to reach him before he got hit by a car but I couldn't get to him fast enough, so I started praying that there would be no cars coming. While I was running as fast as I could, I suddenly saw Christian stop right in the middle of the road and crumpled down on that black top, laying face down crying.

"Christian, get up son! Get up!"

Christian just stayed laid down in the road, shaking his head while screaming back, "No! Ride! Ride!"

Our house was at the top of a hill so if anyone was driving from the bottom, they would never see Christian in time to stop before hitting him, especially now that he was laying down. God heard my prayers and I was able to get to him and pick him up before anyone drove by. We were both crying as I held him, walking back to the house. My tears were from fear, relief, sadness, and happiness all at once.

We had to really watch Christian because it seemed that he had no fear factor at all. Things that he should have been afraid of or careful around, he wasn't. We had to basically protect him from hurting himself unintentionally.

Christian had a hard time dealing with anything that was outside of his normal routine. He couldn't understand what was happening so he would have what we called a "melt-down." It wasn't the normal tantrum a spoiled child would throw when not getting its way, but rather a child falling apart out of fear and confusion. Once his melt-down started it was nearly impossible to get his mind focused on something else to help calm him down.

Our niece, Christina, came down to spend a week or so with us and she was a lot of help with the kids while she was there. One day I had to go shopping in Humble after picking up the boys from school. The only problem was that I realized I had forgotten my cell phone and sunglasses at the house. I already knew we were about to have a fight on our hands with Christian but I needed my cell phone, so I warned Christina before we ever got to the house.

"When we get there, you're going to have to hold Christian down because he's going to try to get out of the car. He knows when we go home that we always get out of the car and go inside. It's going to be a lot easier to just make him stay in the car than it will to let him go in the house and then try making him get back in the car. I'm going to jump out, go in, get my phone, and hurry back to the car so just do your best to hold him."

Just as I predicted, I heard Christian begin to scream, "House! House!" as I ran inside. Christina held him down with all her strength, trying to keep him from opening the door. He screamed all the way to the mall and didn't stop until I managed to get him focused on going to his favorite store. I could tell that Christina's nerves were about shot after wrestling with Christian for nearly thirty minutes in the car. She wasn't as accustomed to his melt-downs as we were, although you never really get used to them.

After Christian completed the school year, they decided to keep him in Pre-K again for the next year since he wasn't ready to go to Kindergarten. He did fine but the next year they figured out that they couldn't just keep him in Pre-K. They made the decision to advance him with his current class since he was already accustomed to those kids and they all already knew Christian. His aide would go with him as he progressed and they would try to keep him included in as much as they could.

The only problem was the first time he went to his new class room, he kept wanting to sneak out, run down the hall to his old room, and cried every time they retrieved him and brought him back. It took a while for him to understand that he had a new room.

Learning how to raise your first child is always a challenge, but when your second comes along and its nothing like the first, it poses another challenge. Autism made that challenge even greater, combined with confusion and frustration, so turning to God was our best and only real option to help us all through it. It just seemed to be getting harder before it got easier. Could we find the light at the end of our tunnel? Was there anything positive in this? Why was our Christian taken from us and could we ever get him back?

A God Moment

How we deal with our struggles in life help define our character and the very outcome of the struggle. Are you getting impatient? Are you at your wit's end? We get to the point where we feel that we're about to snap, but that's when God does His greatest work. He wants us to understand that it's all about Him and what He can do, not about us and what we think we can do. Look at your situation and see what glory God can get out of the end result if we just trust Him. Remember the death of Lazarus? Jesus could have healed him instantly, but He didn't. Why? So God could get the glory of his resurrection and be a testimony to all who witnessed it. What testimony is God creating in your life?

Chapter 45

"I Nacky. . .I Tink!"

"Who Himself bore our sins in His own body on the tree, that we, having died to sins, might live for righteousness—by whose stripes you were healed." 1 Peter 2:24 (NKJV)

Between our family, our new church family, and the school, we were all doing everything we could to help Christian in every way we could. It was a little more difficult than it is now since autism was rarely heard of and not very well known, so we were all pretty much going by trial and error as well as a lot of research online.

Autism was all new to just about everyone so you had to filter through the information. Some advice was pretty radical and hard to believe but when you have a child that you're trying to help, you get desperate for answers no matter how ridiculous it sounds. You get to the point where you'll pay anything, do anything for your child as long as you know it won't hurt them but possibly help them somehow.

Christian still wasn't talking no matter how much therapy he was getting. He either stayed silent, pointed while grunting, or just echoed what you said. We desperately wanted to communicate with our son and everyday life was getting harder with him not speaking.

The school introduced Christian to the Picture Exchange Communication System or P.E.C.S., where he was given a plastic strip with velcro, along with a book of pictures that he could pull out and attach to the plastic strip. It would spell out a simple sentence and Christian would have to approach the person he wanted to communicate with. The person would then read it out loud back to Christian and then he would repeat it back. His teacher made him a book of these cards to help him with his speech and it helped us understand what he wanted more at times, but it didn't seem to help him talk on his own.

We started doing more research concerning his non-verbal state and ran across this new word called "chelation." I had never heard of it but learned that it had been used for years on people who had been exposed to possible harmful environmental elements, like soldiers in Vietnam. There are different methods for chelation but it basically cleanses your blood from any heavy metals, like mercury and lead. We thought as long as it wouldn't hurt him, why not give it a shot, so we made an appointment with an all-natural medicine doctor in Houston.

We learned a lot about heavy metal poisoning, especially mercury, while listening to the doctor. We can get it from past dental work, certain sea foods, and in the preservative called thimerosal used in childhood vaccines. Mothers carry mercury in their systems and pass it on in utero to their babies.

I discovered that both Christian and I had mercury in our blood. That made me think about Daniel and his delay in talking when he was little. Had I passed it on to Daniel too? Money was tight so we knew we had to focus on Christian since Daniel had already seemed to have grown out of the majority of his limitations.

The doctor offered an all-natural chelation treatment that was made of different plant extracts. After placing just two drops of this green liquid under Christian's tongue twice a day, it would naturally work like a magnet, ridding his body slowly of any heavy metals in his blood. Insurance wouldn't cover this treatment so we had to save our money and some of our family gave what they could towards it as well. Just one small bottle cost us $300, but it was well worth it.

We had been praying for a miracle so could this be it? The doctor assured us that this was not a cure but it would help bring him out of a lot of his tendencies and Christian should start talking after about a month's time. We were skeptical but since it wouldn't hurt Christian, we decided to give it a try. We were desperate for anything to help our son and thought this may be our answer.

Just like the doctor ordered, I faithfully gave Christian the drops until the small bottle was emptied. After a month we hadn't really seen much change in Christian like the doctor said we would so I started to slip back into my doubt that anything good was going to come from any of this.

Determined Prayer

Around the time of the chelation treatment, several women from the church went to a conference and I desperately needed a touch from God. I was slowly losing hope and had so many questions that I needed answers to. Dale and I were usually the ones ministering to others so I really wanted and needed to be ministered to this time. I needed to be refreshed in God. To learn to trust and rest in Him and His will for me.

On the second night of the conference, I went to the altar to pray and the Spirit was moving so strongly with me that I couldn't stand up straight. I was totally bent over with my arms out in humbleness, crying out to God.

"I will not let You go until You bless me Father!"

I was determined to receive something from God that night and those words were the only thing that would come to me so I kept repeating them. Suddenly I heard the man who had been leading the worship say something that caught my attention.

"There are some mothers in this place that God wants to say something to. God is saying not to lose hope because your sons and daughters will come back to you. They will come back to you!"

I stopped praying long enough to listen to what he said but then quickly dismissed it since I thought it had nothing to do with me. After all, I had both of my boys at home, but the Holy Spirit spoke to me.

"Yes, Heather, this is for you, too. Christian was taken from you but he will return and come back to you."

I didn't totally understand what God was telling me but I took it that something amazing was in store for us and our Christian. I immediately starting crying out of pure joy, thanking God for hearing our prayers and giving me the blessing that I needed that night.

I found my way back to my seat where the other women from our church were quietly talking after praying themselves. They could tell that I had been crying so as I sat down and bowed over with my face in my hands, they assumed that I was still upset or praying about something serious.

They began earnestly praying over me but what they didn't realize is that my tears had quickly turned to laughter. Somewhere I had transitioned to laughing so hard that they thought I was crying really hard. The joy and love of the Lord had fallen all over me so big, so thick, that I couldn't help but laugh. It wasn't that anything was funny but I hadn't genuinely laughed that hard and that deep in a very long time.

It was like a waterfall of emotions that were quickly washing over me and it felt really good. I knew my Heavenly Father was watching over me and my family. I finally got to the point where I raised my head up to show the ladies that I was alright. Once they saw that I was actually laughing, they all started laughing with me, which made me laugh all the more. Then it started getting funny. Once I could stop long enough to talk, I shared what had happened at the altar and we all rejoiced together and praised God. It was a wonderful moment with those ladies. . .a moment I'll never forget.

And Then It Happened

One thing that I was hoping for was that we could finally get Christian potty trained. After the age of five to six years old, we had just gotten him trained to pee in the potty but we just couldn't get him to do his other business. He kept having accidents and I would have to clean him up.

We still had to use Pull-Ups during the day for his accidents and at night when he wet the bed. Trying to teach him that going to the bathroom in his pants wasn't acceptable behavior wasn't exactly the easiest job so I tried to make it where he understood without making him stressed out.

While cleaning him up I would jokingly say, "You're bottom is nasty. It's stinky. Pew-wee, stinky!"

About a month and a half went by and we had given up all hope that the chelation treatment was going to help, until one day Christian spoke on his own. After another accident in his pants, I took Christian into the bathroom to clean him up, but this time he spoke first.

"I nacky."

I immediately stopped, stunned of what I had just heard. Did he just speak on his own?

I was overjoyed so I said, "Yes, you are nasty."

To which Christian replied, "I tink."

I started laughing as I said, "You got that right silly boy. You stink!"

I was so happy as I looked into his eyes and I could see a glimpse of my son in there. The fact that I was cleaning him up wasn't relevant anymore. Christian spoke on his own for the first time and the fact that he chose those words for his first sentences was absolutely hilarious to me.

I often thought that God has a sense of humor and that day I truly believed it. For the first time in months I had hope. God knew what Dale and I needed, when we needed it. Before we had lost all faith, God gave us something to hold on to.

After that day we tried working with Christian even more. Little by little, we noticed him trying to talk on his own. It was never complex sentences but a word here, a word there, and we were happy with whatever we could get. We also saw him becoming less dependent on his routine and his melt-downs were occurring less often. Christian was slowly becoming more moderate autistic instead of near severe and non-verbal.

A God Moment

God knows what we need and when we need it. It is we who mess things up out of desperation and impatience. Waiting on God is never fun but necessary. His timing isn't our timing. We forget that He is an all-knowing God and we tend to try to tell God how to do

His business, don't we? Through our own stubbornness, we make our lives a lot harder than it could be. God is good, He is faithful and just. Trust that He loves you with an everlasting love that is beyond comprehension and only wants what is truly best for you. Rest in Him. Trust Him.

Chapter 46

Ministry On A New Level

"The Spirit of the Lord is upon Me, because he has anointed
Me to preach the gospel to the poor; He has sent Me to heal the
brokenhearted, to proclaim liberty to the captives and recovery of
sight to the blind, to set at liberty those who are oppressed."
Luke 4:18 (NKJV)

Dale and I had always known what we wanted as a couple and as a ministry team together but we hadn't had the opportunity to fully see it all come together yet. We had such huge visions and different ideas that we were anxious to try and hopefully see the Kingdom of God gain from them.

We've learned through the years that what may work at one church or one area of the country, may not necessarily work as well at another. So far we had only seen success with the few things we had been allowed to implement or try out, so we were excited about the possibility of finally spreading our wings fully in a new place.

At first we had to get used to the new church, it's people, and learning their routine. It wasn't long before Dale started introducing some of his ideas to bring the youth ministry back around at Plum Grove. Everyone else sensed the excitement in us and couldn't wait to get behind us to help in any way they could.

We were immediately introduced to several adults that had previously helped in the youth department. They all got on board with our ideas and we were grateful for their willingness to adapt and stand with us, even with the changes we were about to bring.

There were around five to seven adults that dedicated themselves to the youth department and each had their own special talents that would come in handy later on. We all didn't realize at the time how God was putting an amazing team of people together to build something much bigger than all of us.

Dale and I were grateful for the mutual respect that we all had for one another as youth team leaders. We respected that they were there before we came along and they had already built relationships with the teens. Although we were younger than most of the adult volunteers, they respected us as the new Youth Pastors and trusted our calling. They got behind us with our leadership style and supported us from the very beginning. This mutual respect made our jobs much easier.

Since the church didn't have a permanent place to hold their youth services, we were told that we could use the church's fellowship hall. The only problem with that arrangement was we couldn't permanently decorate the room for the youth. Anything that we brought in to appeal to the décor of our teens would have to be removable.

Dale started collecting different items like hub caps, license plates, metal signs, and even a bumper from an older model truck that he made the lights work when plugged in. He bought 8' x 4' sheets of thick foam board, stuck them together, creating a folding wall and decorated them with different signs and yellow caution tape. We used anything we could think of to decorate the room and it all slowly came together.

Dale had to set up everything and then take it all back down every week, but it was worth all the hard work if it meant reaching one more teen for Christ. We knew that first impressions meant a lot to teenagers, especially if we were going to reach the "un-churched" teens. There had to be something there to attract them—not only to come and see what all the talk was about, but also something to keep them coming back for more.

Between our style of worship, getting the teens to interact together with a little fun, and Dale's way of preaching to them, it all worked out to a winning combination. It wasn't long before we started seeing remarkable growth.

Getting Our Praise On

Dale and I always knew that God would use our talents and interests in music but we wanted to share these gifts with our youth. A praise and worship team made entirely of teenagers for the youth ministry was always a dream of ours and we wanted to make this happen at Plum Grove.

At first, Dale and I carried all the music and singing by Dale playing the electric guitar while I played the keyboard. My keyboard had a sequencer in it so I was able to mix and record all the drums, bass guitar, and other instruments to help make our music sound full. That worked out pretty good at first, but there's nothing like having a live band for a great worship experience. We started announcing our desire for our youth to get involved in this area of their youth ministry.

We soon had several teens that expressed their desire to play or sing in the band. Dale and I quickly filtered through the teens who really weren't going to discipline themselves to make the band a priority and weren't going to dedicate themselves to practicing their instrument or singing.

You'll always have a few that will get caught up in the excitement. They will sign up with the best intentions, but will eventually quit right in the middle of it, most times with no warning or explanation. To keep this from happening, Dale and I set up a special meeting with all the teens for the purpose of sharing our vision, what was expected out of each of them, and the consequences of not following the rules that were clearly laid out. To make sure they understood how serious we were about this, we had them sign contracts.

The contracts specifically listed all of our expectations and rules so there were no excuses of not knowing or having to guess what their roles were. If they broke a rule and then said they didn't know about that rule, then we could bring out the contracts and show them their signatures.

This is one of the biggest areas that most ministries make mistakes in—a breakdown in communication. You have to get past that "small church" mentality of "it's just us" and "that'll do." Being prepared and organized before your first teen shows up and before your service ever starts is very important to a successful youth ministry.

Another part of the contract stated that they were not just band members with talent, but worship leaders, and leaders of any kind are held to a higher standard. If they were a leader in our youth ministry then they were expected to live a life inside and outside the church worthy to be followed.

If they found themselves going through something in their life that was causing them to stray from God or make poor decisions concerning their Christian walk, then it was their responsibility to come to us explaining their situation. Dale and I would then decide whether they should remain on the team while we counseled with them, or if they needed to temporarily step down. If they chose, or were asked, to step down then we prayed and counseled with them concerning whatever it was that they were dealing with until we collectively agreed that they were ready to step back into their leadership role.

The majority of our youth band members had no real experience playing their instruments or singing in front of people but it was their passion and desire to excel in their God-given talent. That made them come together as an amazing praise and worship team. They dedicated themselves to practice at home as well as attend every church rehearsal. That made them all increase in their abilities quickly.

Our youth band was progressing so well that they could be compared to some adult bands that we've heard and we were so proud of them all. It's wonderful to witness a teen, or child, start with something from the very beginning, and then grow to a point of excellence that makes them beam with pride on the inside. A sense of accomplishment and purpose goes a long way in a teen's life and that's not to be underestimated.

It really helped a lot that Dale and I could play several different instruments between us so we took the time to teach them how to play together. It's a big difference playing your instrument at home by yourself, than it is to actually play with others. It really takes a lot of patience to help kids learn how to play and sing together but it is so rewarding when you look at their faces and see the joy of accomplishment on them. Not to mention that they're having a whole lot of fun.

Pushing The Boundaries

When we first started we had around eight teens in attendance. It gradually began to grow as the word got out about the church voting in a new youth pastor. Dale and I noticed that the majority of our youth group consisted of what you would call "church kids," or teens that were pretty much raised in church all their lives. We wanted to reach out to more teens—the ones that needed God in the worst way, so we set out to explore the area and see where God would lead us as we prayed for His direction.

After Dale talked with Bro. Parker about wanting to do an outreach, they both took a drive together. Bro. Parker took him to a sub-division not far from the church that was considered a poor neighborhood. No one really went in there due to rumors of who lived there and what went on. Dale felt drawn to that neighborhood so with the blessing of Bro. Parker, Dale scheduled a meeting with the other leaders of our youth ministry, as well as all the children ministry teachers.

Dale explained that we were about to take several of our youth and leaders to that neighborhood for an outreach, specifically targeting the teens that lived there. He knew that when we invited the teens that their little brothers, sisters, cousins, etc., would want to come, too. Dale warned them that whatever they were doing with their classes, they needed to be prepared ahead of time for a sudden increase.

Dale gave them all about a couple of weeks to prepare and then we went on our first outreach to that area. We made up a simple pamphlet that looked colorful and appealing to a teen. It didn't mention God but just invited them to come be a part of something fun on Wednesday nights at the church.

We could tell that it was the first time for several of our youth to ever do anything like that before, but they were really having a great time. As we went from one house to another, you could see the surprise in everyone's faces as we invited them to join us on Wednesday nights. They weren't used to people wanting to include them in anything but we left each house with everyone smiling.

It was finally the day to see if our hard work paid off and you could feel the excitement in the air. All of our youth leadership team knew what to do and was in place to receive extra teenagers that night. We ran the church van and quickly realized that it was going to take more than one trip to pick them all up. Dale was right. At every stop, a teen had a couple of little kids with them, asking if their little relatives could come, too. Of course, we took every last one of them.

Our youth service that night was the beginning of something amazing for our youth ministry. There was only one problem. The majority of the children teachers weren't quite prepared to handle as many new kids as we picked up, but they didn't make the same mistake the next week.

After a couple of weeks of us picking up even more teens, all the leaders began to notice that the church teens were sitting on one side, while the new teens were sitting on the other. We knew we had to remedy this quickly. We talked with some of our older, faithful youth about purposely sitting with the new teens to help make them feel more welcome. Then we started doing mixers, which are games that get everyone to interact with each other in a fun way.

They all started developing new friendships with each other as Dale preached about reaching out to others, being patient, understanding, and loving every teen that showed up at church, no matter what.

As the youth group continued to grow, Dale and I knew we had to step up our knowledge about running a much bigger ministry than we ever had before. We always had the vision for this but not the experience on how to maintain it all, so we sought out the advice of other youth ministers in the Houston area with much bigger youth groups than ours. We wanted to be ahead of the game and not wait until it was too late.

We were so thankful for the youth ministry seminars that were offered by a group of larger churches. Everyone was so willing to help all of the smaller churches know how to grow their youth ministries. It wasn't like back home where we were used to the majority of the area churches competing against each other. Trying to fellowship with another church, especially if they were of a different denomination, was like pulling teeth. This was a breath of fresh air for us and we loved it. It felt good to be able to ask questions and get a friendly, non-competitive, non-judgmental answer.

With a lot of new ideas to go with the ones that we knew God had already given us, we were even more on fire to see what God was going to do at Plum Grove. After a lot of prayer and careful thought, we started making out a new plan of action that would help our ministry not only continue to grow, but be more excellence-driven and organized as it grew. So did it work?

A God Moment

Whatever God has called you to do, do it with all your might. Never go into anything with the mindset of "that's good enough," whether it's a ministry, your job, your family, etc. If you're called to be in a particular ministry, then begin to pray over it, asking God for His direction. Look for mentors and begin asking a lot of questions. Do research into that ministry. There are lot of great ideas in books, online, seminars, ministry leader retreats, and more. Go all the way, putting your whole heart and soul into whatever you do. You'll never look back in regret if you do!

Chapter 47

Breaking New Ground

*"Blessed is the man who walks not in the counsel of the ungodly,
nor stands in the path of sinners, nor sits in the seat of the
scornful; but his delight is in the law of the LORD, and in his law
he meditates day and night. He shall be like a tree planted by the
rivers of water, that brings forth its fruit in its season, whose leaf
also shall not wither; and whatever he does shall prosper."*
Psalm 1:1-3 (NKJV)

In the first year of our ministry at Plum Grove, the youth group
grew to where we were running between 35-45 consistently every
week. It just seemed that no matter how many new teens showed
up, our total weekly numbers never really increased. Of course,
we knew that all the teens would never all show up at the same
time, but we had to figure out why about half of our youth weren't
being faithful. Some of it was because about half of our youth group
wasn't accustomed to going to church but the rest of the youth were,
so we needed to make a few changes.

Dale decided to issue a challenge that in the next two weeks,
if the youth could get at least fifty teens to show up to Wednesday
night service, that he would dye his hair blue. All the youth thought
that was pretty funny and really wanted to see that happen so they
started figuring out a way to get more teens to show up. While they
were making their plans, we were making our own.

Our youth services were already pretty cool but we wanted to do something special that they had never seen before. One of our youth adult leaders, named Wesley, wanted to help out so we all got together to brain storm. After coming up with an amazing line up for our challenge night, we knew that we couldn't do this just once. The youth were going to have an amazing time but they were going to want more nights like these, so we decided to use this to our advantage.

Ministers of any age are always trying to figure out ways to get more people interested in coming to church. It's harder to get teenagers to invite their friends to come unless they're proud of their youth group. No teen will invite their friend to come to an embarrassing or boring youth group so we came up with the idea of having one night a month that would be a big push for inviting visitors. Everything would be bigger than usual and the message would always be about salvation or rededicating their lives back to God.

We started out by putting up dancing lights, black lights, and a fog machine. Bro. Wesley, Dale, and I dressed up as rock stars, lip synced to a couple of DC Talk songs, while fake playing our guitars. We really played it up for full effect. We knew that the teens would get a kick out of it but we wanted them involved in the night as well, so we got several of our regular youth to perform in black light. After a couple of weeks of heavy advertising to the youth, we couldn't wait to see how our first big night was going to turn out.

The youth successfully packed the fellowship hall with the fifty teens required for Dale's challenge and the night was amazing. Everyone had a great time but now we had to get Dale's hair dyed blue before Sunday.

Trying to get Dale's hair bleached out and then dyed a bright blue was an adventure by itself, but it was worth it. The youth loved his hair but he got a lot of laughs from the adults. Dale had to attend a regional minister's meeting with his blue hair, which really got him a lot of strange looks, but he didn't care. Dale just proudly explained why with a big smile on his face.

Our big nights continued to be a hit with the youth and it caused a lot of excitement where the teens kept inviting more of their friends.

We all realized that we were about to outgrow the fellowship hall as our place to meet.

Dale and I always longed to have a place where we could decorate permanently for our youth ministry, and it was looking like we were about to get it. The Pastor and the board met with Dale to discuss our growing "problem" and it was voted to build a Family Life Center.

We soon broke ground and it was exciting to be a part of a building project from start to finish. The new Family Life Center contained a full size basketball court that also served as a huge fellowship hall, a commercial sized kitchen with a serving window, a large meeting and dining room, upstairs classrooms on one side, and the youth hall upstairs on one end of the gym. The youth hall had a couple of windows that overlooked into the basketball court and an extra room attached for a game room. Dale and I immediately started brainstorming with the youth on how to decorate our new permanent youth hall.

All of our adult leaders each had their own talents to bring to the table when it came to getting the youth hall decorated and ready for our first ministry night in it. We were very fortunate to have two Bro. Wesley's helping us since one was an electrician and the other was a carpenter. Together they built a stage that was clean and professional, and a sound booth. They wired our colored stage lights and disco ball with switches that could be run from the sound booth.

We wanted the room to have that "wow" factor as soon as the youth walked in so we started thinking of ways to decorate that were totally out-of-the-box thinking.

Black lights were placed around the stage so the neon paint on portions of it glowed. I painted a huge mural of an atomic explosion on one of the side walls with our youth name over it, T.N.T. (Teens Night Together), and it turned out amazing. A guy from our church donated bus seats for benches and one of our youth leaders donated huge wooden spools that used to hold cable for tables. The seats and spools were set up for a sitting area and we allowed the teens to write inspirational and positive notes on the spools to leave a legacy for those who came to youth behind them.

We were told that a guy who raced cars wanted to donate the front end clip of his Camaro to our youth group. He heard about our new project and thought his donation would be pretty cool and our guys had the perfect idea for it. Dale and our other leaders got together and painted the front end a beautiful blue and faded it down to purple. Then they found rally wheels to put under the fenders to give the illusion that it was actually drivable. Another leader rigged up toggle switches to make the head lights and park lights work, adding rope lights along the fenders. The final touch was putting our drum set right where the engine went. We hung a sign right above it on the stage that said, "Crank it Up!"

Everywhere you looked there was something cool and different to see. We couldn't wait until we could unveil it all to the youth. For several weeks we made the announcement about our first night in the new room and now it was finally here.

Dale decided to keep everyone out where they all got to experience the reveal at the same time so we had a gym full of teenagers, anxiously waiting for the doors to finally open. First impressions are everything so we had the new sound system pumping with Christian music that rocked. The fog machine made our colored lights and disco ball look even more amazing.

Everything was ready so now it was time to open the doors. Dale wanted to be at the door to see and hear the reactions from the youth as they walked in and it turned out to be a huge success. We loved watching the faces of the youth as they walked in to their new youth hall. It was theirs. Finally, they had a place of their own and they were proud of everything we had done for them.

The teens knew they could invite their friends that didn't go to church anywhere and they wouldn't be embarrassed by what their room looked like. We now had that cool factor that helped draw un-churched teens to visit and eventually stay.

Now that we had the building, we had to have the ministry to keep it all alive and growing. Dale and I wanted to make sure that the youth knew that this ministry was theirs, not ours. If they took ownership of their youth group, then they would be compelled to take care of it and help it grow.

As soon as we saw a teen that was faithful in attendance and growing in God, we wanted to get them plugged in somehow with something they would be interested in and have fun with. This made them feel like they were a part of the ministry, stay involved, and more often than not, they remained committed until they outgrew it.

At that point we planned to train and disciple them how to be future leaders of the church, but we wouldn't get to see that happen to the extent we envisioned.

A God Moment

Now you may be saying, "It shouldn't take all of that just to have a successful youth ministry," and you'd be right. Although it does have it's advantages, it isn't always necessary. Youth can meet in a barn with no decorations at all and be perfectly fine with it as long as they are met with love, given the Word of God on a level they'll understand and retain, mixed with a little fun to hold their very short attention spans, and structure is placed for a smooth service, keeping drama down to a bare minimum. If you have a small group and a small budget, there are a lot of different things you can do to keep your teenagers interested in coming every week. Just get creative and get your teens involved!

Chapter 48

Time To Go

"The Lord our God spoke to us in Horeb, saying: 'You have dwelt long enough at this mountain.'" Deuteronomy 1:6 (NKJV)

After nearly four years of being blessed in our ministry at Plum Grove, God was beginning to change Dale's heart. Everything we had ever wanted in our ministry, God was allowing it all to happen, and then some. We were both so happy and filled with joy as we watched God move through us to touch the youth of our area but Dale was beginning to get burned out.

Dale didn't just help Bro. Parker as the Associate Pastor, as well as being the full-time Youth Pastor. He was also on the praise and worship team, helped with maintenance at the church, and helped the secretary and cleaning lady whenever they needed it as well. Dale pretty much helped out wherever he was wanted or needed and it was all beginning to catch up with him. He was doing too much at once and he was getting tired.

The problem with us being able to do so many things between the two of us was that so much was expected. Since we were paid staff, that meant we were expected to be there unless something major was involved to cause our absence. Of course we always wanted to be at church so that was never really an issue with us, but sometimes you just need a little time as a family to get away.

At one point, I was the teen Sunday School teacher. If the worship leader was out then I was in line to take her place. If the piano player was out, then I took her place. If the drummer was out, then Dale took his place. If the Pastor was out, Dale took his place.

Now you see the problem? It was hard to find a time for us as a family to find time to rest. We had already changed our plans more than once to accommodate other leaders in the church to have their time off, so when we finally made plans to go back home during the 4th of July extended weekend, we were excited.

Suddenly, right before we were scheduled to leave, Bro. Parker informed Dale that he needed us to stay since the drummer was going to be gone that weekend. I had seen Dale aggravated about other things that had happened while we were there but this made him furious. Of course, Dale kept quiet in front of the church leaders but unleashed his fury at home. That's the only place either of us could really open up with our frustrations and hurts so we sat down and talked it out together.

We stayed as Bro. Parker asked but everyone on the praise and worship team could feel the tension with us. We tried to keep everything together but it was easy to see that we were upset about something. I ended up unloading with my friend Karen, the worship leader, but we didn't tell anyone else about our frustrations.

At church the next Wednesday night, two of the deacons, one being the drummer, asked to see us privately. The drummer never even knew about us already having plans and he apologized for us having to change ours because of him. Both deacons were upset with how things were handled and they hoped that we weren't going to quit. We quickly reassured them that if we left it wouldn't be over something like that.

Besides getting weary and tired, Dale felt God leading him in another direction in his calling. For the first time, Dale felt his heart turning away from youth ministry but toward being a Senior Pastor instead. It felt strange so Dale wanted to make sure what he was feeling by continuing to pray and keeping it to himself. Once he felt sure of what God was doing inside of him, we had a serious conversation while laying in bed one night.

I literally cried most of the night after Dale expressed what he felt God telling him.

"You've accomplished what I sent you here to do. It's now time to move back home. I have something else for you to do."

I didn't want to leave. Just a couple of weeks earlier, someone back in Louisiana asked when we were going to move back.

"We're not! Unless God strikes lightening down from heaven and says, 'Move!' then we'll move." I should have kept my mouth shut.

All I could think of was all the wonderful things we had in Splendora. From the amazing school for the boys, to the blessed ministry at the church, and all the friends we had made while we'd been there. We had witnessed God move in so many ways at Plum Grove and for the first time in a long time, we were at peace with very little drama to deal with.

I didn't want to move back home because I remembered why we left. I didn't want to go back home to all of that and I feared that Christian and Daniel would regress in their learning once we enrolled them back in the De Soto Parish school system.

While Dale was praying his prayers, I was praying my own. I knew Dale said that he felt God moving him away from youth ministry but my heart was still there. I didn't understand but I knew my place was to always support and follow my husband. Dale and I both were still unsure so we prayed for God to give us an undeniable sign to help us know His will. We soon got our answer.

A few days later, we got a call from our landlords who lived next door to us. They were very sweet people and the wife had recently received a diagnosis of cancer. They called to tell us that their daughter was going to help the mother through her fight with cancer and we needed to move out of the house. The daughter was going to build another house right where their little rent house sat on their property.

They were very sorry about giving us such short notice but we learned they had known about their daughter's plans for weeks. They couldn't find the heart to tell us that we had to move. We know now that it was all in God's timing.

Dale and I immediately went for a long walk down our street so we could talk about what had just happened. Was this our cue to go back home or just a snag for us to get through? It was only about three weeks until school was going to start so we had to act fast. Not just for the boys but also because I had recently become a school bus driver for the Splendora school district.

I left my floral manager position at a huge Signature Kroger in Conroe, Texas to be a bus driver so I could have more time with Dale at the church and with my boys.

We decided to take a week to look for another house within the Splendora school district that we could afford to rent. If we couldn't find one, we'd move back home to Louisiana. It didn't take us long to figure out that everything available was way above our budget. We were already still paying our house note on our place in Louisiana, plus the rent on the little house we were currently renting so that was right about $1,000 a month that we were already having to pay. We couldn't afford anything higher than that.

The ironic thing about all of this is that Dale had already been moving a few big items back to Louisiana but it was way before he felt God leading him to possibly move back home. Dale just wanted to un-clutter our yard with his old boat that he had been restoring. He really didn't have the time to use it so he figured he would take it to his Dad so he could enjoy it.

Dale also felt led to sell his four-wheeler and pay off one of our vehicles to get our cost of living down. God already knew that we were going to move so He was guiding Dale's hand to prepare us, without us ever knowing about it until much later.

Now that we knew there was no way for us to stay, we had to let our church family know that we would be leaving in two weeks. That was the hardest thing for us to do, especially when we announced it to our youth. The next youth service, Dale and I held services just as we normally would but then we let them know about us leaving at the end. It was so hard watching their faces turn from smiles to tears and looks of unbelief. We reminded them that they built this youth ministry and it was still theirs so it was up to them to not let it die after we left.

We didn't want everything that God had accomplished to fall apart just because we weren't there leading it anymore. That was Dale's design to begin with. . .to help construct a youth ministry that wasn't based on the leadership alone, but mostly on the teens them-selves. This church had already been through that scenario before so we knew we had to make a difference where this youth ministry could continue to run like a well-oiled machine with, or without us.

Dale and I took the time to develop relationships with our adult leaders and trained them so they knew exactly what was expected out of each of them. Every adult knew their job so we were confident that if we ever left, the youth group remained in great hands.

Dale honestly moved to Splendora with a ten-year plan in mind but God had other plans for us. We could actually say that God gave us every opportunity that we had ever wanted while we were there. We felt that we had been blessed to really make a difference, but we didn't quite know how much until we were about to leave.

Preparing For The Transition

Getting ready to pack once again wasn't something that either of us were looking forward to but Dale and I were a little nervous about where God was taking us. We knew we had our house to move back into but the biggest thing on our minds was getting the boys back into school. The Splendora school district had us so spoiled but they also helped us know what our rights were. To try to get a few things ready before we actually moved, I decided to take a quick trip back to Louisiana.

I took all of the files on Christian and Daniel that we had accumulated and showed up at the Special Education Office in De Soto Parish. I noticed that the lady I dealt with before had retired and there was a new lady in charge, which made me a little more hopeful. After telling her everything that we had gone through, especially with Christian, she reassured me that things were different now so we shouldn't have any issues getting both of my boys the help they needed. With that, I gave her all the files of the boys with a declaration.

"We will be moving back in two weeks so I brought y'all some homework. This department left us with a bad taste in our mouths when we left four years ago so I'm hoping that what you say is true about the changes. I may be a preacher's wife but I'm also a mother who has fangs and claws so please don't give me any reason to use them."

As I was leaving, I felt a little bad about that last line. I wasn't used to having to talk to anyone like that but the desperation of a mother with a special needs child was beginning to rear it's ugly head. I wanted the best for my boys, just like any other mother would, and I was learning that sometimes you have to insist for what your children need before they're going to get it.

Now that I had the boys enrolled into school, I had to get back to Texas to start packing. There was so much that needed to be done before we left and time was flying by too quickly. Dale and I knew we had to leave but our hearts were still longing to be with our church family in Splendora. We had made so many close and lasting friendships there.

Just as with any of our past youth groups, all of our youth had become our "babies" and we had the privilege of watching many of them grow. We knew that leaving was going to be hard, but we didn't know it would be this hard.

Bro. Parker and many of our friends at Plum Grove put together a going-away party for our last weekend there. That Saturday they had a nice fellowship at the church where we could all spend time together.

One of our youth leaders, Patsy, along with several of our youth, had already talked with many about writing a note or letter to us to put into a big picture album that they were putting together for us. They wanted us to have something special where we would never forget our amazing four years there at Plum Grove. The album was loaded with pictures, notes, cards, and hand-written letters from so many of our youth and adult friends. We cherished that gift so much and we still have it in our church office today.

After seeing that Dale and I were trying to read some of the letters and notes in our new memory album, one of our youth, Gary, told us to wait until we left before reading his. Of course, that made us curious so we ended up reading it together at the hotel where the church put us up for the night. I'll let you know about the letter in the next section.

Dale had the honor of preaching that Sunday morning for one last time and he gave an amazing message. I couldn't remember when I'd felt more proud of him. After the service was over, Bro. Parker asked the four of us to come up to the front to allow the church to say goodbye to us. That ended up being harder than we thought. We loved every one of them and I ended up crying like a baby the whole time.

Several invited us out to lunch so we could be together one last time and we all had a great time. After our final goodbye, it felt strange during the drive home. What was going to happen now? Only God knew.

To Save A Life

Sometimes you never really know the impact you have on some people until years later. There are even times when you may pour your heart and life into an individual and may never get the opportunity to see the fruit of your labor in that person.

Every now and then, God gives us those times where we can be encouraged by seeing someone's life change for the better because of the time, effort, prayer, finances, etc. that you've provided to help them. Dale and I have been blessed by getting to watch so many teenagers grow in God in so many ways through the years. Even today we still have close and distant relationships with those same teens who are now adults with their own children.

Although there are many with amazing stories that I could share, I want to tell you about how good God is by introducing you to a brother and sister that lived directly across the street from us in Splendora named Gary and Christina.

Christina was the older sister and seemed quiet and guarded. We had the privilege of meeting her shortly after we moved in but didn't see her much after that. Gary, on the other hand, loved being outside either riding his bike or his skate board down our little black top road.

Gary was often around when Dale came home from working at the church and picking up the boys from school so Dale stopped and talked to Gary. Dale always made sure to invite Gary to our youth group but Gary never came. Gary was always nice and seemed to like talking with him so Dale tried to build a relationship with him, whether he ever came to church or not.

One day, Gary said he would finally come to church with us. Gary came faithfully every week and wanted to get involved in our youth band. He liked that Dale was a musician and found a common bond with him when it came to playing the bass guitar. He asked Dale to show him a few things on the bass and Gary was a natural. Gary took off with a true passion for learning the bass and quickly ended up being our bass guitar player for the youth band.

Not too long after that, Gary started teaching himself how to play the electric guitar and got so good that he took over as the electric guitar player for the youth band instead of the bass. We loved how faithful and on fire Gary was becoming for God and his sister took notice to the changes in his life as well.

Gary invited Christina to come to youth and I think it was more out of curiosity, but we were glad she came. At first you could tell Christina just wanted to stay on the sidelines but it wasn't long before God got a hold of her heart in a big way. She soon asked to be a part of the youth band as well, but as a singer.

I already knew that Christina could sing because I heard her in the back seat of my car, singing to whatever I had playing every time we picked her and Gary up for church. Then one day I was listening to her and I heard her singing harmony instead of lead. I had no idea she had an ear for harmony and evidently she didn't either because when I asked her if she knew what she was singing, she didn't really know.

I started working with her and Sarah to see if I could teach them how to sing both parts of the harmony while I sang the lead. Neither of them desired to be the lead singer but really enjoyed singing back-up so we worked on getting our sound tight and our voices blended well.

Now that I've given you the back story, here's where it ties in with Gary's letter to us. When we got back to the hotel, Dale and I started reading all the notes and letters. Many of them made us cry but none of them shocked us as much as Gary's letter. Gary had kept a portion of his life a secret until now and it brought back so many memories that we had with him and Christina, but now it was with a different perspective.

In the letter, Gary shared that he had been going through a rough patch in his life. One day he made up his mind that he was going to commit suicide but he kept thinking of Dale and some of the things he said during their short visits in our driveway. Dale took time to stop and have conversations with him, befriending him from day one. This particular day, Gary wanted to give up but he decided to pray and challenge God.

Gary's prayer went something like this: "God, I'm not sure what to do anymore but if you have something for me to do in my life, then make Mr. Dale stop this afternoon when he comes home and invite me to church one more time. If he asks me to go, then I'll go and I won't kill myself tonight."

Gary knew about what time Dale got home with the boys so he purposely rode his bike around, waiting for him to pull up. He was getting nervous as he waited for Dale. Would he stop like he normally did? Would he ask him to go to church again, even though he's already asked so many times before? As Dale pulled up, Gary tried not to look like he was waiting for him but wanted to make sure he was close enough to talk if Dale wanted to visit.

Dale stopped and started talking with Gary about his day but he was specifically waiting for Dale to invite him to church. Eventually, Dale did ask him toward the end of their conversation and Gary lit up with a big smile. That's what he was waiting to hear. Dale had no idea how big of a deal it was with him inviting Gary to church again.

Gary never spoke of that day until he poured his heart out in his letter to us. He basically said that Dale saved his life that day, in more ways than one. Dale and I both cried that night, so thankful for what God did in Gary's life through us. Thanks be to God that Dale was obedient to the leading of the Holy Spirit that day or this story may have had a very different ending.

A God Moment

You never know whose lives you can touch or change just by simply living out your Christian walk before others. God opens up opportunities daily for us to minister to others, whether it's through a spoken word or action that reflects Him, His love, His mercy. Don't allow fear to rob you of the blessing of being a blessing to someone else. Become that vessel that God can fill up with His Spirit, only to be poured out into another life. He has called us to be a light in a dark world so get out there and go change it for the glory of God! You may just save a life.

Chapter 49

Back In Louisiana

"If you abide in Me, and My words abide in you, you will ask what you desire, and it shall be done for you." John 15:7 (NKJV)

Took a lot of work getting settled back into our house in Louisiana but it felt good to be back in our own home. We wondered how the boys felt about the move, especially Christian, but they both took everything pretty well. They liked having a much bigger bedroom with plenty of space to play, as well as plenty of land outside to ride around on. Our biggest problem was going to be getting our house back into shape after renters nearly destroyed it.

Our last renters turned out great but the ones we had before them literally tore up the house. While we were away in Splendora, we depended on my in-laws to keep a watch over our property. Everything went good at first but when our niece and nephew, Christina and Josh, visited our renters frequently, Mom and Dad English simply asked them how the house looked since they had been there. The kids always said that everything looked fine so Mom and Dad English didn't worry.

For reasons I can't remember now, the young couple that rented from us suddenly moved out. It was then that my in-laws went back to the house and found a horrible sight. They had been tearing down walls, building other walls, painting, making so many changes and all without our permission. Some of the things I had done to decorate the house, if they didn't like it, they changed it. The worst thing about the changes was that it was all done with cheap materials and poorly done. Everything looked horrible.

Another thing we didn't know is they raised two mastiff dogs and multiple cats inside the house, which left a horrible stench. They had found pieces of old carpet and pieced them together to cover the floor of one of the back rooms. The carpet already had some stains in it, but then the animals used the bathroom all over it. The rest of the house still had the original hard wood flooring so we could see everywhere the dogs had urinated and where they failed to clean it up before it ruined the floor.

One of the stipulations of them renting from us was that they were not to mess with my Great Grandmother's cherry finished, upright piano that I had to leave behind since we didn't have the room in the small home we rented in Texas. When we moved back, I discovered that our renters had allowed the dogs to chew on the legs of the piano and stool, as well as urinate on it. I was livid!

We also discovered where they had several farm type animals, but instead of using the acreage around the house to hold them, they built small fenced in areas attached to the house itself. The odor of animal feces and urine was so strong right around the house, the yard, and the whole place was infested with fleas.

We didn't know about the flea problem until we all walked back to the house for a quick inspection right before we moved every-thing back in. We had walked around the perimeter of the yard and then through the house when Christian suddenly started yelling, "Ouch! Ouch!"

I looked down and saw several moving black dots all over his legs and immediately thought they were ants. As I started trying to quickly knock them off of him, I noticed they weren't going any-where. After looking closer, I discovered they were fleas.

Christian was the only one wearing shorts so when we all looked at our own pants legs, we saw hundreds of fleas, climbing up our legs. Some had already reached our waste. We all ran outside screaming, stopping every few feet to try to knock off as many fleas as possible before running a little more toward Mom and Dad English's house. We managed to get the majority of them off but just in case, we stripped down at the back door of the English's home and all jumped in a tub with bleach.

Later on, Mom English went back to the house to spread Seven Dust around before we showed up with all of our furniture to move in. We already called a pest control company to come spray but she wanted to make sure that we didn't have any problems. When she got in the living room, she noticed a big pile of something on the floor that resembled dog poop.

Mom English knew she had already cleaned up the house so she found it odd. She decided to finish spreading the Seven Dust around and then clean up the mess afterward but when some of the dust hit the pile of "poop" it suddenly scattered. It was a huge pile of fleas! Needless to say, Mom English ran out of the house and called the pest control people to come back.

While it was nice to be back in our own home again, it took me a while to get used to the idea of us having to start all over in remodeling our home. It was going to take a lot of money to get our house looking good again and money was something we didn't have a whole lot of.

God Always Provides

After moving back, Dale only had his last check from being employed at Plum Grove so we both needed to move fast on trying to find work. Dale was putting his resume and applications in everywhere he could think of but no one seemed to be hiring.

It wasn't long before I found a job working in the office of a motorcycle and ATV dealership/shop in Mansfield. I was a little out of my element but it was a job and I've always been good at business and administration type work. My boss was a nice Christian guy who I had known for quite a while so that made working there a lot easier.

A few months after me working there, a lady that owned a local newspaper came in to see my boss about advertising. After talking with me for a few minutes, she wanted to offer me a job working for her so we arranged a meeting.

When we met I talked with her and her daughter, who also worked at the paper. I answered all their questions and they thought adding me as their advertising manager would be a good fit. It meant more money for me, which we desperately needed since Dale still had not found a job yet.

I didn't want to leave my boss at the motorcycle place but I had to do what was best for my family so I gave him my resignation and began working for the local newspaper. I've always been good at selling so that part I knew I could do, but I had never worked for a newspaper and it took me a little while to get used to how things were done.

I had heard rumors of how my new boss was and some of it wasn't that good, but I've never been one to listen to gossip and make judgment calls on someone without knowing facts from personal experience. I dismissed the rumors and decided to make the best out of what I was given.

Things were always very busy at the newspaper office so there wasn't very much time to make lasting friendships, however the lady that did the majority of the computer layout for the paper and I got along great. The daughter seemed hard to get close to and my boss was hard to impress but I worked hard regardless. There were times of laughter and times of sheer aggravation, but it paid the bills. Well, sort of.

I could tell Dale was getting frustrated that I found two jobs immediately and he still couldn't find any places hiring. In the mean time, we both prayed and made sure we paid our tithes faithfully, no matter how much money we had.

From past experience, we knew that God blessed those who were faithful with their tithing and giving. We also knew from experience that if you withhold from God and live in disobedience in this area, God withholds His blessings. Things start happening around you where that same amount of money, or even more, will unexpectedly leave your wallet. Dale and I both didn't want to live in disobedience and wanted to remain faithful, trusting in God for everything.

Being in a situation like this really makes you have to trust in God. We were financially in a place where we had to totally rely on God's help and provision, and He was indeed faithful to His word.

Dale has never been a lazy person so, although he couldn't find a job, he never just sat around waiting for a phone call. He actively searched out anything he could do to support us from bush hogging to helping with roofing jobs. My parents called and asked him to finish putting up the vinyl siding on their big house since they hadn't had the time to do it themselves. They agreed to pay him for the job and it helped us more than they'll ever know.

Around six months after we had moved, Hendrix Manufacturing in Mansfield, Louisiana finally called Dale in for a maintenance position and we both immediately praised God. It was just in time. We were slightly behind on several of our bills but they always got paid because God showed up just in time, every time. Fully trusting in God for everything can be a scary place, but it can also be a very rewarding time where your relationship with Him becomes more real than ever before.

Not long after Dale got hired at Hendrix, I got another job offer at the local Hibernia National Bank in Logansport. The way things were going at the local newspaper, I figured this would be a better option for me, with a chance of advancement, a better and steady paycheck, as well as benefits. After praying about the job offer, I felt it was a good move so I started the necessary steps to making it happen. I quickly got a call from Hibernia and before long, I was in training and on my way to becoming a teller.

I started out being a floater when they were about to permanently assign me to one of the biggest branches in Shreveport. I had been praying for God to move me closer to the house somehow so when I got a call that a promotional position came open at the Logansport branch, I screamed for joy. Not only was I much closer to the house, but I was also going to be the vault teller, which meant more responsibility and a small raise in salary.

It was exciting to start my new job and I loved everyone I was working with. Not long after that, we learned that Hibernia was being bought out by Capital One. I stayed with them for over seven years while slowly moving up the ladder to eventually become the "platform" person at our branch. My responsibilities were opening all accounts, debit card and account maintenance, loan officer, helping the tellers during busy times, and filling in for our manager, Kristi, when she was out.

I really enjoyed my job but I loved interacting with the people even more. I made so many friends by working at the bank and found that I was ministering to many of them as opportunities presented themselves. Sometimes people would come to sit at my desk just to talk about God or ask for prayer as they shared their hearts with me. As long as I didn't have a customer or something important pending, I didn't mind at all. I saw how God was using my position there to help many different people and I loved it.

Dale stayed with Hendrix for a while when he heard of another job offer at the International Paper Company just outside of Mansfield, Louisiana. He applied and got on with the maintenance crew, making a little more money an hour. After a while, he was offered the oil and lube position for Paper Machine #1. This meant a raise, a steady route on the job, no shift work, off on weekends, and he would be an actual I.P. employee instead of the company over the maintenance crew. This was a blessing in so many ways. This position allowed him to be available for the ministry when he needed to be off and with every advancement of his training, he received more raises.

As I look back, I can see how God took care of us, through every door He opened. As long as we remained obedient and faithful in every area of our lives as best as we could, God continued to keep His protective hand over us and His blessings kept coming. But there was another area of our lives that we weren't very certain about.

A God Moment

We hear people complain about how God isn't answering their prayers, but when you ask them about their lives, their faithfulness to God, their obedience to His Word, then their countenance suddenly changes. No one wants to think about that. No one likes to own up to their own selfish and sinful ways. We are all prone to it, none of us immune to it. We need to depend on God, asking for His forgiveness as well as His Holy Spirit to guide us through this life. We want to live our lives like we want to but expect God to turn his eye on those areas and grant us our every wish. It doesn't work that way. God's Word explains that our prayers can be hindered through our disobedience. I encourage you to seek out His Word on what you can do to help your prayer life as well as your relationship with God.

Chapter 50

Taking A Break

"For the vision is yet for an appointed time; but at the end it will speak, and it will not lie. Though it tarries, wait for it; because it will surely come, it will not tarry." Habakkuk 2:3 (NKJV)

While we were trying to figure everything out on the financial side of things after moving back to Louisiana, there was another issue we were faced with. What would we do now when it came to ministry? What church would we go to? There were so many questions going through our minds. We had always held a position in every church we were at, only because that was our calling, but we were uncertain what God was wanting us to do at that time.

Naturally, Mom and Dad English wanted us to come back home to Family Worship Center in Logansport so we started attending there, but they soon approached Dale with a different proposal.

With them both getting older and dealing with several health problems between them, Mom and Dad English were considering retiring from their pastoral positions. That's when they asked Dale if he wanted to take over as the pastor of Family Worship Center.

Dale wanted to pray about it and talk with me before making a decision. We knew that we were going to have some struggles with certain issues but Dale decided to accept the position.

One of the problems we had was Mom and Dad English remained at the church, which sometimes presented a problem for the congregation on who to look to as their leaders. They had their former pastors, as well as their current pastors, serving together in the same church. That can sometimes be confusing.

Another problem, which was the same one we had before, was our ideas and ways of doing ministry was totally different from Mom and Dad English's. We all loved each other very much but it was getting obvious that all of us trying to pastor a church together wasn't going to work. After much thought and prayer, Dale resigned before the church suffered in any way and Mom and Dad English went back to being the pastors as before.

Dale and I both wanted to see Family Worship Center flourish but we knew being there wasn't in God's timing for us right then. It was during this time that Dale slowed down long enough to realize that he wasn't fit for spiritual service. He was hurt, tired, and spiritually burned out. I, too, was very hurt and tired so we decided to take a break from ministry altogether. We needed a chance to rest, as well as heal emotionally and spiritually.

So now what? Where would we go? This was new territory for us. We decided to start visiting some area churches where we either had friends or family. It was so different being able to leave the house later on Sunday mornings with nothing to have to do once we arrived at church, but it felt nice.

We were always made to feel welcome when we arrived at every church we visited, but if they knew us, then they knew what we could do, they knew our history. Dale and I were asked if we would stay and help them with either their youth program or with their worship. We were surprised at how many local churches were interested in bringing in the contemporary praise and worship to their church, especially since the majority of them had always been on the traditional side with their music.

On one hand we felt honored and humbled that they asked us to be a part of their church's ministry, but on the other, we were wondering secretly to ourselves, "Can't you just like us coming to your church for who we are and not necessarily for what we can do?"

We knew they all didn't mean it that way but it felt like they were only wanting us to come to their church for what we could possibly do for their church. We just wanted to rest for a while and were in desperate need of a good friend. We politely declined their offers and kept visiting different churches.

One Sunday we decided to go visit a church in Joaquin, Texas where Dale had family attending there. We didn't get to see these family members very often so we thought it would be nice to visit them and their church. Just like the others, we were welcomed by all who knew us. No one openly asked us to do anything at the church so we decided to come back the next Sunday.

Although we hadn't met the pastor or his wife, we liked his preaching. It was that Sunday or the next when a friend introduced us to the worship leader and youth pastor. Our friend explained what all we could do, or had done for other churches in the past. The youth pastor kindly explained that they didn't allow anyone to serve in the church who hadn't faithfully attended there for at least three months. Dale and I agreed with their church policy and were relieved that we could sit back and rest while still serving God faithfully by attending church.

We decided to start going to that church but after a couple of months, we started feeling restless. We weren't used to only sitting in the pews and not having anything to do. Dale and I needed time to heal and rest, both spiritually and physically, but now we felt God leading us to get back into the swing of things. During our time of rest, we still had a few people approach us about singing or playing an instrument but we always politely declined. Now we were getting that itch again.

One day the youth pastor asked us about possibly playing and singing on the praise and worship team, as well as sharing some of our knowledge and experience in youth ministry. Dale and I both agreed to meet with him and the pastor to talk about it. This was the first time that the pastor took the time to talk with us. The pastor asked us a few questions and wanted to see how well we played and sung. After a few minutes of playing, we got the approval and it wasn't long before we were introduced to the others on the praise team.

We enjoyed being a part of the praise and worship team, as well as working with the youth pastor in his youth ministry. Dale and I were having a great time but Dale felt God leading him to do something else.

While lying in bed one night Dale said, "How do you feel about us starting our own praise and worship band that would travel and minister at other churches or events?"

Of course I was all on board with that idea. Anything dealing with music or singing had always been my heart and soul.

Intensify

Dale and I both could sing and play different instruments but now we had to decide what we would play and who else would play or sing with us. We put the word out about what we wanted to do and set a time and place for anyone interested to come. We were excited at how many showed up. We had such a great time playing around but it was time to make the hard decision of who would minister with us.

We decided that I would sing lead or back-up harmony as well as play the keyboard. Dale would sing and play the acoustic guitar. Our son, Daniel, would play the drums. A young guy, named Virgil, would play the electric guitar. Another young guy, named Tim, would play the bass guitar. Finally, a young lady, named Lachelle, would also sing with us so we would have three-part harmony.

Dale and I knew that we needed a place to practice so we cleaned out what used to be a room we used for an office and utility room. We also needed some serious drums since the only set Dale used to have was messed up by his nephew a few years before. I found a beautiful set of Yamaha Stage Custom Series in a natural wood grain and gave them to Dale for Christmas. Of course, he loved them but it seemed that Daniel had his own plans with them.

Before we go any further, I'll have to give you the back story on our son, Daniel. Daniel was always very quiet and shy but one day after church, we heard him playing around on the drum set. Dale quickly went over and showed him how to hold the sticks and play the basics. Daniel got it on the first try and he had a steady rhythm. Dale and I looked at each other in amazement. We were excited about the possibilities of Daniel being musically gifted, especially since he was only around five years old.

We felt God reminding us of how Dale and I laid Daniel on the altar at the church when he was only a week old, dedicating Daniel to God and His service. We prayed that God would bless Daniel with something that he could in turn bless God back with someday. Although music was always a part of me and Dale, we didn't get specific with our prayers for Daniel, but we both hoped that he would at least be interested in music at some level. Now we were seeing that Daniel had a natural ability on the drums.

Daniel kept learning quickly about how to play on the drums but one day he saw a drummer on TV and how they play in front of people. In the past, Daniel got sick at the thought of having to be in front of a crowd, even if his entire class was doing something, he didn't care. He wasn't doing it. He cried and begged us not to make him get in front of anybody. Now after Daniel had seen that drummers have to play in front of an audience, he put the drumsticks down and wouldn't touch them until years later.

Dale and I were frustrated since we knew God had blessed him with a gift of playing drums but we couldn't push him into it. Every now and then we tried to encourage him, but he still refused. After Daniel got old enough to join the youth department at the church in Texas where Dale and I were helping at, his heart began to change.

One day Daniel came up to Dale and asked if he would teach him how to play the bass guitar.

"Absolutely, son! Go get Daddy's bass!"

Both of us had a glimmer of hope that Daniel would be following in his parents' footsteps when it came to music. Music had always been a major part of our lives so having Daniel join the club was a bonus blessing. I loved sitting back and watching Dale and Daniel play together.

Daniel picked up playing the bass quickly and was doing so well that Dale and I agreed to buy him his own bass guitar and amp if he stuck with it. That Christmas Daniel was excited to see that he finally had his own bass guitar that was his own size.

After working with the bass player at the church, as well as the youth pastor, Daniel was asked to be the bass player for the youth band. I didn't know how well Daniel would be with playing in front of his peers but he seemed to handle it well. Dale and I were thrilled that he was pushing past his fears and honoring God with his gift.

Not long after that, Daniel came back to Dale and asked if he would teach him how to play the electric guitar. Just like before, Dale agreed and told him to bring his guitar into the living room. Daniel ran to get Dale's guitar and they worked on it for about thirty minutes.

"I'm just going to show you these two chords for right now because I don't want to overwhelm you with too much at once."

Daniel looked like he was disappointed but he was happy that Dale got him started.

The next day after Daniel got home from school, the first thing he said as soon as he walked through the front door was, "Mom, where is that book that has all the guitar chords in it?"

I knew what he was going to do. He wasn't going to wait on his Daddy. I started hearing him in his room, playing away as best as he could. Daniel steadily practiced all his new chords that he taught himself for about a couple of hours. When Dale came home, he heard a guitar being played.

"Is that Daniel?"

"Yeah, he's not waiting on you," I said laughing.

"I can't believe that's him playing. How long has he been practicing?"

"Just a couple of hours. He's doing very well considering. He's got a gift for this. It didn't take him long to learn the bass either."

"He's doing great!"

When I bought Dale his new drum set, you would have thought that we bought them for Daniel. He immediately became comfortably attached to them and played like he had never quit. He was doing things on the drums that most people that have played for years couldn't do.

Dale and I were so proud of him and made sure that we continued to encourage him with his new-found talents. After we knew how good he was, that's when we asked if he wanted to be our drummer for the new band.

After we got the band established, we had to come up with an amazing name. After a lot of thought and prayer, we decided on "Intensify" as the perfect name for our praise and worship band. It was simple and described what we wanted out of our ministry which was to encourage everyone to intensify every aspect of their life with God.

We all got along great and had so much fun together as we started getting booked for different events, concerts, or revivals. During our time ministering together there were a few changes in the band. Lachelle had to leave so another lady, named Robin, joined us with her beautiful harmony. Not long after that, Robin and her husband introduced us to a couple that had just moved to our area. Justin and Lana were good friends with them when they all lived in Utah together, but now they moved in with Robin and her family until they got settled and established on their own.

We were told that Justin was an amazing electric guitar player and used to tour in his younger years. We all decided to invite Justin and Lana over for one of our practices and he fit in quite nicely. Not only did he add even more to our band musically but we figured out that he was just as crazy as the rest of us. As you can imagine, we had a lot of fun at our practices.

Just as we were all getting used to each other, Robin and her family had to move due to her husband getting another job opportunity in another state. That meant we had to search for another singer, again. Stacy sang on the praise and worship team at the church we were attending in Texas and I knew she had a great harmony voice. After Dale and I talked about it, we asked Stacy if she'd like to sing with us. God put a great team together and we were all having a wonderful time ministering to others with the gifts God gave us to use for His glory. God was about to change everything for all of us.

A God Moment

When God blesses you with a gift or ministry, you definitely feel a nagging pull on your heart when you're not fulfilling that call, or using that gift, for His honor and glory. We all have that nudge, that feeling deep inside of us that leads us to do the things we were born for. Be careful how the world can move in on that territory of your life and lead you to do things that bring *you* glory, or even pull you away from God altogether. If you're not using the gifts that God has blessed you with, or possibly using it for your own gain instead of honoring Him, I challenge you to come back to the One Who blessed you with those gifts. Time is running out so what are you waiting for? Fulfill your spiritual purpose while you still have the chance to make a difference.

Chapter 51

No Fear Like This

"So we may boldly say: 'The Lord is my helper; I will not fear. What can man do to me?'" Hebrews 13:6 (NKJV)

I want to share one of the scariest days of my life. Don't get me wrong, I've had a lot of scary moments, but I can't remember ever feeling fear to the level I did on this particular day. This was supposed to be a weekend full of fun with my boys, but it turned in an instant.

Before Daniel graduated into the youth department at the church we were attending, he was involved in their children ministry, as well as their Discipleship program. This group of older kids met for intense Bible study and discipleship training. Every year this group of kids got to go on a trip to Schlitterbaun Water Park for a day of fun. Then each kid was given a $100 bill for a day of shopping the next day.

Parents that were willing to go and chaperone were welcome to bring any of their other children on the trip as well, so that meant I could go and bring Christian along. When we got to the water park, a few of us tried to stick together for the most part, moving from one side of the park to the other. About half of the day had gone by and we were all having a great time when we decided to go back to the original side of the park.

At this particular water park, there was a natural running, small river that went through the park. It was beautifully kept with concrete and stone walls along the way. I noticed that every now and then there were steps built where you could enter or exit the water at different places if you didn't want to walk, float, or swim the entire length. We saw several people floating down the small river in their tubes.

One of the parents suggested that instead of walking the entire way around to the other side of the park, that we could take a shortcut through the river instead. She had been at the water park before and I hadn't so I thought it would be alright. It looked shallow and the water wasn't flowing that fast so we all decided to walk through the river.

The water was much colder than the park's water slides but it felt good as we walked through it. We had a little trouble walking through some parts of it because of the natural river rocks. The rocks were slippery and at some places, the water current was a little stronger so I made sure I held onto both Daniel's and Christian's hands. I didn't want either one of them falling down and getting swept away with the current.

Everything was going fine until we realized that we were on the wrong side of the small river and needed to cross over somewhere. We had two choices at this point. We could all try to walk back where we had just come from and risk falling down against the current, or swim across one place that didn't look that far or unsafe. One of the parents started walking across to see how deep it was and she quickly discovered that it was above our heads.

After discussing it, we all decided that it would be better to swim across. Although he wasn't a strong swimmer, Daniel could swim across on his own but a couple of his friends said they would stick with him to make sure he got across. Christian couldn't swim that well so I decided to carry him on my back since I was a strong swimmer. I had never carried anyone like that but I figured it couldn't be that hard and Christian didn't weigh that much.

Since a couple of the other parents said they would swim close by just in case I got tired, we all felt confident that we could make it across with no problems. We all started swimming across and at first, everything was going fine. I was almost half way across when I suddenly felt my arms and legs getting very weak. It came on me quickly and I began to struggle just to keep myself and Christian above water.

I instantly knew we were in trouble and I had to do something quick, so as I was sinking under the water, I kept pushing Christian up so he could breath. I managed to pull myself up one more time to get a breath of air.

"Someone grab him! Please!"

I went back under the water, trying to keep Christian above it and I felt like I was about to drown. I made a decision that I was going to drown but my baby was not. I would sacrifice my life to make sure that Christian lived.

Just when I was about to give up, I felt God whisper to me that I couldn't save Christian if I was dead myself. I needed to fight to save us both. God wasn't through with me yet.

I felt someone grab Christian so I gave all I had to pull myself back up. I could barely keep my head above water but I heard the other ladies say they had Christian. I had more fear about not being able to put my eyes on both of my boys to make sure they were safe than me fighting for my life.

Suddenly I looked across and saw a set of steps not far from me but on both sides was just tall concrete walls. That was my target. I had to try to get to the steps. As I continued to struggle I noticed that the current was taking me faster than I anticipated. I knew that I was about to miss the steps. Panic struck me as my very weak body couldn't swim against the current and I reached out for the steps, just missing them. Now what? I finally reached the concrete wall and my fingers found a groove that I could barely grasp onto and I was literally clinging on for life.

I lost grip and my arms were giving out when one of them went down and I felt something just under the water. It was a small ledge about one foot wide. I strained to pull enough of my body onto the ledge and then collapsed in sheer exhaustion. A huge relief swept over me as I laid there trying to catch my breath.

"Are my boys alright?"

The other ladies rushed over to make sure that I was alright as they reassured me that both of my boys made it safely.

My emotions were everywhere at once and I felt like I was in shock. I could tell the other parents that witnessed the whole thing were terrified right along with me but none of us said much. It was like we were all scared to talk about it or we would all probably break down and cry. All I could think about was what went wrong.

Through all the years that I had swam, nothing like that had ever happened to me. Why did I suddenly get so weak? Because I was carrying Christian, I was not able to get as deep of a breath as I needed. I couldn't breathe properly so I wasn't getting enough oxygen to my muscles, therefore making my muscles shut down.

After I rested a few minutes and caught my breath, we all walked to the other side of the park together. I was still traumatized by what had just happened but I wasn't going to break down in front of my boys, so I kept a strong front. The other ladies asked if I was alright and I knew they were concerned but I told them I was fine, although I really wasn't.

I decided for the remainder of the day that the boys and I would just float down the park's lazy river together with some of the other kids. That would be safe and relaxing, giving me time to calm my nerves. The rest of the day turned out fine but I stayed on the quiet side for hours. I had never been that close to death or losing one of my boys before. It was very humbling.

Later that day we all went back to our hotel to clean up and get ready for dinner together at a local restaurant. It was there that some of us finally opened up and started talking about what had happened. A couple of the ladies that were with me said they were really concerned about me, whether I was going to have a nervous break down or something because they hadn't seen much emotion out of me. I had managed to lock it up inside for the time being.

The rest of the trip went well and everyone had a great time. After arriving home I told Dale what had happened. I still hadn't released all the emotion inside of me. The next morning while taking my shower, something broke inside me and I suddenly started crying uncontrollably. It hurt but felt good at the same time to let it all go. I thought I had moved past it. I hadn't planned on losing it in the shower that morning but sometimes the very thing we try to hide away will always find its way out.

I was so thankful that both Christian and I had survived that day. I thanked God for speaking to me under the water and reminding me not to give up. Sometimes you have to fight for what you want or need. When bad things happen, that's not the time to throw in the towel. It's time to fight. God is good!

A God Moment

Through the years I've talked to people that felt life was too hard and wasn't worth living, wanting to end their life. Life is a precious gift from God and not ours to take. We all go through hard times and it's God that gives us the strength to endure if we only trust Him. He promised that He would not leave us during these trials but be there with us through it all. Jesus knows how it feels to be human so He completely understands right where you are and what you're going through. Satan's job is to lie to you, telling you that your life means nothing to no one, but don't listen to him. He only wants to destroy you. Fight back, take back your life, and put it in God's hands where it belongs. You are certainly worth it!

Chapter 52

Following God's Will

*"My soul, wait silently for God alone,
for my expectation is from Him." Psalm 62:5 (NKJV)*

While we were still attending the church in Joaquin, Texas, we continued to minister at other places with our band, Intensify. We were invited to minister at a small local church in Logansport for a special singing after their normal church service one weekend. Dale and I heard that the pastor from another local church, along with his wife and some of his congregation, were going to come hear us.

At first we thought that maybe they heard of us having a band now and wanted to hear how good we were before possibly inviting us to their church. Everyone seemed to enjoy our music and God moved in a big way that day, but things got more interesting as we were packing up all of our equipment.

People usually come up to us after a service to say how much they appreciated our ministry, maybe talk a few minutes, and then leave, but we noticed the visiting pastor and his wife stayed longer than usual. They stuck with Dale and me during the entire time of us tearing down and packing up the equipment. While we were talking, Dale and I could tell that they were there for a reason and it finally came out.

They were hinting around that they were wanting to bring contemporary praise and worship music to their newly founded church but needed help getting it started. They also didn't have anyone attending their church that could play or lead that kind of music. They were thinking that we could possibly fill that void.

We had a great time visiting with them and before we said our goodbyes, they invited us to come visit their church. Dale and I talked about what happened that day and agreed to both be in prayer about the whole thing. After a week of prayer and more talking, we agreed to visit their church to maybe have the opportunity to talk with the pastor and his wife again.

Dale and I had already felt God pulling us from the church in Texas for several reasons so it felt good to be going to another church that day. We hadn't made a decision about anything but we felt at peace when we drove up to the little church. The pastor was welcoming people at the door of the tiny little building they were meeting in at the time and he suddenly saw us coming from our car. As we got closer, he had a big smile on his face.

"We were praying we would see you all here today and here you are. So happy to see you."

The pastor, along with a hand full of people, started this church together and they were a fairly new congregation. Since they didn't have a church building to meet in yet, their sanctuary was an old deer camp. They had also bought a couple of portable buildings that were placed behind it for Sunday School classrooms.

Everyone there was friendly and the service was great. Dale and I had several people visit with us after service, including the pastor and his wife again. We were invited to come back that evening to see how they were putting together their annual outdoor Christmas production so we decided to check it out. When we arrived at the rodeo arena, there were already several people working or hanging around a fire pit, trying to stay warm.

Dale and I enjoyed watching Daniel and Christian hanging around some of the teens they had going there. Some were very friendly while others didn't want to have much to do with the new boys. We were hoping that our boys would be accepted and get to be a part of a good group of young people.

It wasn't long that we were officially approached with a couple of propositions. The church wanted us to bring in contemporary praise and worship into their services as well as help getting their youth program running and successful. They already had several kids and teens attending but needed help getting those ministries to grow and be more organized. After talking with them, Dale and I went home to discuss everything and agreed to be in prayer about it all.

Since this important decision didn't just effect Dale and me, we talked to both of the boys about leaving the church in Texas to start helping with the ministry at this new church. Christian is usually game for just about anything but it would mean Daniel leaving the youth band and his current youth group. After he learned that he would be helping us play music for the new church and they also had teens for him to hang with, Daniel agreed to us moving our family to the other church.

Dale and I already felt good about the decision but now we had to tell the worship leader and youth pastor at the church in Texas that we would be leaving their church within a couple of weeks. Although we had a great time there with our many friends, we felt the pastor didn't really like us being there. I know Dale tried to befriend him as a fellow minister but he wasn't really what you'd call a "people person." I never felt right whenever I was around him either and always ended up saying all the wrong things. There's a lot I could say about that whole situation, but I think I'll keep being positive about my writing.

We said our good-byes to everyone and looked forward to a new journey, with our calling to serve God wherever He led us as a family. Dale had time to finally heal spiritually and felt the Lord leading him to preach again so he was anxious to see what God had for him now. We quickly settled into our new church home and were already working behind the scenes in their Christmas production.

While trying to jump start their youth ministry, it didn't take us long to figure out that this group of teens were different from any other youth group that we'd ever been over. This group was all about horses, rodeos, country music, and they weren't much for outsiders that weren't into what they were. Nearly everything we tried to do that we had great success with everywhere else wasn't really catching the majority of the teens' attention. We could tell that a couple of them really liked what we were doing but the rest were making it hard on us.

Trying to introduce the contemporary praise and worship wasn't going to be easy either. The church as a whole wasn't used to it. They had their established piano player and loved singing the hymns. We had to be careful how we tried to make the transition. Although the pastor wanted it, we didn't want to hurt anyone in the process of incorporating new music, mixing it with the old, creating a blended style of worship.

We enjoyed being a part of their ministry. We were asked to participate in their drama productions, fill in as teachers for Sunday School classes when needed, and help with the construction process of their new church building just down the road. We made a lot of friends while we were there and formed a wonderful relationship with the pastor and his sweet wife. It's not often when ministers can find another ministry couple that they can just let down their hair and have fun together with. We found that in this couple.

Although there were some bumpy moments while we were there, nothing major ever happened to discourage us completely from doing what we felt God leading us to do. We were fighting an uphill battle with the youth group since the majority of the youth were kin to each other. There were also clique and drama issues, but we weren't going to give up on them.

Before long, the church grew to the point where we needed to go to two services every Sunday morning. This is where we came in with the music. The pastor decided to designate the early service as the contemporary service and keep the later one as it's original classic service.

The newness wore off quickly. Most people didn't like the idea of getting up earlier on Sunday mornings so there weren't many who showed up for the early service. Of course that was discouraging but we were still having a blessed time.

Another Church Came Calling

One day we got a phone call out of no where from another pastor over a church in Mansfield. He asked if he could meet with us concerning needing our help with something and a possible proposition. Dale and I didn't know what to think about this but we decided to meet with him to at least hear what he had to say.

Dale had been feeling God leading his heart to preach again. Not as a youth pastor, but as a pastor of his own church. God had been preparing him for this next step in his ministry for several months. Now it was up to Dale to listen to God's voice concerning when and where.

Dale and I both felt great at the church we were currently at but we both knew that we wouldn't stay there forever since God was moving Dale toward becoming a Senior Pastor. We weren't considered Associate Pastors and we certainly weren't going to try to take away the Pastor's position either. That wasn't our calling and that's not how God does things. Our goal was to follow wherever God was leading us so we agreed to meet with this other Pastor for that reason. We had no idea where God was going to take us but we were willing to do whatever, and go wherever, He led us.

Dale and I met with the Pastor and one of his members at a restaurant to hear them out. The conversation went a little something like this:

"I have cancer and I'm currently going through radiation treatments, which make me very sick and weak. I realize that my time here as Pastor is limited so I'm offering you a position. I'd like for you to be the Associate Pastor for a while and eventually becoming the Senior Pastor of my church. We are a small congregation at the moment but we're hoping that you and your family can help with that by bringing new life into the church. We would love for y'all to bring your musical talents so we can have anointed praise and worship again. We currently don't have any youth but with your experience, we hope to remedy that. All we have is a hand full of kids but we don't have a children ministry program in place either. We were hoping that you could help with that as well. After some time I will step down and this congregation will be yours to shepherd."

After a lot of questions and a lengthy conversation, we thanked them for the dinner and told them we would be in prayer over their proposal. It sounded like a great offer but we had a few concerns. We also wanted to make sure we were in God's will so we talked together and prayed a lot for the next several days.

On one hand, we felt uncomfortable about taking over as Pastors at this particular church but we did feel God leading us to start attending there and begin implementing a few changes that would help the church to grow. Dale and I both felt that we were being sent there for a reason but it wouldn't be a long term stay.

The bad part was having to tell our current church family and Pastors. That was something we weren't looking forward to. We had made many friends there and didn't want to upset anyone but we knew that was going to be hard to do.

Some didn't understand and acted almost mad that we were leaving. Thankfully the Pastor and his wife understood why, although they didn't want us to leave. I remember them praying with us and saying that it was going to be hard not to pray selfishly. We all got a good laugh as we tearfully hugged each other and promised to keep in touch, lifting each other up in prayer.

A God Moment

God always has a plan and purpose for your life. Even when things look dark, or even confusing at times, He is still on the Throne. Just trust Him. After all, He knows a whole lot more than we do. If He is our Heavenly Father, isn't our best interest as His children at His very heart? Of course it is! When He speaks to you with that small, still voice, listen to Him. Then respond with a big, "Yes, Lord! Here am I! Send me."

Chapter 53

Church On The Rock

"If you extend your soul to the hungry and satisfy the afflicted soul, then your light shall dawn in the darkness, and your darkness shall be as the noonday. The Lord will guide you continually, and satify your soul in drought, and strengthen your bones; you shall be like a watered garden, and like a spring of water, whose waters do not fail." Isaiah 58:10-11 (NKJV)

When we first started at the new church in Mansfield we were welcomed with open arms and they were ready for anything we suggested. There was a new excitement in the air and people were ready to work. We quickly got the praise and worship team up and running, so the next step was to work with their youth and children ministries. It wasn't long before those two ministries were going in full swing as well.

Dale and I also learned that they had a private Christian school right there at the church. That peaked our interests since Daniel was having so many problems at his current school. After a lot of prayer and consideration, we had Daniel transferred there right after he started his sophomore year in high school. Daniel seemed to like the smaller class, more one-on-one time, and the Christian atmosphere there. He had just gotten his driver's license and his own truck that his Pawpaw had given him so he was able to drive back and forth everyday.

Christian was doing well at Stanley High School and we were pleased at the teachers he had working with him. He was assigned his personal aide and they all enjoyed working with him. Christian made many friends and they all protected him from anyone bullying him. That made Dale and I feel good about us not being able to be there to watch over him.

As far as the church was concerned, things were going well and the church began to slowly grow. The Pastor suddenly began to change his attitude toward us and everything we were trying to do, which made us confused. He was all behind us, then he didn't want to agree with different ideas we had. He didn't want to approve funding toward different things that would help the children and youth ministries grow anymore.

Through speaking with him, Dale and I quickly figured out that it wasn't anything that we had done. It was simply that he wasn't ready to let go and step down as the Pastor. We also later found out that this would be a pattern for him. We knew God had us there for a reason, even if it was only temporary, so we stuck it out, making a difference wherever we could.

A few months later, we were visiting with Mom and Dad English at their house when they began talking about retiring from full-time ministry. They both were having more health issues and it was getting harder for them to keep up physically with all of the demands that being a pastor of a church can bring. Their congregation had slowly faded to a fairly small group at that time, but they didn't want to close the doors to the church that they had started over twenty years ago.

They knew that Dale and I would take very good care of the church if we took it over but we agreed to pray about it, to make sure this was the door God wanted us to step through. Dale and I talked a lot about the possibilities of becoming the Senior Pastors there. Dale knew that he would have to make some drastic changes and stipulations if he did. We also had the issue of us helping at the Mansfield church. Did we need to stay or did we need to go?

Dale and I wanted to be totally in God's will with everything we did so we didn't rush into the decision. We took our time in prayer together. About a week later we had our answer and we both felt at peace with it.

Dale preached his last message at the church in Mansfield and began praying over the direction God wanted him to take with the church in Logansport as the new Senior Pastor. The church in Mansfield is still struggling today.

Dale, his parents, and his sister, Lisa, talked together about the changes coming to all of us. We all already knew from experience that having two Pastors in one church, the former and the current, just doesn't work.

Lisa took an offer to be the piano player at a Methodist church close to Converse, Louisiana so Mom and Dad English started going to church there with her. They all quickly made several friends at their new church home and got actively involved. Dad and Mom English still preached from time to time whenever another church needed them to fill in and that made them both happy.

Before they officially left the church, Dale and I started attending just as part of the congregation for about a month so we could introduce ourselves to the people who were still attending. It was shortly announced about the change that was coming and it had a two-fold effect.

A couple of the older people weren't interested in any changes so they decided to leave before we ever had the chance to take over. On the other hand, some of the younger people were excited and started inviting others to come.

The first change Dale wanted to implement was the name of the church. He wanted a fresh, clean start to a place that had so much history, both good and bad.

The church was originally built in 1924 and had changed hands, as well as denominations, several times through the years. Dale wanted a church that wasn't identified or attached to any one certain denomination. He wanted a place where anyone could freely come and worship with no expectations of what people were generally used to when you went to church. A place where anyone could come, no matter how they were dressed, their economic status, what denomination they were raised in, what their past was, or even their present. They could come without being looked down upon or judged unfairly, but loved with a God kind of love.

Dale decided on a new name that best reflected the mission of the church: Church On The Rock. Taken from the verse in Matthew 16:18 which says, ". . .on this rock I will build my church, and the gates of hell will not overcome it."

Jesus would be our foundation, not a denomination. This church was going to be a spiritual hospital, not a country club or museum for Christians. Our vision together was for it to be a place of refuge, for worship, for community, for prayer, outreach, and service, with a huge focus on children and teenagers.

Dale's vision was quickly coming together and I hadn't seen him so focused and happy like this in a long time. We both knew we were centered in the will of God and it felt good. The fact that we both knew this was going to be our spiritual home and ministry for a long time felt great! We were finally home. Both of us felt in our spirits that God was going to do some pretty amazing things through this ministry and we were all thrilled just to be a part of it.

With us having hearts for teenagers, one of the first things we prayed over was who to bring in to be children pastors and youth pastors. We met a young couple at the Mansfield church that were interested in youth ministry but never had the opportunity. Dale and I told them that if they felt God leading them to help us, we would train and mentor them every step of the way.

There was another young couple that had just started attending our church right before we took over as Pastors. We watched carefully how the young lady interacted with children and learned that she was a certified day care worker/teacher. We both prayed about asking her to be our children pastor and she excitedly agreed.

Things were coming together nicely. Since we were such a small congregation starting out, we didn't have a deacon board, or a lot of people "in charge", and definitely not a bunch of committees. Whenever we had something to decide that was considered major, we simply took it before the church body for a vote. With everything else, Dale made the necessary decisions as he allowed God to direct him. Dale didn't place himself on a higher shelf than everybody else either. There were no big "I's" or little "you's" and he wanted to keep it that way.

As soon as we knew that we would be the Pastors of the church, Dale and I, as well as the rest of the worship band "Intensify", knew that we couldn't do both full time. While Virgil and Tim stayed at their churches, Justin and his family decided to start attending church at Church On The Rock and play in the worship band there. We all stayed in our respective roles but I took over as the worship leader of the church. Our Youth Pastor's wife started singing with us and I loved how our voices matched so well. It was hard after several months to find out that they were moving.

Now what would we do about the youth ministry? While God had changed and moved Dale's heart away from youth ministry, my heart never left the youth. I was still drawn to ministering to them, counseling with them. I had a God-given skill set when it came to talking to teenagers and relating to them.

"I don't think God is through with me in this ministry just yet. My heart is still with them. Right now, you and I are the only two in this small congregation that are qualified to do youth ministry. It can't be you so I'll step up and do it until God sends someone else and calls me out of it."

Dale agreed and said he would support me in every way but he was concerned that I may overload myself with too much.

Of all people, Dale knew how demanding and exhausting youth ministry can be when it's done right. We both wanted a successful youth ministry but we had to be careful to make sure we didn't push ourselves too far and too hard. If I took over the youth ministry then that meant there would be three major ministries in our house: pastor and wife, youth ministry, and worship leader. It's hard enough being the Senior Pastor of a church, but when you have that many major ministries in one household, it can effect your marriage and family life if you don't protect them.

At first, Dale had a plan as to who he envisioned would come help us build our church but God showed us within the first year that He had better plans. It didn't take Dale long to let go and let God do His thing. We both started praying that God would bring the people He knew we needed to be an effective ministry team to reach our community. People with the same heart and vision that we did. Once we moved our own agenda aside, God began to move and people started showing up out of the strangest of circumstances.

As I worked for the local Capital One Bank in Logansport, I had the privilege of meeting a lot of wonderful people. Some came to sit at my desk just to visit and talk about the Bible, God, or ask for counseling and prayer. I believe God put me in that position, at that bank to meet a lot of people that I would have never had the opportunity to meet otherwise. It gave me the ability to witness and invite people to church frequently, and sometimes they would actually show up.

I'm happy to say that we never solicited people to come from other churches. We have never been about trying to build our congregation out of taking them from other churches. You don't build the Kingdom of God by shuffling people from church to church. It's all about reaching the lost, the hurting, and raising up disciples for Christ.

The majority of our congregation were people who weren't currently going to church anywhere. Some had either been hurt at a church in the past, or the idea of going to church anywhere was a bad afterthought. We were getting known for how different, loving, and non-judgmental we were at Church On The Rock and people started coming to check us out.

God kept sending us wonderful people, too many to personally name or list, who were not only hungry for God but also wanted to be used as His servants for the Kingdom. Dale and I felt so blessed to be a part of something so amazing once again. We watched it grow from the very beginning when we officially started on July 12, 2009. We were about to have to take another step outside of the normal box when it came to church related stuff.

Since Dale worked for International Paper outside of Mansfield, whenever they decided to have a one-day shutdown, it always fell on a Wednesday. That kept Dale from being able to be at church. I always stepped up and filled in for him but whenever I had to take over the youth ministry, I couldn't do that anymore. We didn't exactly have anyone qualified to take his place that wasn't already tied up with their own ministry positions so we had to make a change.

We asked everyone how they felt about having our mid-week services on Thursday nights instead. Who said that church had to be on Wednesday nights anyway? Everyone was all for it and that decision actually helped our church grow in every department, especially our youth ministry.

A God Moment

It's amazing to watch the handy work of God's hands on something that He has privileged you to be a part of. The only problem with success in anything that God is doing is that it makes the devil mad and he will do anything to destroy it and stop it. Be watchful for wolves in sheep's clothing, the gossips, and those who love to create or stir up drama. Be in prayer over yourself, your family, and your ministry at all times. There will always be a storm that will try to rise up but do not fear in the middle of it. God is always there with you so trust Him to pull you through it victorious on the other side.

Chapter 54

Youth Ministry One More Time

"I can do all things through Christ who strengthens me."
Philippians 4:13 (NKJV)

When we decided for me to take over the youth ministry, I had to basically start over. The young couple we were training were picking up teens from the Mansfield area where they lived. We told them they needed to do local outreaches in order to attract teens in our own area around the church. Just as soon as they moved, the teens they were picking up from their area stopped coming since they no longer had a way to come. Now we were back to square one.

All we had were my two boys, Daniel and Christian, but we had to start somewhere. You can never get ready for a youth service with the attitude of, "Well, it's just us."

You have to design your youth service as if you have a room full of teens, even if you only have two or three. You have to get creative with things when you have a small group but you can still have a great time. Your youth service and how it's designed to flow changes, just as your youth ministry grows. We've seen where youth ministries stayed small because of their "small church" mentality. You can't minister to a group of fifty teens the same way you can with fifteen.

We started meeting in the extra building to the side of the main church building. We could get as loud as we wanted without disturbing the adults while they had their bible study together.

The first couple of weeks it was just my boys. Then Daniel started dating a girl named Britney and she started coming. Britney then invited her cousin and his girlfriend. They in turn invited even more and it just snowballed from there. Within six months time we were running an average of about forty teens every week and it was only getting bigger.

We soon realized that the youth couldn't meet in the extra building anymore and we had to come up with another plan of action. The only place that made sense was to move the youth to the main sanctuary and the adults would meet downstairs in the fellowship hall for their bible study. Although we couldn't permanently decorate to make the atmosphere more inviting to teens, it didn't seem to matter to them. We made up for it in other ways.

As soon as teens show up for church on Thursdays they are greeted by at least two adult leaders outside, instructing them to come inside immediately. This is not only for their safety but to prevent any trouble that can occur in the parking lot.

Once inside the foyer of the church they are greeted again by a teen youth leader who directs them to the sign-in table. At the table are two more teens who take attendance, give out tickets, and direct them to another teen leader who helps them fill out a visitor information sheet if it's their first time.

After they're through with that, the teens are greeted once again by another teen youth leader who welcomes them inside the main sanctuary. Now that they're inside they will hear either cool Christian music with slides on the TV, or a video being shown that is entertaining until service starts. The teens love hanging out and having fun while at least two other adults, as well as more teen youth leaders, are watching over them and making them feel welcome.

All of our adult and teen youth leaders are trained twice a year, and watched carefully how they handle themselves, inside and outside the church walls. Being a teen youth leader is a privilege and they are rewarded for their faithfulness and hard work.

I've always told my youth that this youth ministry is theirs, not mine. If it grows, it'll be because of them inviting their peers and making them feel welcome after they've arrived. All the ministering opportunities aren't just my job either, but theirs as well. They're trained how to pray with one another and how to minister to each other.

There's an atmosphere of fellowship and family, not cliques. When dealing with more than one teenager, there are always opportunities for drama so you have to be prepared on how to handle it when it shows it's ugly head.

To change things up a bit, we have one night a month that we focus on inviting friends, salvation, and coming back to God. This night is similar to what we had in Splendora. We call this our "Big Thursday" because the free stuff that we give away are bigger and better, we introduce a mixer game that gets them to interact with one another, and there's usually a theme for the night that allows them to dress up accordingly.

Although we always have a great time, we want every minute we have with them to count. We only have a couple of hours each week to make an impact on these teens' lives so we give them as much of the Word of God as possible.

My adult leaders help out in a big way every week but not just in crowd control. I try to back off and allow them to do all the extra stuff before the preaching begins. They help with youth small groups, cell phone surrender, games, and judging the best dressed for our theme nights.

They also help with other ministry teams like our "Holy Hands." This group of teens learn beautifully choreographed sign language to Christian songs, all done in black light.

"Spotlight On God's Word" is where one scripture is highlighted for the night and all the teens are given an index card and a pen to copy it down. They're encouraged to put it somewhere so they can see it every day that week to help them memorize it and allow it to minister to them that day.

All of our leaders do an amazing job of stepping wherever they're needed. Our youth ministry runs like a well-oiled machine because everyone knows exactly what their role is for the night and they all jump in wherever they see an extra need. The entire service is laid out in order, down to the minute, so there's no guessing as to what comes next for my workers, unless the Holy Spirit moves in a different direction and then everything is subject to change.

As the worship leader for the main church, I wanted to work with the youth and teach them how to put their talents together to form an amazing worship band for their youth ministry. There are a lot of teenagers that have talent and love music but no one to really work with them, especially when it comes to serving the Lord with their talents. They need the experience before they ever reach adulthood. When they get to that age, they're all ready to step into a position to serve in their church, whether it's ours or somewhere else that God has called them to.

I can teach all the main instruments except for guitar but I get others who are skilled in their instruments to help teach the other teens as well. Most teens can play their instrument well in the solitude of their bedrooms but when you try to get them to play with others, it's a whole different ball game. They have to learn how to play with others and I love the look on their faces when they realize that they're playing as part of a group in an actual band. You get that full band sound effect and it's awesome to hear for the first time. Right now we have several singers and musicians in the youth band and they are all doing a great job.

We encourage fellowship with other churches and we welcome teens that actually attend other churches on Sundays and Wednesdays but want to come to ours on Thursday nights. Coming together with other churches for different events has always been a lot of fun and our youth love the fellowship, as well as our adults.

Church On The Rock is already well-known for it's active youth ministry and we want to make an even bigger impact on our community in the future. We're continuing to create opportunities for our youth to serve others in our area. We want them to understand what it means to have a servant's heart as described in the Bible.

Trying to teach our youth how to serve others less fortunate than them has always been a focus in our youth ministry and for several years we took them on mission trips. Every trip was so wonderfully impacting to all who went but in the last couple of years, Dale and I felt God leading us in another direction.

Instead of raising a bunch of money to travel somewhere else, we are now saving that money by staying in our own communities and helping those in need around us locally. We are able to spend that money on fixing problems in homes and yards of the elderly, the widows, those down on their luck, etc.

Another new thing we've done just this year is take our youth leadership to Hot Springs, Arkansas in order to tour the facilities of the orphanage and young mothers' housing. Our youth decided to sponsor one teen boy and one teen girl by sending them monetary support as well as letters and treats. Our group had a wonderful time and they can't wait to go back.

It has been prophesied over our church that our youth ministry would produce many pastors, youth pastors, and other ministry leaders and we can already see that coming to pass. There are several who are college age and in high school that we are currently mentoring and training due to a calling on their lives in a ministry. We give them the avenue to plant their feet, as well as spread their wings, in their gifting or calling. We are training up disciples for Christ and as long as we're here, we will continue to do this for the cause of Christ. Not to build up our church, but to build up His kingdom.

I haven't spelled out everything we do in our youth ministry but I hope what I have shared may help spark some interest, or maybe even some hope, concerning the youth ministry at your own church. We've offered youth ministry seminars in the past so we could share a lot of different information and ideas that could help others and we're still willing to do the same now. Just contact us and we'll be more than happy to talk and share with you.

Is It Worth It? Absolutely!

With all the stress and headache that come with ministry in general, especially working with teenagers and the drama that comes with them, one may wonder why someone would subject themselves to such torture. Why would anyone sacrifice so much of their time away from their own families to help someone's child and their problems? Why would anyone spend so much of their own money just to make sure that a teenager had what they needed, or even wanted? Why do we accept those texts, messages, and phone calls at all hours of the night? Why do we come running when they're crying out that they need us? Because we're the hands and feet of God. It is our heart, our passion.

We've had to deal with a lot through the years but God has always been there to help us through it all. No one ever warned us that we'd have more trouble dealing with parents than with the teens themselves. We've been gossiped about and had more lies told on us than I care to count, by both parents, disgruntled teens, and even people who we've never met, but the truth always seems to find it's way out. God always takes care of things much better than we ever could anyway, right?

Dale and I have seen youth ministry drastically change through the years. We went from no cell phones to every kid having one. Social media didn't exist when we first started but look at where we're at now. We use social media for ministry purposes mostly and it's a good tool to get the word out concerning events and what's happening at the church. It's also the best way to keep up with your youth, sending them reminders, and ministering to them through short posts.

Although I can recall a couple of incidents where we were targets of a smear campaign on Facebook, I'll have to say the majority of what's floating around in our area concerning our church is positive. We don't want people seeing me, Dale, or any other leader at our church. We want them to see Jesus working through us. We're losing our young people to the world and all it has to offer so fast. It's up to all of us to reach them by any, and all means possible.

Dale and I, as well as the rest of the Church On The Rock family, vow to continue our quest to invest in our children and teenagers with everything we have in order to equip and train them to be disciples of Christ everywhere they go. No matter how much time it takes, how much it costs, or what other sacrifices have to be made, we will not give up on this upcoming generation! This is our calling and we will not take it lightly.

A God Moment

Youth ministry is one of the hardest ministries there is so if you're impatient, quick-tempered, lazy, easily offended, lack compassion, or don't have a heart for troubled teenagers, then don't get into it. You've really got your hands full in today's society when dealing with these teens but it's so amazing to watch them turn to God and be healed from their pasts. One soul coming to God is worth all the headache you may go through. Youth ministry may be hard, but it's also one of the most rewarding ministries to be a part of. If God called you to it, He will certainly bring you through it!

Chapter 55

So What Now?

"Therefore by Him let us continually offer the sacrifice of praise to God, that is, the fruit of our lips, giving thanks to His name."
Hebrews 13:15 (NKJV)

As I'm sitting here typing this, it's 2015. It's taken me over two years to write this book. Finding time to sit down, collect my thoughts, and put words to paper is no easy task with my busy schedule, but now it's here. This is the final chapter of the book but I'm not sure how to end it. So much has happened in my short forty-five years on this planet. Maybe I'll catch you up on the most recent events and family. Most of all, I want to leave you feeling spiritually empowered and encouraged.

Dale and I just built onto our house by closing in our car port to make a bigger living room. We finished remodeling the entire outside of the house so now it's time to start on the inside. It's taking a while to do it all since we're remodeling as we have the time and the money, which we lack a lot in both departments, but God has been good to us. We can't wait until we can sit back and say, "We're finished!"

This year marks twenty-seven years of marriage for Dale and I and we're closer now than we've ever been. I'll never forget what the kids did for us at our twenty-five year anniversary. When I say "the kids" I mean Daniel, Christian, Stephanie, and a teen boy who was living with us at the time.

They took our dining table out to our front yard, decorated it beautifully, and dug holes all over the yard to hold tall candles everywhere. They cooked us a home made meal and had us facing the sunset. We were served and then allowed to be alone together to enjoy the romantic moment they had created for us, all in candle-light. It was beautiful and they made sure to take plenty of pictures to capture the moment.

Our sixth year anniversary at Church On The Rock has just passed and God has continued to bless us. We were able to purchase the existing property and are currently purchasing more land by the church. The new land will be for our large youth center and extra parking. After we finish the youth center, we plan to build a new sanctuary. It will include a large children center for our expanding kids' ministries.

God has also brought us a wonderful young couple from Shreveport as our new Youth Pastors. They were both called into youth ministry as teenagers and have been actively serving as youth leaders and working at many youth camps. God arranged for them to now join our ministry team and we can't wait to see what God is about to do with our youth ministry.

Have I quit youth ministry? Not quite. I'm still in the background for now. The youth band is still my baby and I'm putting more focus on them, as well as on the praise and worship for the church as a whole.

Daniel and Christian recently turned twenty-three and twenty years old. Am I really that old, because I certainly don't feel it? Speaking of the boys, a lot of milestones have happened to them and we couldn't be prouder.

Daniel

Daniel finished high school and put himself through dental assisting school thinking that would be a good career start and it wouldn't take him out of church. All went well for a while but he realized that there aren't many jobs to be found in that field.

While working other jobs he joined a contemporary/rock Christian band called Alive By Sunrise where he recorded and toured with them for about a year as their drummer. He really enjoyed having the opportunity to use his talents for the Lord. It's always been his dream to be a part of a Christian rock band. After some time they all agreed that since the band was trying to go in a different direction that Daniel wasn't really in favor of, that he would leave the band. Daniel felt better about leaving since they knew of another drummer that could slide right into his place.

Daniel still has dreams of a music career but he knew that he had to put that on hold for a while. He needed to start thinking about a career that would support his future family. After dating his sweetheart of three years, Stephanie Dees, they planned to get married, so out of nowhere he decided that being a truck driver was the career for him. At first it surprised us but then I remembered that it's in his blood on my father's side, three generations now.

Daniel put himself through Diesel Driving Academy in Shreveport at night while he worked at a local veterinary clinic during the day. After thirty weeks he finally graduated and was hired immediately by a well-known trucking company. Shortly after that he asked Stephanie to marry him and they got hitched this past April. The wedding was beautiful and I was proud that she chose to wear my wedding dress. She looked so beautiful in it and it brought back a lot of memories of my own wedding. They're both doing well and have their own house not far from us.

Although Daniel stays on the road a lot right now, Stephanie is able to help us out at the church and we're very proud of the young lady she has grown to be since we've known her. She currently serves as a youth leader, sings and/or plays bass guitar in both praise and worship bands, and is the director/choreographer of our youth Holy Hands Team. She signs to music so beautifully. God has blessed her with the ability to teach others how to come together as a group and sign in black light for the glory of God. She has been such an asset to our ministry but we love the fact that she is now a part of our family even more.

Daniel still plays in the church band and helps in the youth ministry when he's home. Dale and I appreciate his faithfulness to the work of the church and serving God with his life. We are all so proud of the Godly young man he has become.

In a world with rare Godly morals, Daniel has stood against the flow and kept his integrity. We've never had to worry about him getting drunk, using tobacco products or drugs, using filthy language, getting a girl pregnant outside of marriage, or catching a sexually transmitted disease. He made it to his wedding night pure. Is my son perfect? Of course not, but he's amazing in our book. To God be the glory!

Christian

Christian received a lot of attention his Senior year in high school concerning his prom. Several of our youth suggested that we make a video of Christian asking Sadie Robertson to the prom to see if she would actually come. Out of fun, we made the video and posted it on Facebook and YouTube, but we weren't expecting the outcome we received.

People started sharing it and a local news channel asked for an interview. Christian was excited about being on television, even though we never heard from Sadie. Young girls and their parents started flooding the news station, as well as us personally, with requests to take Christian to the prom.

Dale and I didn't want to pick just anyone so we prayed over all the requests. We settled on a sweet, Christian young lady from Bossier City named Breanne, who had a younger autistic brother. Her letter touched our hearts so much that we arranged a meeting for them to get to know each other a week before the prom.

We started getting offers for free professional photography, car rental and gas, tuxedo rental, flowers, and dinner. Both Christian and Breanne looked amazing and the local news came back to do a follow-up story.

A young couple from our youth teamed up with Christian and Breanne at the prom to watch over him since I wasn't allowed to go. Christian danced the night away and was voted Prom King! It was truly a night that he will never forget and we're so thankful to everyone who made it all possible.

Christian graduated high school last year and everyone was so happy and proud of him. We've had several say that the school just isn't the same without seeing Christian on campus. He was famous for his hugs and sweet smile. He loved picking around with certain coaches and teachers that knew him well. Christian still gets to visit with some of his classmates at church when they come.

Christian currently helps us out a lot at the church and around our property, taking care of the animals of our fast-growing farm we're building. We already have a donkey and chickens, but we plan to soon acquire some goats, turkeys, and possibly a calf or two. Christian also likes to help Daniel and Stephanie out by taking care of their cat, Pit Bull, and Great Dane whenever they're gone and need his help. He is so good with animals and he loves taking care of them.

Another favorite thing he likes to do is ride his four-wheeler around our property. It's an automatic so it's easy for him to drive. We figured it's the next best thing since he will never be able to drive a car. He also loves watching his movies whenever he can. It's never a boring moment around our house because we never know what each day holds for us, but Christian has gotten used to it and takes it all in a stride.

What About The Rest Of The Family?

Mom and Dad still happily live on the Funny Farm and they're both loving the retired life. We all go visit when we can and it's always a lot of fun when all of us "kids" and our families show up together for a great time. Sometimes we have jam sessions since several of us can either sing or play an instrument. Life on the Funny Farm has changed a lot through the years but it'll always be our favorite place to be due to all the wonderful memories. Right now, we're having fun making new ones.

Bill remarried a wonderful lady that he met through his singles Sunday School class at his church. Barbara had never been married before and she reminds me a lot of my Mom. Her and Bill are great for each other and we love going to visit with them when we can at their house they built together. I had the privilege of singing at their wedding and making Barbara's flower bouquet.

I've been given the honor to sing at many weddings, as well as funerals. It's so hard to sing at either because I get so emotional either way. I cry when I'm sad, mad, and glad so basically it doesn't take much to make me cry. The only problem with that is you can't sing when you're crying. We have buried all of my grandparents, except for Bill's mother, and I sang at their funerals.

So what about my siblings? Amy and Ronnie have just moved their house back on the Funny Farm after living in Shreveport all these years, while their twins, Justin and Eliza Rae are now twenty years old and doing well.

Mary and Glenn are still living on the Funny Farm and have their hands full with their first-born, Faith, getting married this year, Hope working, and Sam graduating from high school this past May. They all faithfully attend a church in Texas together and serve there faithfully.

Stacey remarried to a guy named William from the Shreveport area. He has helped Stacey raise her two daughters, Amore' Sierra and Hannah, and they just recently moved to the Funny Farm as well. Stacey, William, and the girls have all started attending Church On The Rock since they moved back to this area.

Joey married his high school sweetheart, Amanda, and together they have three children: Dayton, Alyssa, and Seth. Joey served in the National Guard before, and during, the Iraq war, fighting for our freedom for a year tour before returning home. He has worked for the De Soto Parish Sheriff's Department for many years and is currently a Sergeant on the force. Joey has worn many "hats" for the DPSD including, S.W.A.T., Firearms Instructor, and now the Helicopter Division. Joey, Amanda, and the kids currently live in Logansport and all attend Church On The Rock.

Dale's brother, Dennis, and his family are all doing well. He and Patsy are enjoying being grandparents of four beautiful grandchildren—two from Chris and two from Crystal. They still currently live in the Bossier/Benton area.

Dale's sister, Lisa, lives beside Mom and Dad English and they all help each other out a lot. Lisa is also enjoying being a grandmother of three grandchildren—one from Christina and her husband, Jacob, and two from Josh and his wife, Samantha. Lisa is still faithfully serving as the piano player in her church as well as other areas where she's needed.

There are a lot more family members that I haven't mentioned and because there are so many, there's no way that I can list them all, so I apologize in advance. Just know that you are all loved very much.

Not The End

This may be the closing chapter of this book but it's certainly not the end of my journey. Throughout my life I can look back and see where God had His loving hand on me the entire time. He never left my side and I'm thankful and humbled. We all have lessons to live and learn so what have you learned lately?

Remember that our lives have meaning—we have a purpose. You are important in the eyes of God, no matter what anybody else says. You were personally created and crafted by the Master and He certainly doesn't make mistakes. He couldn't make a mistake even if He tried so look up, get up, and get on with your life where you can make a difference in someone else.

It always come full circle. We reap what we sow, or as everyone seems to say today: "karma!" But what about the things that we don't cause for ourselves? The things that we didn't deserve but we certainly got? God can turn those around for your good and His glory, if we let Him. Let go of your past and hang on tight to your new future in Christ. His ways are much better than ours anyway.

A lot of great things are happening with me, my family, and our ministry so I feel very blessed. I pray that this book has been a blessing to you in some way and if you ever need prayer, just reach out to us on Facebook or email.

As far as the church goes, God is still blessing and we continue forward with the huge vision that God has placed in both of us. God has sent us an amazing group of people that love God and share our vision so we can't wait to see what else He has in store for us at Church On The Rock.

Our current church service times are Sunday mornings at 10:30, Thursday nights at 6:30 for youth and 7:00 for adult bible study and kids' church. Church On The Rock is currently located at 301 S. 3rd St., Logansport, LA. All are welcome to join us! We'd love to meet you personally.

Look us up on Facebook under Heather West English, Church OnThe Rock, Rock Solid Youth, or Kidz' Rock Kids. My email is heather.englishpfs@yahoo.com and our church website is cotrlogansport.com. May God bless you!

"The Lord bless you and keep you; the LORD make His face shine upon you, and be gracious to you; the LORD lift up His countenance upon you, and give you peace." Numbers 6:24-26 (NKJV)

CPSIA information can be obtained
at www.ICGtesting.com
Printed in the USA
FFOW03n1450020216
21043FF